WANDERING THROUGH WINTER

THE AMERICAN SEASONS

THE FIRST SEASON

NORTH WITH THE SPRING

THE SECOND SEASON

JOURNEY INTO SUMMER

THE THIRD SEASON

AUTUMN ACROSS AMERICA

THE FOURTH SEASON

WANDERING THROUGH WINTER

WANDERING THROUGH WINTER

EDWIN WAY TEALE

A NATURALIST'S RECORD OF A 20,000-MILE JOURNEY
THROUGH THE NORTH AMERICAN WINTER.
WITH PHOTOGRAPHS BY THE AUTHOR

INTRODUCTION BY ANN H. ZWINGER

ST. MARTIN'S PRESS
NEW YORK

Library of Congress Cataloging-in-Publication Data

Teale, Edwin Way
        Wandering through winter : a naturalist's 20,000-mile journey
through summer / Edwin Way Teale.
                p.   cm.
        Reprint. Originally published: New York : Dodd, Mead, 1981. (The
American seasons ; 4th season).
        ISBN 0-312-04458-5
        1. Winter—United States.   2. Natural history—United States.
3. Natural history—Outdoor books.   I. Title.   II. Series: Teale,
Edwin Way   American seasons ; 4th season.
QH104.T355   1990 4th season
574.5'43'0973 s—dc20   90-8006
[574.5'43]   CIP

First published in the United States by Dodd, Mead & Co.

Dedicated to
DAVID
Who Traveled with
Us in Our Hearts

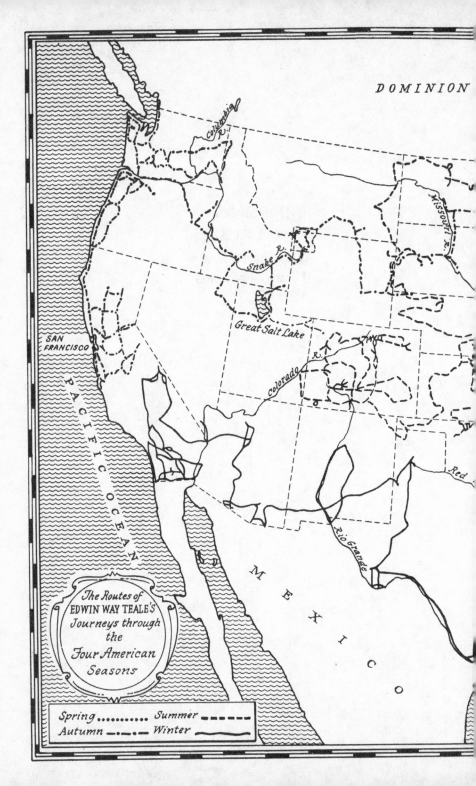

The Routes of
EDWIN WAY TEALE'S
Journeys through
the
Four American
Seasons

Spring .... Summer - - - -
Autumn -..-..- Winter

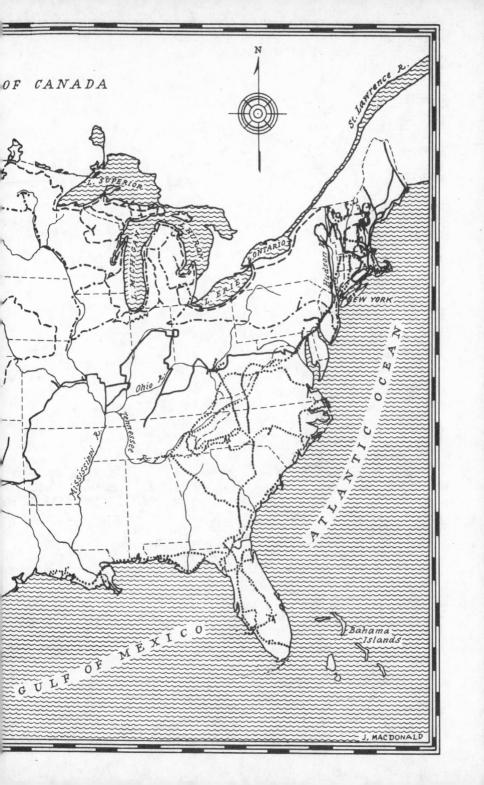

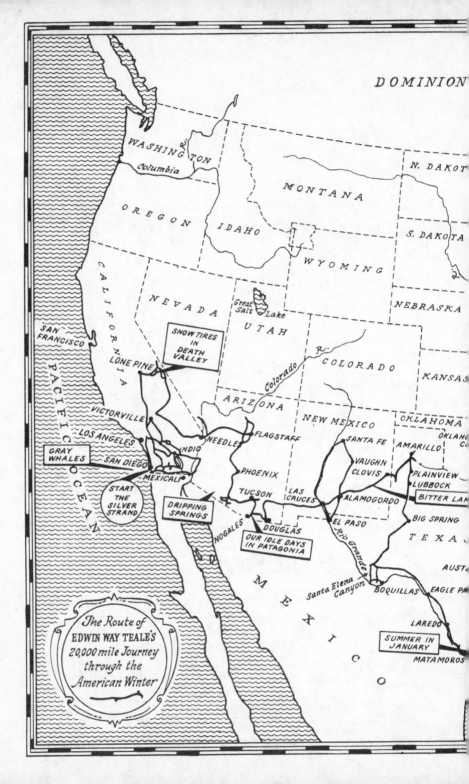

The Route of
EDWIN WAY TEALE'S
20,000 mile Journey
through the
American Winter

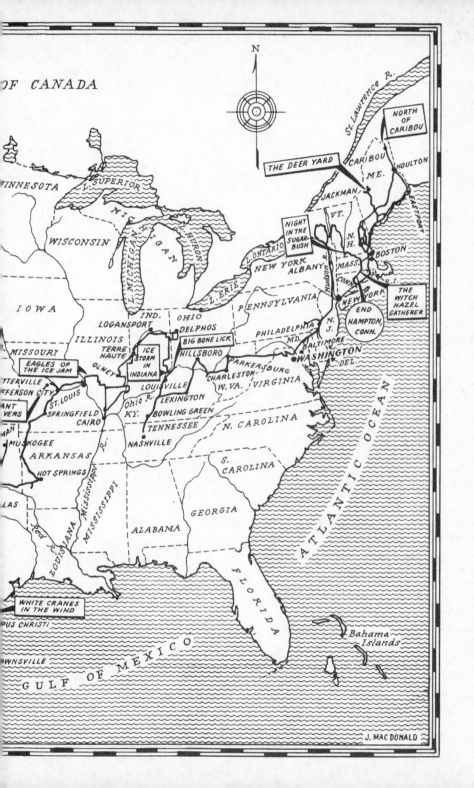

ACKNOWLEDGMENTS

ON a summer day, more than twenty years ago, I set down on a sheet of yellow paper a plan for following the spring north, keeping pace with its fifteen-mile-a-day progress up the map from lower Florida to Canada. Four years went by before, in 1947, this dreamed-of journey could be realized and another four years passed before the book, *North With the Spring*, appeared in 1951. The following year, 1952, we crossed the continent through autumn; in 1957 we journeyed into summer; during the winter of 1961–1962 we traveled from coast to coast through the fourth and final season.

Autumn Across America was issued in 1956, *Journey into Summer* in 1960, and now, in 1965, more than two decades after this survey of the natural history of the American seasons began, I bring it to a close with the publication of *Wandering Through Winter*.

During this time, including return trips to portions of our routes for checking facts or obtaining additional information, we have traveled well over 100,000 miles by automobile, airplane, ferry, mudboat, snow Weasel, scout car, Jeep, cog railway, canoe, on foot and on snowshoes. Counting our return from California at the end of the autumn trip, when we followed the same general route east, the total distance traveled through winter exceeds 35,000 miles.

Everywhere we went during this adventure with a season we accumulated a debt of gratitude to those who, from coast to coast, assisted us in innumerable ways. For such help I am under obligation to:

Mrs. I. D. Acord, Dean Amadon, Charles M. Bogert, Sharon Brown, John Bull, William Bullard, Lee and Ida Cantwell, Ralph Chapman, Mrs. Kennedy N. Clapp, Howard P. Clemens, Roland Clement, Clarence Cottam, John Cronan, Allan and Helen Cruickshank, Marvin Davis, Wendell and Alison Davis, Henry Duquette, Loren Eiseley, William Fitzgerald, Robert Garrett, Raymond M. Gilmore, Stanislaw Gula, Connie Hagar, Walter Harding, Mrs. Everett Harlow, William Harrison, Merton E. Hinshaw, Gregory Hitchcock, Homer Hoffman, Edmund C. Jaeger, Pauline James, Riley and Bonnie Kaufman, Don Greame Kelley, John and Margaret Kieran, Edgar Kincaid, Alexander B. Klots, Joseph Wood Krutch, Richard and Ruth Launer, George W. Leetch, Ruth Lengelsen, Tilford McAllister, Rowland R. McElvare, Sibyl Means, Howard A. Millar, Henry Scott Miller, Mike Milonski, Charles E. Mohr, Ann Haven Morgan, Henry Mullins, John Murphree, Philip B. Myers, James Neal, Josephine Newman, J. d'Arcy Northwood, Harry C. Oberholser, Leslie and Dorotha Peltier, Richard H. Pough, Roger Tory Peterson, James Pickering, George Ranney, Harold W. Rickett, Herbert Ruckes, C. Bertrand Schultz, Harry and Ann Sopp, Hal Sorter, Edson and Isabel Stocking, Warren Stone, Edwin Sutton, George Miksch Sutton, Thomas Tippit, Hobart Van Deusen, John Wanamaker, Farida A. Wiley, Warren Winslow.

I am especially indebted to William Fitzgerald, Edmund C. Jaeger, J. d'Arcy Northwood and Leslie Peltier for reading chapters in manuscript form and to Harry Sopp for his help in arranging our Weasel ride to the deer yard in Maine. Benjamin T. Richards, who showed us the Great Smokies in the spring, has again, as in previous volumes, been of invaluable assistance in copy-editing the manuscript and reading galleys and page-proofs.

Portions of Chapter Twenty originally appeared in *The Atlantic*. Prior to book publication, Chapter Fifteen and Chapter Twenty-Four appeared in *Audubon Magazine* and Chapter Four in *Natural History*. To the editors of these publications I wish to express my thanks for permission to include the material in the present volume.

Nellie, my wife, not only accompanied me on the trip but accompanied me in re-living the journey while writing the book, reading the chapters a number of times as they evolved from the mass of fieldnotes and reminiscences. In both these journeys her help has been inestimable.

For more than a quarter of a century, as book has followed book, I have been well aware of my indebtedness to members of the Dodd, Mead staff for their valued contributions to editing and publishing the successive volumes. My grateful acknowledgment is particularly due to Edward H. Dodd, Jr., Raymond T. Bond, S. Phelps Platt, Jr., John Blair, Helen M. Winfield and Mary McPartland.

Trail Wood
May 1, 1965
EDWIN WAY TEALE

INTRODUCTION

---

*E*DWIN Way Teale sits in the stern of the canoe, paddle hooked under the thwart in front of him. A small spiral notebook rests on his right knee, stubby pencil in hand, recording the immediate details of what he has just seen in a few words, or perhaps noting something to look up, or even jotting down a philosophical comment on the beauty he sees but, always, catching the freshness of the moment. This picture is indelible for me not only because I saw him so often in this pose when we worked together on a book about the Assabet and Sudbury rivers in Massachusetts, but because it catches the quintessence of Teale as the ultimate meticulous nature writer.

Edwin Way Teale's shirt pocket notebook was always with him, a lifelong habit that turned trips anywhere into vivid and lively accounts. When he translated his notes into finished text, he fretted about the "bridges" needed to join disparate passages. It was that concern for smooth reading that gave his writing such a seamless, deceptively effortless quality and allowed his words to fall with great calmness on the page.

Dr. Teale left assignment magazine writing in October 1941 to become what he had set his heart on, a nature writer, and forever after celebrated his "freedom day." He had prepared for a career in nature writing for years, neatly and methodically as he did almost everything in his life. As an uncommonly good black-and-white photographer, he made the lens an extension of his learning. He began by writing about the world close by, and widened his horizons through the years, culminating in the four books in which he followed the seasons throughout the United States.

Although the first Earth Day in 1970 came eleven years before Dr. Teale's death, his writing never left the center of the pure nature writing tradition. Although he was an ardent champion to Rachel Carson's *Silent Spring* and was deeply disturbed by the damage he saw being done to the environment, his books never became "environmental writing." During his forty-year career of writing and editing more than thirty volumes, all embellished with his fresh insights and lucid prose, he won both the John Burroughs Award and, for *Wandering through Winter,* a Pulitzer Prize in 1966, the first in more than fifty years given to a nature book.

His books on the seasons are as expansive in design and character as Edwin Way Teale was. He always saw them as a whole, and that is how they read, despite the years between their publication: spring, 1951, summer, 1960, autumn, 1956, and winter, 1965. His delightful and beloved Nellie accompanied him on all these trips through "the great days of our lives," and all four books are dedicated to "DAVID, Who Traveled with Us in Our Hearts," their only son, who was lost in World War II.

The itineraries for each trip were thoroughly organized through months of extensive and meticulous research of who and what to see where and when, yet he was always able to take advantage of the unexpected adventure. He kept notes of every single travel day and transcribed them on a portable typewriter at night, turning skeletal observations into sentences and paragraphs of near-perfect prose. At the end of each book he had the typescript pages bound into volumes that now reside at the Rare Books Room in the Library of the University of Connecticut. They are voluminous, Herculean accomplishments of devotion and self-discipline; they have to be leafed through to understand the care and attention to detail that went into them, and the sheer labor, all accomplished while driving about 17,000 miles per book.

We find reassurance as well as pleasure in reading these books today, for Teale's values are rooted in the natural world. He writes of green leaves and clear summer skies over the lakes of Minnesota, of the glossy ibis and a spring sunset over Lake Okeechobee, of an ice storm in Indiana and a flooding Ohio River, of a luminous larva on a barrier beach and fireflies lighting the dusk, of harvester ants foraging on the Little Bighorn battlefield in Montana.

The seasons herein are not only those of the countryside, but seasons of the heart. We reap a pleasure in the reading from a goodness of the heart, a keenness of the mind, and an excellence of the writing.

—Ann Haymond Zwinger
Colorado Springs, Colorado

CONTENTS

bird—Our day of eagles—Keenness of avian vision—
The rare tree sparrow—Ice cakes—Ducks and eagles
—Virgin prairie—"The Bird of Washington"—Eagle
with a silver bracelet—The hanging valley—Path of
the eagles—The years of persecution—Tumbling
through the air—The weight of feathers—Eagle
fever—The last silhouette.

rows on the heath—The closeness of ancient men—
Our highway disappears—The Ohio in flood—Detours
—The flood gates—Rock slides—Hill country in flood
time—Wolf Summit—Molehill into Mountain—Parade of the telephone trucks—We tear another sheet
from the calendar.

survivor—Alexander Kathan's almanacs—Boiling sap
—A craving for sour foods—Sugar sand—A traveler's
misconception—The taste of buds—First run sap—
Cinderella Boots—Sign of the moth millers.

Scent and memory—The dusty weeds—Smell and
emotions—The scent of coal smoke—A memory of
the Hall of Fame—The evocative scents of winter—
Rainbows on muddy spray—Witch-hazel factory—An
Indian lotion—Brushmen—The witch-hazel gatherer—
Crooked growth—A botanical individualist—The last
flower of the year—Projectile seeds—An inquisitive
fox—Deer and dogs—Snow fleas—Winter buds—
"Thoughts for the morrow."

Ancient wildness—Work of the glaciers—Pussywillows
—Holly berries—The artificial vine—Primitive cat-tail
—Cat-tails as food—Cocoons and woodpeckers—A mu-
sical mouse—Mice in birdhouses—Benefits of cold—
Blue shadows—Beauty of the Maine winter—Snowshoe
maker—Trapper's cabin—The green trees of winter—
Red Paint People—The Forty-Mile Woods—Moose
River.

The Weasel—Across the forest drifts—Burnt Jacket
Mountain—Meal at a lumber camp—How Slidedown
Mountain got its name—Pressure of ice—Snowshoe
hare—Wildcat crossings—The great revealer—Deer
yard—Mechanical sounds and deer—Snowshoes in the
forest—Deer-yard trails—The browse line—Squeaking
snow—The pileated woodpecker—Rising wind—The
sunning deer.

The long shoreline—An unusual naturalist—On being
alone—Irish moss—An old New England custom—
Fragments of conversation—The soaring eagle—Meddybemps—Butterfly lighthouse—Lincoln of Lincoln's
sparrow—Eastport—The greater tides—Birds in a winter gale—The cautious Down-Easter—"Fowle of divers
kinds"—Blue pools—Effects of temperature—The one-
tree orchard—Red snowshoes—Maine's potato empire—The final miles to Caribou.

CONTENTS

ILLUSTRATIONS

WANDERING THROUGH WINTER

ONE

THE SILVER STRAND

IN THE far southwestern corner of mainland America, where California joins Mexico and the land meets the sea, we watched the shortest day of the year come to an end. Lazy swells, silky smooth, drifted in from the open Pacific. Across the sheen of the wet tide line, behind each retreating wave, running sandpipers imprinted the winding ribbons of their bill marks. The air was rich with the tang of salt and seaweed.

Away to the north, off to the south, extended the Silver Strand, that narrow barrier against the sea that forms the western boundary of San Diego Bay. Here, walking in the sunset, Nellie and I saw for the only time in our lives that rare phenomenon known to the ancients as "living light" or "the green flash." Out where the sun had met the level horizon line of the sea, the brilliance of its light contracted like the expiring image on a television screen. It concentrated, through abnormal conditions of refraction, into a sudden flaring spot of the intensest emerald green. Then it was gone. With that fleeting apparition, once considered a lucky omen, our long adventure with the winter began.

Nearly ten years before, my wife and I had stood on the towering headland of Point Reyes, north of San Francisco, and watched the final sundown of autumn. Now, on this same coast, hundreds of miles to the south, we were taking up for a last time the thread of our seasonal wanderings. More than twenty years—a good part of a lifetime—had gone into that naturalist's dream, our grand project of following all the four seasons across the face of America. We had come *North With the Spring*, keeping pace with its advance from the tip of Florida to the Canadian line. We had wandered through the north woods, over the Great Plains and among the Rockies on a *Journey Into Summer*. We had spanned the continent, from Cape Cod to Point Reyes, traveling through *Autumn Across America*. Now, in another continent-wide sweep, the fourth and final season stretched before us.

To meet the spring, we had driven from Long Island down the Atlantic Coast to lower Florida. To keep this rendezvous with winter's beginning, we had ridden from coast to coast. On Thanksgiving morning, when snow was falling, we had locked the door of our home in the hill country of northeastern Connecticut, near the village of Hampton, and had headed west. When we would turn that lock again, the season would be spring.

Darkness comes swiftly in the Long Night Moon of December. At the end of this twenty-first day of the month, this shortest day of the year, this time when, in other ages, men lit bonfires to strengthen the expiring sun, the Silver Strand faded rapidly from sight. Picture yourself standing with us in the gathering dusk. The evening mist increases. The low rumor of waves sweeping across sand is in our ears. My wrist watch ticks on. Its hands touch 6:20 P.M. The year has reached the instant of the winter solstice. In that moment, the northern hemisphere leans farthest away from the sun. A season dies; a season is born. We took one breath in autumn, the next in winter.

As we climbed into our white car, where the trunk and rear seat were crammed with cameras and binoculars and field guides and jackets and snowshoes, where maps had been laid out in zones across the continent, we looked inland from the sea. Before us stretched all the unguessed experiences of 20,000 miles of wanderings. A new season extended away untouched, a book of blank pages, to be filled with the events of successive days. The zigzag of our eastward path would carry us from this far southwestern corner of the land to the far northeastern corner, above Caribou, in Maine. It would complete that web of trails that our passage through the four seasons was tracing on the map.

Traveling east through lengthening days, we would experience all the wild diversity that comprises the North American winter. There are seasons within seasons. Winter is a hundred seasons in one. We would observe it in the desert, in the mountains, on the plains, along the Gulf Coast, in the north woods. We would see it in a land of kit foxes and green jays, white squirrels and giant beavers. And for me the wandering freedom that lay ahead took on added appeal because it would be shared by the finest of all companions for any season of the year.

Dorothy Wordsworth, in October 1802, wrote in her journal: "It is a pleasure to the real lover of Nature to give winter all the glory he can, for summer *will* make its own way, and speak its own praises." Of the four seasons, spring entices, summer makes you welcome, autumn gives you a lingering farewell, but winter remains aloof. We think of it as harsh and uncompromising. We speak of the dead months, the night of the year, the return of the ice age, the *winter* of our discontent.

Yet, paradoxically, in its own way, winter is a time of superlative life. Frosty air sets our blood to racing. The nip of the wind quickens our step. Creatures abroad at this season of the year live intensely, stimulated by cold, using all their powers, all their capacities, to survive. Gone is the languor of August heat waves. Winter provides the testing months, the time of fortitude and courage. For innumerable seeds and insect eggs, this period of cold is essential to sprouting or hatching. For trees, winter is a time of rest. It is also a season of hope. The days are lengthening. The sun is returning. The whole year is beginning. All nature, with bud and seed and egg, looks forward with optimism.

Alone among the seasons, winter extends across the boundary line into two calendars. It is the double season. We meet it twice in each twelve months. It embraces the end and the beginning of the year. It includes the great holiday times of Christmas and New Year's. Alone among the seasons it retains its original Anglo-Saxon spelling. Spring began as *springen*, literally "to spring" as the grass springs up; summer as *sumer*; and fall as *feallan*, referring to the falling leaves. But winter was always *winter*.

This fourth season of the year, this final act in the "eternal drama," this time when nights are longer than days, this season means many things in many places. In the California deserts, it means more rainfall. In the high Rockies, it means blizzards. In New England, it means skating and skiing. It means toboggan rides and hockey games and fishing through the ice. It means the beauty of snowflakes and trees mantled in white.

Here, in the region of the Silver Strand, it has another meaning. Here it signifies the beginning of a unique sport, the sport of whale-watching. Down from the Bering Sea, swimming on a migration equivalent to a quarter of the way around the globe, gray whales begin passing along the coast during the earliest days of the new season. Before we turned inland toward the east, Nellie and I rode out to join these migrants in our first adventure of the winter.

TWO

GRAY WHALES

TENSELY we waited. Sunshine glittered on the waves around us. Heermann's gulls, black of tail and white of head and brilliant red of bill, slanted by. Hardly 150 feet from the boat's rail against which we leaned, the water suddenly paled to a light green. It grew more gray. With a rush and a long, audible "swoosh" of pent-up air, a forty-foot whale shouldered up out of the sea into the sunshine.

Thirty-five cubic feet of air—a single exhalation greater than that expelled by 1,000 men in normal breathing—rushed from twin nostrils on the top of its head. Coming warm and moist from the lungs of the ocean mammal, it condensed in the cooler atmosphere. A fountain of mist shot upward. It hung in the air, drifted aside, slowly dissolved. Three times the gray whale emptied and filled its lungs. Then it submerged. The water closed over it, and only a widening slick marked the spot where it had so suddenly materialized. I found I had been holding my breath. I let it out and inhaled deeply.

We were just north of the Silver Strand, a mile or more at sea. Our guide, Dr. Raymond M. Gilmore, had spent more time studying gray whales than any other scientist on earth. Season after season, while biologist for the U.S. Fish and Wildlife Service, he had followed the whales south and observed them on their ancient wintering grounds along the coast of Baja California. With us, also, were Don Greame

Kelly and his wife, Marion, who had shared our last full day of autumn at Point Reyes, and Merton E. Hinshaw, who had shown us white-tailed kites along the Salinas River and sea otters in the surf below a headland south of Carmel. These three had been part of the ending of autumn. Now, years later, coming south for a short reunion, they were part of the beginning of winter.

From La Jolla to the Silver Strand, we cruised along the highway of the journeying whales. We would pick up one migrant and follow it south, then turn north and repeat the process. Thus we traveled with them on a short segment of their long descent from the Arctic. On one occasion, we saw mist fountains rising ten or fifteen feet into the air above three whales that had surfaced at the same time. As a rule, the travelers are not gregarious going south. Most migrate singly. But once, for miles, we kept pace with two that swam side by side, rhythmically diving and reappearing together. Each submergence lasted almost exactly seven minutes. A gray whale spends about eighty-five per cent of its time under water. Usually, each dive lasts between three and seven minutes. Sometimes, but only rarely, a particular whale will remain submerged for ten minutes. Of all the thousands of descents Gilmore has timed, the record stands at twelve minutes and forty seconds.

Each time we fell in line beside a new whale, Gilmore would flick on his stop watch. Different whales have different rhythms in their breathing. Once he has clocked its underwater period, he can tell almost precisely when a given whale will reappear. To avoid alarming our quarry by changes in the sound of the engine, the speed of our boat was kept uniform. While the whale was submerged, we used up excess speed by swinging wide or advancing in a letter S or even doubling back in a figure 8. Then, when the stop watch indicated that the time for surfacing was near, we pulled back into position. Several times, we were hardly more than a boat's length away when the leviathan rose among the waves.

Our first glimpse of a gray whale had come in that previous winter when, at the end of our autumn trip, we had followed the California coast south into the misty redwoods of the Big Sur, among citrus groves yellow with lemons, through miles of nodding oil-well pumps at Signal Hill and past eucalyptus trees and poinsettia fields running in great splashes of color to the brown base of the coastal mountains. Off the harbor at La Jolla, our glasses had picked up a tiny fountain of mist shining in the morning sun. For a moment, far off, we saw the gleaming curve of a mottled body. On that day, the migrants had been remote. Their huge forms had been made tiny by distance. Now we saw them immense, close up. We rode in the very midst of the whale migration.

Like the sea otters that Hinshaw had pointed out among the kelp beds of the northern coast, the gray whales were making a dramatic comeback from the edge of extinction. Hardly more than a quarter of a century before, they had seemed close to the point of no return. Along this same California coast, in the 1840's, there had moved an armada of migrating whales estimated to have been between 25,000 and 50,000 strong. Each year—then, as now—the great mammals swim as much as 14,000 miles on a round-trip migration between the Bering Sea and the warm coastal bays where they winter and breed and bear their calves.

Gold brought the forty-niners to California. The next year, in 1850, the state was admitted to the Union. Around the Horn sailed a parade of whaling ships. Lookout stations rose on all the headlands down the coast. The migrants were hunted going south and going north. The relentless pursuit went on while their numbers dwindled. Then a fresh calamity overtook the persecuted migrants.

On an evil day for the whales, a Yankee whaling captain, Charles M. Scammon, discovered what is now known as Scammon's Lagoon. As his ship sailed down the coast of Baja

California, sometime in the 1850's, a lookout sighted the impossible—whales spouting on land. The columns of vapor appeared to be rising in the midst of sandhills. Investigating, Scammon came upon a hidden inlet. It led him to a wide saltwater lagoon swarming with gray whales. This was one of the chief goals of the southward-moving migrants.

For a time, Scammon's discovery was kept secret. Then other captains learned of his whale-oil bonanza. There followed a period of butchery unequalled except among the bison herds of the Great Plains. The bay became a vast slaughterhouse. Trapped within its confines, the maddened whales, swimming through water stained with blood, attacked and smashed small boats on sight. Normally peaceful and unaggressive, they became known to their persecutors as "devil fish."

In less than a decade, the gray whale became so scarce along the West Coast that hunting it was no longer profitable. The lookout towers stood abandoned. The ships sailed away. The vast armada of whales seemed gone forever. Many people believed the sea mammals had been entirely exterminated. But gradually the whales drew back from the brink of complete destruction. Slowly their numbers increased. Then, in the 1920's and 1930's, they were overwhelmed by a second massacre. A new breed of whalers, using factory ships, harpoon cannon and high-speed pursuit boats, roamed the seas. In Scammon's Lagoon, winter after winter, they fell upon the gray whales. When the killing ended, the species once more was so reduced in numbers that there appeared little hope for its recovery. Another chapter seemed to have been written in the long record of public loss for private gain.

On the other side of the Pacific, a second herd of gray whales, never mingling with the North American migrants and following the coast of Asia, had met a similar fate. So things stood in 1938. In that year, an international treaty, signed by Canada, Mexico, the Soviet Union and the United

States, outlawed the killing of the gray whale. The hard-pressed sea migrants at last received protection. But had it come too late?

Happily the answer is no. On this day when, in the winter sunshine, we rode beyond the kelp beds of the coastal shallows, along the ancient ocean highway of the whales, Gilmore estimated that 6,000 migrants now pass the Silver Strand each year. It is his belief that their numbers will rise to about 15,000 before they level off. In the region of San Diego, one of the few indications that winter has come is the arrival of the barnacle-encrusted travelers. Whale-watching is the sport that ushers in the season.

We had just passed through an area where lobster pots were sunk to a depth of 150 feet and had watched our wake set the red, black and yellow marking buoys bobbing, when an old-timer among the whales broke the surface a few hundred feet away. We moved along the rail for a better view. Its head was white with encrusting barnacles. Even its flukes were patched and mottled with these marine crustaceans. It is the barnacle, in fact, that is largely responsible for the gray whale being called gray. Actually, its skin is dark, sometimes almost black. But it is dappled with unpigmented areas and patches of white barnacles. The latter increase with age. The older the swimmer, the more it resembles Moby Dick.

When it has reached its full growth, a gray whale may weigh more than thirty tons and have a length of forty-five feet. It is a baleen whale, a member of the group that includes the 100-foot blue whale, the largest animal, past or present, known to man. I asked Dr. Gilmore about the gray whale's life span. At one time, this was believed to be a century. Now, the maximum is thought to be between thirty and forty years. As we watched, through our binoculars, the old whale rhythmically appearing and disappearing, we noticed that a great nick had been cut from one of its flukes. These fleshy tail fins have a span of ten or twelve feet and may weigh 400 pounds. Gilmore told me of one whale he encountered that had lost almost half of one fluke. It was swimming along with no apparent trouble. He pointed out the row of bumps running along the back toward the flukes. These knobs or knuckles vary with individuals. They may provide the sea mammals with a means of recognition. For among the questions that still puzzle scientists are: How do whales keep together? How do they find one another? How do they communicate? The animals have no vocal cords. Yet naval technicians have recorded various sounds made by whales while swimming under water. One resembled the noise produced by a child beating with a tin cup on a table.

On one occasion, a whale emerged so close to our boat that we seemed to be looking down on its back. The mammal became uneasy. The next time it rose, it resorted to what is known as evasive swimming. No longer did it break the surface with a rush. No longer did it send up a high fountain of mist into the air. It remained mostly submerged and breathed out slowly. Only a telltale slick on the surface of the sea showed where it had come up for air.

When a whale is really alarmed, it sounds, plunging deeply and often veering off its course. We witnessed this awesome sight once when a small speedboat charged in, with a sudden roaring of its engine, to let one of its passengers try for a close-up snapshot. The whale sounded. All around it, the water foamed and boiled as it tilted steeply downward. Its immense flukes lifted high in the air, carrying aloft masses of seaweed. Water streamed away in cascades. The sun played across it as across a series of waterfalls. Then the whale was gone, and swirling foam and a widening whirlpool remained. The overwhelming impression of drive and bulk and power is still vivid in our minds.

Between whales, we reminisced about the autumn days and watched the sea birds. Once Don Kelly noticed an airy

SPLIT MOUNTAIN in the Anza-Borrego Desert of California is divided by this dramatic chasm nearly three miles long.

SLENDER trunks and bunched treetop foliage characterize
the eucalyptus introduced from Australia into California.

arctic tern dancing in the uneven air. Another time, a gray, gull-size bird new to our experience, a tube-nosed fulmar, swung from side to side as it soared for several miles in our wake. Through our glasses, we watched it scale away toward the open sea. Then whale excitement returned. We swung south again and fell in beside what appeared to be a tiring migrant.

It was nearing the end of an immense journey, 6,000 or 7,000 miles long, a journey that consumes between three and a half and four months. During all this time, the gray whale apparently never stops to eat, and sleeps no more than four hours out of the twenty-four. At times when the moon is full, the whales swim night and day without halting. For some reason still uncertain, a migration will occasionally dam up farther north and then suddenly release a wave of whales. At such times, a hundred may plow past Point Loma and the Silver Strand in the course of a single day.

Looking toward the slant of the sun, we watched the ponderous body of the weary migrant appearing and disappearing in the midst of glittering wavelets. The maximum speed of the gray whale is ten knots. Its usual cruising speed during migration is four. This individual was hardly making two. Perhaps it was heavy with young. For the vanguard of the migration, reaching the San Diego region in the first days of winter, between the twenty-second and the twenty-seventh of December, is always made up of females. Larger than the males, they breed on the wintering ground every two years. Gestation takes almost a year. About half the females that return to Baja California bear their calves soon after their arrival. At birth, the baby whale may weigh 3,000 pounds and measure seventeen feet in length. It grows rapidly on the rich milk its mother supplies. By as early as February, it is ready to start the long migration northward to the Bering Sea.

Going north and coming south, along the ancestral sea lanes of their kind, the whales apparently make use of the contours of the ocean bed to guide them. They may also employ landmarks such as high headlands along the coast. Their eyesight is excellent. On occasions, Dr. Gilmore has seen these immense mammals hurling themselves straight up, towering twenty feet in the air, momentarily standing on their tails, while they reconnoitered their surroundings.

Before our boat turned toward home that day, and we said good-bye to our friends, Nellie and I were training our glasses on the very spot where the last whale we saw broke the surface. To our magnified vision, the water cascading over its barnacle-splotched head appeared but an arm's length away. Its eye—which alternately meets the watery dimness of the depths and the glare of the open sunshine—seemed staring directly into mine. We looked at each other across a couple of hundred feet of tumbling water and across immeasurable gulfs of evolutionary time. How far back it was that our mammalian ancestors had taken different roads! How unfathomable was the chasm that separated our ways of life! For this great creature that looked at me while I looked at it, what was existence like? This insatiable desire to be inside other forms of life, to see the things that I see with their eyes and their minds—this is a thread that has run through all our seasonal wanderings. A thousand reincarnations, each as a different form of life, would be too few to satisfy this curiosity. Thoreau understood it when he wrote of the calling of the Concord frogs:

"So the frogs dream, would that I knew what!"

That night we slept for a last time beside the Pacific. We had known it in two seasons. We had followed its twisting coast from Neah Bay at the northwest tip of Washington to Imperial Beach near the Mexican border. We had seen its rain forests and its redwoods, its tide pools and its butterfly trees, its otter surf and its gray whales. Early the next morning, we turned inland. Once more, as amid the goldenrod of Monomoy at the start of the autumn trip, the width of the continent lay before us. Now we were spanning it in the opposite direction, by a new trail and in a new season. Henceforth, no matter how our route wound or twisted or zigzagged to this side or that, our course was set toward the east. It was set toward another ocean—a winter away.

THREE

SPLIT MOUNTAIN

FROM the sea to the desert, from gray whales to elephant trees, from The Silver Strand to Split Mountain and the Mud Hills, to ocotillo and circus beetle and desert shrimp and Christmas dawn at Yaqui Well—so our eastward trail commenced.

We left the overpopulated highways of the coast. We climbed, first through citrus groves, then through rangeland, then up valleys rich in live oaks. We came out among the ponderosa pines of the high country. Beyond we descended into a different world. Less than 100 miles from the ocean, we dropped behind the wall of the coastal range, down the dry side of the mountains. The desert spread away before us.

To one accustomed to the comfortable, companionable, green-clad hills of the East, the desert, at first meeting, appears unfriendly and forbidding. It is stark and harsh. The land seems lifeless. Its arid mountains resemble the slag heaps of creation. You feel a long way from home. Such was our first impression.

But the desert country, we realized, is not known in a day and a night. It makes no concessions. You approach it on its own terms. It possesses a kind of reticence that only long acquaintance overcomes. Yet, for us, as the initial strangeness wore off, as we felt more at ease, it became comparable to some person we greatly desired to know intimately. With increasing frequency, as we looked about us amid its far-

spreading expanses, the thought of Shakespeare's King John
came to mind:

"Ay, marry, now my soul hath elbow-room."

In a swing to the east and north and west and south again,
our route tracing a rough rectangle, we roamed across what
Mary Austin called "The Land of Little Rain." We crossed
the irrigated Imperial Valley, dipped below sea level near
El Centro and traveled east close to the Mexican line. West
of Yuma, we found ourselves among billowing dunes that
extended away in flowing lines. Although we had never visited
the spot, we had seen those dunes before. For this is the
Sahara of Hollywood movies. A lonely road beyond the Arizona line, a road with one filling station in seventy-five miles,
led us north to Quartzsite. Then west again, across the Colorado Desert where, as late as 1890, travelers sometimes encountered camels roaming wild.

When we reached Mecca and Coachella and Indio, north
of the Salton Sea, we were in a different kind of desert. Here,
where the year is usually without frost, where the annual
growing season is almost 365 days long, where irrigation
ditches supply ample moisture, we were among cultivated
fields and groves and vineyards. Date palms ran for miles
beside the road. Fresh dates, date crystals, date butter, date
ice cream were for sale. Nellie restrained herself. But I was
carried away. I topped off lunch with a super-rich date chocolate malted milk.

The night before, rain had fallen. What could be more
welcome in the desert? The answer appeared to be: almost
anything—at least in this region. Here moisture is under
strict control. Specialized watering is adapted to specialized
crops. Instead of rejoicing in rain, the people I talked to
seemed to wish nature would mind its own business and quit
interfering with their well-laid plans.

All the desert towns we came to, those days, were gay with
lights and decorations. Christmas was almost here. Winter's

great holiday season was at hand. Shoppers crowded the stores. Strangers wished us merry Christmas. On our way to circle the Salton Sea, we pulled into a filling station bedecked with red and green and white. As he pumped fuel into our tank, the owner remarked:

"To me, Christmas decorations mean that spring is just around the corner."

For wildflowers begin blooming in February in the vicinity of this strange sea below the level of the sea. Thirty miles long and between eight and fourteen miles wide, a lake without an inlet or an outlet, it was created between 1905 and 1907 when rampaging waters from the Colorado River poured into the lowland of the Salton Trough. Along the roads following its shore, we watched black phoebes and Say's phoebes hawking for insects nearly 200 feet below sea level.

When we turned west again it was toward California's vast, protected desert wilderness, the largest state park in America, Anza-Borrego. We climbed to 100 feet below sea level, then to sea level, then, in the Borrego Valley, to more than 400 feet above sea level. Up to now, we had experienced the desert in general. We had seen its width. Now we would see it in greater detail, observe it in depth, change from the wide-angle view to the close-up.

That close-up began at dawn the next day. With Jim Neal, headquarters ranger, we climbed into an International Harvester Scout car. Thirty miles to the south, we joined outpost ranger George W. Leetch and his wife, Dorothy, for a day-before-Christmas roaming along dry washes through a desert region that appeared little changed since the stagecoaches of the Butterfield Overland Mail crossed it. We met no one. We saw no signs of anyone. We had the whole desert to ourselves.

In the first sunshine of that morning, we clambered over boulders out of a sandy wash to visit one of the rarest of American trees. With silvery bark, contorted branches and swollen lower trunks, elephant trees, *Bursera microphylla*, lifted above a jumble of rocks. About the time of the Civil War, this tree was first reported from northern Mexico. Half a century later, in 1910, not far from where we stood in the Fish Creek region of the Anza Desert, a western botanist discovered the first specimens growing north of the border. Only here, and in a few remote stands across the line in Arizona, is this desert tree native to the United States. Usually it is rooted among boulders. All the elephant trees growing in the Anza-Borrego Desert State Park are confined to fewer than 1,000 of its 470,000 acres. Exactly how many trees are rooted here nobody knows. No count has ever been made, but estimates run between 500 and 1,000.

When we grasped one of the heavy branches, suggesting an elephant's trunk, it flopped up and down as though made of rubber. Unlike oaks and maples, the elephant tree has neither strong longitudinal fibers nor annual growth rings. The interior of both the branches and the dropsical trunk is corky and filled with resin and latex-like fluid. The sprawling limbs have no set design. Each tree follows its own individual, wayward pattern of growth.

After rains, both in summer and in winter, the elephant tree is clothed with small, multiple, richly green leaves. In winter this paradoxical tree bears its fruit. Around us, on many of the twigs, we saw these winter fruits amid the winter leaves. Only about a quarter of an inch long, they suggest, at first glance, tiny, wine-red figs.

Frankincense, frequently mentioned in the Bible, is obtained from an Old World relative of the elephant tree. This relationship is evident in a pleasing aroma that often surrounds these trees of the California desert. Their sap, their resin, their leaves all are aromatic. On some of the twigs and branches we noted scars. They were left by the knives of thoughtless visitors who had slashed the bark to test an old superstition of the region. This is the belief that from such a gash an elephant tree will bleed white sap on one side and red sap on the other. As a matter of fact, its sap invariably is tinted red. Except for all the innumerable other things to see, we could have spent the better part of our day among these strange, perfumed, red-blooded trees.

Leetch's home, and the headquarters for his outpost patrol that ranges in elevation from 240 to 3,000 feet, is a trailer located close to the mouth of a three-mile chasm. This is Split Mountain, one of the unforgettable landmarks of this desert. The impression is that a whole mountain has split in two, with the halves pulled slightly apart. Geologists believe that this titanic gash, now floored with sand, was created along a fault by ages of running water.

With Leetch's Jeep leading the way, we started through the chasm. Walls of reddish-yellow rock rose out of sight on either hand. On a night when the full moon fills the canyon with silver light, Leetch told us, the walls appear to shine or glow in unearthly beauty. At one time, Fish Creek ran through the canyon. Fish swam here. Now there are no creek, no fish. But when rains fall, the fleeting pools they form often swarm with tiny desert shrimp. These branch-footed crustaceans hatch from hardy eggs that lie dormant in dry ground. We stopped beside one depression about the size of a shallow dishpan. The clay at the bottom was baked and hard. When we bent close, we saw, sprinkled all across it, the minute forms of the short-lived shrimp. I extracted a small magnifying glass from my pocket. Through its lens, the black and desiccated bodies brought to mind miniature trilobites embedded in prehistoric rock.

Where a twist in the gorge brought sunshine streaming in slanting rays down one wall, we noticed dark stains on the cliff side thirty-five or forty feet above us. They followed a crevice that provided a home for bats. It was not far from here, a few years before, that two friends of ours from Hampton, Edson and Isabel Stocking, had come upon the sooty-brown body of a dead mastiff bat. This is North America's largest species. It rides through the air on wings that have an expanse of as much as twenty-one inches.

We advanced slowly down the winding length of the canyon, pausing frequently. Beside the wheel tracks of the primitive road, desert asters rose among the rocks in dry, pale-tan clumps. In one cluster, surrounded by dead stalks, half a dozen strikingly blue, faintly purple flowers still bloomed. This, we were told, was the Jaeger's aster, named for its discoverer, the dean of desert scientists, Dr. Edmund C. Jaeger, of Riverside. I examined it with special interest. It was part of a dramatic double discovery made some years before at Split Mountain.

Different species of the day-flying heliothid moths often are associated with particular species of asters. After he had discovered this new wildflower at Split Mountain, the thought occurred to Dr. Jaeger that this new species of aster might be associated with a new species of moth. An entomologist friend, John Sperry, of Riverside, visited the canyon, caught a moth on a clump of the Jaeger's aster, compared it with described species and found it was unknown to science. The blue flowers we gazed at had even greater interest for me because Dr. Jaeger, a valued friend, had volunteered to take me camping at the scene of another, even more dramatic, discovery he had made among the Chuckwalla Mountains, north and east of the Salton Sea.

No sooner had we emerged from the narrow passage of Split Mountain than we found ourselves among the strangely shaped mounds and all the bizarre formations of the Mud Hills. Their tops seemed to have moved like glaciers and their sides to have slipped downward during periods of rain. The skin of the hills appeared to be sloughing off.

On rainless days the roads of the desert are its dry washes. Like forest streams, they lead the wanderer into new country and bring him home again. For much of this day we followed the winding trail of one dry wash after another. And along their length from time to time we moved among the low clouds of the gray smoke trees. Although they were bare of leaves, their fine, multitudinous twigs, each covered with a dense, feltlike coating of hairs, combined into puffs and plumes that gave them the appearance of being enveloped in delicate masses of foliage. In the case of the smoke tree, *Dalea spinosa*, these thorny twigs take over the function of leaves. Nowhere else in the world except in sandy, rock-strewn desert washes do such trees flourish. They require the tumbling waters and grinding stones of flash floods to groove and weaken their hard seeds and enable them to sprout.

Noon found us near the edge of the Mud Hills. Beside a little slope of sand, we climbed down from the Scout car and Neal produced our lunch. All around us, as we ate, the elongated noontime shadows of the hills and rocks wrote on the desert floor the first definition of winter given by Webster's Dictionary: "The season of the year, in any region, in which the noonday sun shines most obliquely." Here, even the most slanting rays of the sun are hot. From May to September the average daytime temperature in the Anza-Borrego Desert is 112 degrees F. One elderly visitor, who arrived at the park in July, told Leetch as he was leaving:

"Young man, in my opinion, the most interesting thing you can show me in this region is a patch of shade."

Winter or summer, to both Leetch and Neal, the desert is one of the most fascinating places on earth. Leetch had just bought a Scout car of his own to go exploring in his free time. For him, the life of a remote, outpost ranger was the world's prize job. In his movements I noticed a smooth, cat-like speed. At one time he had risen high in the West Coast prize ring. His fighting name, bestowed on him by sports-writers, was "Gentleman George." We found him reflective, interested in books, responsive to the beauty of the desert and with a mind stored with observations and adventures of the past. While we ate he recalled a time when he had ridden

with a Mexican friend in a small boat off the coast of Baja
California. Two killer whales had circled around and around.
His friend sat in the stern with a lighted cigarette in one
hand and a stick of dynamite in the other, ready to ignite the
fuse and toss the explosive overboard if the swimming predators attacked.

We had come to the end of the tuna-fish sandwiches,
cookies and apples Neal had brought along when a movement
on the sand caught my eye. Advancing laboriously over the
bare ground moved a swollen, jet-black beetle. It was an inch
or more in length. Nellie and I bent close to examine it.
Disturbed, it stopped, lifted its body almost vertically in the
air, balanced itself on long, katydid-like hind legs and stood
on its head in the sand. We were seeing the famed circus or
pinacate beetle of the dry Southwest. With its wing covers
fused together, this tenebrionid, *Eloedes armata*, is flightless.
Watching the insect as it remained motionless, minute after
minute, I detected a curious mushroomy smell. To ward off
enemies, this beetle exudes an offensive fluid. I picked it up
and put it near a hole beside a brittlebush. It promptly scrambled inside.

In its way, the desert brittlebush was as interesting as the
desert beetle. I ran my fingers along the gray-green leaves.
They were hairy and insulated against the drying action of
wind and heat. Across the tops of several clumps of this
drought-resistant member of the sunflower family extended
a thin scattering of yellow blooms. In one place, where a
stem was broken, a globule of orange-yellow resin had oozed
from the fracture. Indians used to collect this material, heat
it and smear it on their bodies to relieve pain. They also
chewed it as gum. I tried a little. It had a pleasant, wild taste
and produced a copious flow of saliva. In the early Spanish
missions of the Southwest, this aromatic resin was burned as
incense. When I held a match beneath one fragment, a rich
fragrance rose into the air. For hours after I had handled the

broken stem, my fingers were strongly scented.

Everywhere we went on this day, we had questions and our questions had answers. We encountered other exotic plants—the spiny herb, only an inch or so tall, cactus-like but not a member of the cactus family, an inhabitant of the most dry, cracked and barren portions of the desert; the perfumed desert lavender; the wild apricot, which produces a thin fruit enclosing a huge seed; and the red sand-mat, a relative of the poinsettia which becomes a mass of glittering droplets of collected moisture after a rain. We stopped beside the cat's-claw, whose curved spines give it the nicknames of "tear-blanket" and "wait-a-minute bush." In the spring its branches become festooned with fluffy yellow catkins of flowers that form one of the chief sources of nectar for desert honeybees.

High on the face of a cream-colored cliff in Sandstone Canyon, that afternoon, we saw a colony of these wild bees. An overhang of rock protected their exposed, heart-shaped combs. Some were new and white; others old, discolored, chocolate-brown. For more than thirty-five years this same colony has occupied this identical site. During these winter days the insects were obtaining most of their nectar from the small flowers of the desert lavender.

Exactly where we went, on that day before Christmas, I know but vaguely. I know we crossed the widespread Hapaha Flats. I know we went twisting among boulders down the length of Sandstone Canyon. I know we ascended knife-edged ridges high above a badlands. I remember we looked for fragments of Indian pottery at the site of an old encampment. There was one unnamed hill that Dorothy Leetch, who shares her husband's intense interest in the desert, had christened Yonder Bluff. I remember there was a mountain with a window in it, a hole near the top through which we could see the blue of the sky. And I remember it was already dark—the dark of Christmas Eve—when we got back to the outpost trailer, bid the Leetches good-bye and merry Christmas, and started with Neal on the run north to Borrego Springs.

That night we dined on pepper steaks, in a Quonset hut, at a Chinese-American restaurant called The Bean Bandit. As we rode back to our motel, past colored Christmas lights strung on living wands of ocotillo, we recalled the many people we had met on our trails through the preceding seasons. We wondered where they were and what they were doing as this night before Christmas fell all across the land. We went early to bed on this holiday night. For Christmas morning was to be unlike any we had ever known.

It began with a blue mirage. We were away at sunrise, driving south, then west to Yaqui Well. Looking east toward the Salton Sea, across the California Painted Desert, we became aware of what appeared to be a range of distant mountains, bluish and banded. As we watched, they altered shape. The higher peaks became lower. The skyline changed. At times, we seemed to see trees and buildings, all vague and wavering, as though glimpsed through blue water. By the time we turned away, the long mirage had begun to dissolve into vertical bands of lighter and darker blue.

Beyond Yaqui Pass and Tamarisk Grove, before we came to Grapevine Canyon, near the far western boundary of the park, we turned aside on a rocky spur. When we stopped, we were in the midst of a cluster of ironwood trees shaggy with mistletoe. Cupped in its little valley, the oasis of Yaqui Well lay in shadow. Far above us we saw the earliest sunshine of Christmas day flooding across the brown, boulder-strewn slopes of mountains. Slowly it crept downward. It touched the tops of the ironwoods. Then it filled the little valley. It lighted the mistletoe that hung from the trees like thick ornamented draperies, adorned from top to bottom with the tiny globes of the rich, red fruit.

This particular species, *Phoradendron californica*, produces berries that range from white through pink to red. Here all were red. On ironwood, this desert semi-parasite oftentimes produces swellings and deformities of the trunk and branches. Although it manufactures its own food, it drains water and obtains minerals from its host and, in time, may cause its death.

Through a long succession of centuries, from the time when the ancient Druids sought mistletoe on the sixth night after the full moon, this semi-parasitic plant has been linked with witchcraft and primitive religion. In Scandinavia, uncounted generations of men kindled "Balder's balefires" on hilltops at Midsummer's Eve in remembrance of the good and beautiful Norse god Balder, who, according to the prose *Edda*, met his death through the malign magic of mistletoe. It was the mistletoe that provided Sir James G. Frazer with the title for his classic study of primitive religious beliefs, *The Golden Bough*.

As we walked among the hanging curtains of this plant, I picked off one of the berries and squeezed it between my thumb and forefinger. When I tried to flip the seed away, it stuck tight. I scraped it off with the forefinger of my other hand. It then glued itself to that. I tried to snap it away with a thumbnail. It fastened itself to the nail. This game went on for minutes before I was able to free myself of the seed. One of nature's most effective adhesives is the pulp of the mistletoe berry. The continuation of the species, to a considerable extent, depends upon it. Where it cements a seed to a twig or branch, the pulp dries, the glue hardens, and rarely is the seed dislodged. It germinates there. A small sucker pushes inward among the fibers of the host and the life of a new mistletoe begins. Birds are the chief distributing agency of the seeds. Wiping their bills on branches, after feeding on the fruit, they leave the seeds solidly cemented in place.

And birds were everywhere around us in the desert chill of that Christmas dawn. At Yaqui Well, weed seeds are plentiful and the juicy fruit of the mistletoe provides fluid as well as food. Robins, mockingbirds, linnets, California thrashers, blue-gray gnatcatchers, white-crowned sparrows flitted among the bushes or dashed from tree to tree. We watched an Anna's hummingbird hover before the red flowers of a chuparosa. And out from a mass of mistletoe darted a gray-bodied, yellow-headed little beauty, a verdin. Mourning doves cut by, flying straight and swift. In early times, the dawn and evening movements of these birds led pioneers to desert water holes. Once we looked up and saw, no more than fifty feet away, twenty valley quail, with forward-nodding plumes, sunning themselves among low bushes. One Christmas gift of this oasis was a new bird, clad in grays and browns, with a dark "stickpin" spot on its breast, our first sage sparrow.

But the bird most in evidence that day was one whose staple food is mistletoe berries, one that frequently nests in mistletoe, one so often associated with this plant it might be called The Mistletoe Bird. This is the silky flvcatcher or phainopepla, *Phainopepla nitens*. Like the wood stork, it is the only representative of its family in North America.

One peculiarity of the species is the fact that the male does most of the work of nest-building and much of the incubation. We saw the males, crested, glossy black with white wing patches, and the grayer females, appearing and disappearing among the trees in easy, butterfly-like flight. Their plumage shone with a satiny sheen. Throughout the deserts of the Southwest, whenever we encountered concentrations of mistletoe, we looked for and almost always found the phainopepla.

Several times, as we followed sandy trails under the iron-wood trees, we came upon empty snail shells, pure white, weathered, frail and almost translucent. And in every open space, dense stands of the shadscale or saltbush, *Atriplex*, lifted masses of pale tan or cream-colored seeds that suggested dry oatmeal. At a touch they rained down with a fine sound like that of falling sand.

The sun was high when we left this desert oasis, traveling first west, then north, by way of Scissors Crossing and Banner Canyon, past Palomar observatory and the rolling hills of Temecula. Skirting around Los Angeles—no easy thing to do—we reached Monrovia and the home of Fred Stryker, a friend from boyhood. When we turned east again, fruit from his kumquat tree rode with us.

What I looked forward to, as we approached San Bernardino, were the pepper trees. Years before, on my first trip to California, I had come down from the high desert on a Santa Fe train early on a winter morning. Suddenly we were in San Bernardino. The air was soft and perfumed. The feathery foliage of exotic trees, pepper trees, swayed in green luxuriance. This was California! So I have remembered it how many thousand times! Now I saw it again. The city had expanded, changed. But the same pepper trees flowed in the breeze in the same fluid lines I recalled from that first, unforgettable meeting, three decades before.

Climbing over Cajon Pass, beside the Santa Fe right-of-way down which I had ridden, we headed out among the Joshua trees of the high Mojave Desert. Somewhere amid these yuccas we caught sight of a desert rabbit so pale in hue that Nellie described it as having "lots of cream in its coffee." East of Victorville, traveling through a region of "champagne climate and caviar scenery"—according to the reticence of a California billboard—we reached Lucerne Valley. There, on a desert slope overlooking a vast expanse of lower ground, friends of ours, Riley and Bonnie Kaufman, had built their modern home.

During the following days, we watched a surprising variety of birds come to drink the sweet, red-tinted fluid put out for hummingbirds. At these feeders, the Kaufmans have recorded orioles, black-headed grosbeaks, chickadees, linnets, desert sparrows and cactus wrens. One evening, at Lucerne Valley, Riley brewed medicinal-tasting Mormon tea from a desert plant, the naked joint fir. And it was there, while Nellie remained to watch the Kaufman birds, that I stowed away a sleeping bag and climbed into a green Jeep beside Dr. Edmund C. Jaeger and his early hiking companion, Gregory Hitchcock. We buckled our safety belts and waved good-bye. We were off for the Chuckwalla Mountains, seventy-five miles away, for a night on the desert floor and for a memorable visit to a small but historic canyon.

FOUR

THE DESERT WIND

"SWALLOWS certainly sleep all winter. A number of them conglobulate together, by flying round and round, and then all in a heap throw themselves under the water, and lie in the bed of the river."

Thus, in the year 1768, Samuel Johnson explained the disappearance of these birds in fall to his biographer, Boswell. He was expressing—with Johnsonian finality—the prevalent belief of his time. In *The Natural History of Selborne*, Johnson's contemporary, Gilbert White, noted that one eminent Swedish naturalist of the period talked "as familiarly of swallows going under water in the beginning of September as he would of his poultry going to roost a little before sunset." With the passage of time, the absurdity of this idea grew obvious. A better understanding of migration explained the mystifying disappearance of birds in fall and Johnson's "conglobulating" swallows became recognized as a classic misconception. Through the nineteenth century and the first decades of the twentieth, the belief in hibernating birds stood as a symbol of human credulity.

It was against this background that Dr. Edmund C. Jaeger, in the Chuckwalla Mountains of the Colorado Desert, on December 29, 1946, discovered a hibernating bird.

On this December day of a later year, with Gregory Hitchcock at the wheel, we were returning to the scene of this discovery. We ran east from Lucerne Valley to Twenty-Nine

Palms, turned south through the Joshua Tree National Monument, then swung east again toward Desert Center.

In one of his books, Dr. Jaeger has observed that "the desert landscape is monotonous only to the uninformed." Mile by mile as we advanced, our surroundings became more interesting by virtue of his comments and explanations. They were drawn from a lifetime of desert study. In his mid-seventies, the recognized authority in his field, he retains all the passionate interest in the interrelating life of these dry lands that has guided his activity for more than half a century.

Almost every week-end, he heads for the desert. Over a period of more than thirty years, he once calculated, he had spent at least two or three nights of every week in his sleeping bag. Formerly Chairman of the Department of Zoology at Riverside Junior College, he usually takes along on his trips two advanced students. By preference, one is a good cook, the other proficient in the handling and repair of automobiles. Thus he is left free for his studies.

Aside from having a bed in the back of his Jeep, he has little interest in the usual refinements of camping. Food tastes best to him cooked over a campfire. In fact, during the summer, he not infrequently prepares his meals over an open fire in his backyard in Riverside. He makes a habit of drinking a good deal of water while in the desert. Once, on a camping trip, when he felt dehydrated, he drank eleven glasses in one evening. His rule of eating less and walking more as he has grown older has left him sturdy and active at seventy-five.

To him, a rickety house in the desert is a better house than a new one. It will fall down sooner. When Hitchcock mentioned that some place was near a certain ranch, he replied: "I don't know where ranches are." With considerable logic, he pointed out that if the plural of mouse is mice and the plural of louse is lice, the plural of house should be hice. Over the years, each time I have received a card or letter from him, I have marveled at the copperplate quality of his handwriting.

I mentioned it now. He recalled that in high school he had been a miserable writer. One day he determined to improve. He bought a penmanship book with "Emulate all that is good" written at the top of each page. Slowly, letter by letter, he copied it. He kept on copying it for 500 times before he was satisfied. Since then, during more than half a century, his handwriting has changed hardly at all.

Loup City, about forty miles north of the Platte River in Nebraska, was his birthplace. At fifteen he was graduated from high school and began his teaching career. Moving west to California in 1906, he obtained a B.S. degree from Occidental College—which later bestowed on him an honorary doctor's degree—and continued his teaching. As a result of carrying heavy back-packs on rough mountain trails, about this time, he broke the arch of one foot. A friend told him of a small desert village where a teacher was needed and where he did not have to walk but could ride a burro to school. The village was Palm Springs. For several years he lived in a tiny one-room shelter that stood on land now occupied by the luxurious Tennis Club in the heart of this exclusive resort city. From time to time, as we advanced south through the Joshua Tree Monument, he recognized rock masses where he had camped more than forty years before. Then he had wandered alone with a burro over all this region. When, in 1936, the government added 870 square miles of this desert to the National Park System, Dr. Jaeger was one of those consulted on what areas to include.

In his absorption with the desert, Dr. Jaeger represents a type of natural-history specialist that is coming to have increasing importance in science. Instead of specializing vertically, as in a lifetime spent on a restricted subject like duckweed or moss animals or feather mites, such an authority will specialize horizontally. All life within an environment will be his province. He will devote himself to every aspect of his chosen area—meadow, timberline, swamp or mesa—as Dr.

Jaeger has devoted himself to the life of the desert.

We had been gradually descending as we advanced. East of the Little San Bernardino Mountains, we left the Mojave behind. We were in the lower Colorado Desert when we swung off the highway onto wheel tracks that led us across a dry, flat land broken here and there by immense mounds or hills of jumbled reddish rock. In the sunset, they stretched long shadows toward the higher masses of the barren Chuck-wallas.

When we made camp in the protection of one of the larger piles of weathered rock, dusk had almost fallen. We fed dry twigs from creosote bushes to a campfire and added branches from a dead paloverde tree. The fragrance of wood smoke was all around us as we ate our supper of pea soup, turkey sandwiches, hot tea and cocoa. The night came quickly. The chill of the desert increased. I slipped on a sweater, then a plaid flannel shirt, then a fleece-lined jacket. I even pulled down the ear flaps of my woolen cap. Dr. Jaeger was reminded of an old Chinese who divided winter weather into "one-shirt, two-shirt and three-shirt days." Stars were out when we washed the dishes. Each time we piled wood on the fire the glare of the mounting flames danced in flickering light across the great rocks behind us.

In this light, we inflated our air mattresses and unrolled our sleeping bags. For more than an hour, before we went to bed, Hitchcock and I wandered down sandy washes, beside the steep foothills of the mountains, under the stars, in the still, glimmering beauty of the desert night. The glowing dot of the campfire was the beacon that would lead us home. But when, at last, we turned back, the flames had died down and the glow had all but disappeared.

When I crawled into my sleeping bag that night, I kept on my woolen socks, my sweater and my woolen cap, with the ear flaps down. Snug as a snail in its shell, I lay on my back looking up at the brilliant ceiling of the stars. In the dry air of the desert, they drew close. At times, the illusion was strong that they were within reach of an outstretched hand. So the hours of the night went by while I watched the parade of the winter constellations move across the sky. I was too elated, too happy, to sleep. I was alone, but alone in a wonderful way. Each moment seemed one I would recall vividly as long as memory lasted.

The desert, it has been said, is all geology by day and all astronomy by night. And I was seeing its sky in winter, in the season of stars. To most people, the winter constellations are the most familiar. We see them then in clearer air, in a time of earlier darkness, when foliage is off the trees. Here the Great Dipper was below the horizon and Orion shone higher in the sky than at home. Lying there, I stared at the Pleiades above me and at the blue star, Sirius, in Canis Major, the brightest in the night sky. Several times meteors drew swift lines of flame among the stars. I lay remembering that August night when Nellie and I stood in the dust of a lonely Kansas road while the meteor trails of a summer Perseid shower crossed and crisscrossed in the sky above us.

The night was intensely still. Once I heard a high yipping squawl or bark some way off. It probably was the voice of the smallest of our foxes, the desert creature I wanted most to see, the kit fox. Dr. Jaeger has been fortunate enough to observe these graceful, large-eared little animals digging their burrows. With forefeet placed together, using them as shovels, they send the sand streaming out between their hind legs. In the morning, beside a dead paloverde tree less than a hundred yards from camp, we discovered the used burrow of a kit fox.

After three o'clock that morning, my mind was occupied largely with the mystery of the birth and death of the desert wind. During the early part of the night, the air was calm. Then, virtually without warning, gales of erratic wind began to blow. They came in a long sequence, reaching a peak, dying away entirely, then rushing upon us once more. What brought them into being, what caused them to stop, I could not fathom. Although I have questioned many people since, the mechanics of that strange night wind remains a riddle. The broken surface of the desert floor, the proximity of the bare rock of the mountains, the innumerable canyons nearby—all these probably played a part.

On and above the surface of dry land, the rapid fluctuations of temperature produce violently shifting air currents. Wind is so much a part of desert life that a number of creatures have developed special adaptations in consequence. On the Mojave Desert, Dr. Jaeger has noted a small blue butterfly, *Philotes speciosa*, alighting on a windy day and hooking the three legs on one side to a pebble, letting the gusts blow it over parallel with the ground. In this position it offers the least resistance to the wind.

We had made our camp on the south side of the mass of rocks. Gregory Hitchcock had tied a large section of heavy canvas to the side of the Jeep and we lay with our heads against this cloth wall. Thus we were doubly protected from the north. But the gusts blew not from that direction but from the west. At times, they must have struck at a speed of fifty miles an hour. I was first in line, rocked and cuffed and pummeled in the recurring gales.

The pressure exerted by moving air mounts rapidly as the velocity of the wind increases. At fifteen miles an hour it is slightly more than one and a tenth pounds to the square foot. At thirty miles, it is four and a half pounds; at forty, eight pounds; at fifty, twelve and a half pounds; and at sixty, eighteen pounds. It has been calculated that a fifty-mile-an-hour wind pushes against a cliff half a mile long and a hundred feet high with a pressure of 33,000,000 pounds. I was a noticeably smaller object. But in the heavier onslaughts I seemed on the verge of rolling away, tumbleweedwise, in my sleeping bag.

During some of the lulls, I fumbled about and fished from my shirt pocket a small spiral-ring notebook and the stub of a pencil. Inside my sleeping bag, sight unseen, I jotted down notes. The experiment was less than a complete success. Next day when I looked at what I had written, I found I had gone forward a few pages, then back over the same pages. In the maze of writing on writing, only a few words were legible.

Toward the end of each lull, I could hear the new wind coming like an onrushing train. I would snuggle farther into my sleeping bag, pull in my neck like a turtle, and let the gale pound me as it rushed by. I timed the lulls between the gusts as the stars paled and a faint pink flush spread up from the east. They lasted about half a minute. When six o'clock came, I waited for the beginning of a lull, then leaped out of my sleeping bag, jumped into my trousers, yanked on my fleece-lined jacket and was pulling on my shoes when the next cold blast struck. Fifty yards downwind, I retrieved my plaid flannel shirt from a creosote bush. I was up and dressed in record time. A new day had begun.

That day—like the night that had preceded it—was no ordinary one. It comes back in memory, as it always will, as the day of the poorwill canyon. We ate a breakfast of scrambled eggs cooked over a windblown campfire. Then we started off. We wandered on foot among the widely scattered paloverde and smoke trees, out over the desert, along the broken front of the Chuckwallas. The night wind blew itself out. Fresh diggings in the earth and marks of paws sliding in sand showed where a kit fox had hunted in the night.

There were few signs of the season around us. Throughout much of the year, the desert has a bare and wintry look. Even living plants appear parched and yellow. We bent to examine the curiously swollen stem of a desert trumpet, *Eriogonum inflatum*. The plant, which rain would turn green again, was dry and parchmentlike. One of the small hunting wasps employs the inflated stems of this wild buckwheat as storage chambers for the paralyzed insects on which its larvae feed. It bores a hole near the top of a stem, fills the lower part of the cavity with tiny pebbles, then deposits its prey and its eggs. Over them it places more pebbles and sand. Under such strange conditions the young wasp hatches, grows, transforms into an adult and makes its way to freedom.

Also dead-appearing in their dry surroundings were many of the slender wands of spiny ocotillo which rose in clusters from the desert floor. All through the year, in a series of short growing seasons following rains, these rodlike, unbranched stems put forth small leaves. Each time, as drought conditions return, the leaves change from green to red and fall away. Once we came upon a clump in which each wand was still clothed from top to bottom with red-tinged foliage.

In pioneer times, ranchers sometimes improvised stock-proof fences around corrals by cutting off the thorny stems of ocotillo and planting them in the ground where they took root. Under favorable conditions one of these wands may rise to a height of twelve or even fifteen feet. Its bark is rich in resinlike wax. One of its common names, candlewood, is derived from the fact that it burns with a steady deep yellow flame. It is in the spring, when all the wands are tipped with scarlet flowers, that the ocotillo most deserves the *splendens* of its scientific name, *Fouquieria splendens*.

Another curious wand, gray-green, smooth, waxy and limber, rose at times higher than my head from among rock jumbles of the mountainside. When prospectors roamed the western deserts with burros, these stems, strong and pliable, were used as whips. I noticed that where the skin of one wand was broken near the tip, thick, milky sap was oozing out. The gray-green wands formed the complete plant of the desert milkweed, *Asclepias albicans*. As I was looking at this naked plant, and accepting the fact that it *was* a milkweed, my mind returned—as it did more than once during these desert days—to the words of the White Queen, who remarked to

Alice behind the looking-glass:

"Why, sometimes, I've believed as many as six impossible things before breakfast."

Past a dozen clusters of these slender wands, we worked our way upward among tumbled boulders that choked the mouth of a small ravine. At the top we came out on a floor of pale-gray sand between walls of granite. At the opposite end of the canyon, the entrance was even more dramatic. On one side of this mountain portal, a pinnacle, a spire of reddish rock, towered in the air. On the other, a titanic mass of similar stone had weathered into the form of a sitting woman. Only a hundred yards or so in length, only a few yards wide at the bottom, this small canyon seemed specially marked by nature as though in anticipation of some noteworthy event in which the ravine would play a part.

That event had already occurred. It had taken place in 1946. For the ravine was the site of Dr. Jaeger's historic discovery. By the merest chance, on that late-December afternoon, as he and two of his students passed through the canyon, they had caught sight of a western relative of the whippoorwill, a Nuttall's poorwill, lost in its winter sleep.

I had imagined the bird was found in some deep fissure, well hidden from sight. But when Dr. Jaeger pointed out the spot, I was amazed to see it was only a small concave depression in the granite wall, hardly larger than my cupped hand. I measured it when, on a later day, I came here again to show Nellie the poorwill canyon. It was roughly five inches high, four and a half inches wide and four inches deep. Into this rounded depression, with its head up and its tail down, the bird had pressed itself. Its mottled gray and black plumage almost perfectly matched the coloring of the rough granite.

A thing may be found many times and still be lost. It must be recognized as well as seen. The chance discovery of the poorwill was important. But a comprehension of the significance of what was found was more important. Prospectors, Indians, children, hunters, all may have come upon sleeping poorwills in the desert. The winter dormancy of the bird apparently was known to the Hopi Indians. Their name for the poorwill is "The Sleeping One."

But Dr. Jaeger was not only the first scientist to see the bird in hibernation, the first to comprehend the importance of what he found. He also followed up his discovery with careful, detailed studies. He photographed, measured, weighed and banded the bird. He returned to the canyon for additional observations many times and over a period of four winters.

On this first encounter, he touched the poorwill, stroked its feathers, even picked it up without disturbing its torpor. As he was returning it to its niche, it slowly opened one eye and sleepily closed it again. That, Dr. Jaeger told me, was the only sign he had that it was a living bird. During four hibernating seasons, extending from 1946 to 1950, the canyon was the scene of additional scientific study. The numbered aluminum band revealed that the same individual was returning year after year to sleep the winter away in the same niche in the same small ravine.

The normal temperature of a Nuttall's poorwill is about 106 degrees F. When fortnightly temperature readings were taken over a period of six weeks in 1947, they showed the body heat of the hibernating bird had sunk to 60.4 degrees. Its breathing was so shallow and infequent that no movement of the chest walls could be noted, and when a cold metal mirror was held close to its nostrils, no moisture collected on it. Even when using a stethoscope, Dr. Jaeger was unable to detect the slighest sound of a heartbeat. So low had the flame of life sunk that bodily functions had all but ceased.

In the sand below the niche in which the poorwill had spent successive winters, I noticed the tracks of coyotes. Apparently, the narrow canyon formed a regular path followed by these predators. When I measured the distance, I found the niche was hardly more than two feet above the sand. Yet, so effective was the bird's camouflage that it had been passed and repassed while virtually on an eye level with the hunting coyotes. In its torpid state, with its organs barely functioning, it apparently gave off virtually no odor.

By night as well as by day, Dr. Jaeger studied the occupant of this poorwill canyon. On one nocturnal visit, he found the dormant bird with one of its eyes wide open. From a distance of two inches, he shone the narrow beam of a flashlight directly into the pupil of the eye. Even this violent stimulus brought no response. The eye remained unblinking and unseeing. So deep was the torpor of the bird's hibernation that a violent storm of sleet and hail—although it left some of its feathers noticeably battered—failed to arouse it. By weighing the bird repeatedly during one season of dormancy, Dr. Jaeger found that, in spite of its extremely low rate of metabolism, its weight gradually but steadily lessened. Whether all poorwills hibernate or whether only some individuals do, the rest migrating south like other members of the goatsucker family, is a question still to be answered.

Everywhere we wandered that day, I unconsciously looked into small openings, peered into crevices, hoped in vain for another miracle, another poorwill in the midst of hibernation. The chances against seeing it were astronomical. Dr. Jaeger noted that in more than forty years of wandering in the desert he had encountered only this single dormant bird. "It is doubtful," he added, "that I will see another." Only a very few persons ever encounter this ornithological rarity. Yet Nellie and I were among that lucky few.

Seven years after Dr. Jaeger made his initial discovery, we were riding home at the end of our autumn trip across America. At Tucson, Arizona, we stopped to see Joseph Wood Krutch. Not long before, two workmen, while digging up an agave in the Silverbell Mountains, northwest of the city, had come upon a torpid poorwill. When we saw it, it was resting on mesquite bark in a box set half underground and covered with a sheet of glass. The weather had turned unseasonably warm for January. The day before, the thermometer had risen to eighty-seven degrees. In this abnormal warmth, the poorwill showed signs of awakening. From time to time, it would open its eyes sleepily. But soon the lids would droop and it would fall once more into the deep stupor of its hibernation. Altogether, about thirty instances of hibernating poorwills have been recorded. Some of the birds have been found sleeping between stones in the open desert, others among the mountains. Most have been reported hibernating in clefts in rocks.

For a long time, Dr. Jaeger, Gregory Hitchcock and I wandered about the poorwill canyon—which, since then, appropriately has been set aside, with 160 surrounding acres, as the Edmund C. Jaeger Nature Sanctuary. We examined the thick, leathery leaves of the goatnut. We noted the trails of pack rats under the overhanging rocks. Dr. Jaeger recalled that once, while sleeping in the desert, he was awakened by one of these animals tugging at his hair as it gathered material for building its nest. We rested on a flat rock where the scraggly branches of an ironwood overarched the ravine. And from the topmost boulder, up which we had scrambled, we surveyed the open desert spread out below us with giant heaps of rock scattered across the flat expanse like the stumps of mountains. When, at last, we descended and began crossing the expanse to break camp, I kept looking back. I wanted to see as long as possible that remarkable spot, remarkable in its singular character, in its surrounding scenery, in its association with a dramatic discovery in natural history.

FIVE

SNOW TIRES IN DEATH VALLEY

DECEMBER was nearly over when we rode north from Barstow across the Mojave Desert. Beyond the shaggy, uplifted arms of the Joshua trees, our eyes swept over illimitable stretches of arid landscape. Here we saw none of the dramatic changes so often encountered elsewhere. No forests had been felled, no sheep pastured, no irrigation ditches dug. The land seemed unchanged since the long-past days when "desert rats" with dusty burros toiled through the heat looking for gold.

Yet such areas are easy to alter. They recover slowly. I remember Jim Neal pointing out a bare rectangle, miles away, on the slope of the Borrego Valley. Thirty years before, it had been cleared and the vegetation burned. The scar was still unhealed. A bush flattened by a passing Jeep in the desert does not spring up again as it would in a more humid climate. A stretch of desert wrecked by an army maneuver involving 100,000 men and heavy military equipment stays wrecked for half a century. This arid land, where growth and recovery are painfully slow, always is in need of special protection.

U.S. Highway 6—the road we had crossed coming north with the spring, the road we had met and re-met in our summer wanderings, the road that had carried us on the first miles of our travels with autumn across America, the road that passes within three miles of our home on the other side of the continent—this same highway now led us up the west side of the Owens Valley, under the wall of the southern Sierra Nevada. It brought us, at the end of the day, to Lone Pine. There, in the deepening shadows of Mt. Whitney, lights were going on. Away to the south, below the horizon, the Chuckwalla Mountains and their poorwill canyon also were sinking into the night. They lay 300 miles behind us.

We quenched our thirst that evening with snow water piped from 14,490-foot Mt. Whitney. Outside Alaska, this is the loftiest peak in the United States. Fewer than 100 miles separate this high point of the West from the lowest point in the nation, Death Valley's Bad Water, more than 280 feet below sea level. Those miles we covered next day. We crossed the Panamint Valley on a ruler-straight road. We twisted up to mile-high Townes Pass. Death Valley, with its dunes, its salt pools, its alluvial fans, its volcanic craters, its waves of chemical deposits sweeping like white breakers along its floor —all enclosed within the colors of scarred and eroded mountains—lay outspread below us. As we descended in sweeping curves of hard-topped road, we tried to imagine ourselves, a century before, riding in a heavy-wheeled covered wagon, advancing slowly, pulled by oxen, traversing that awesome chasm. The early menace of the land is reflected in such names as Bad Water, Funeral Peak, Desolation Mountains, Starvation Canyon, Furnace Creek, and Jubilee Pass.

We dropped a vertical mile to sea level at Stovepipe Wells. When we reached Furnace Creek, we were 178 feet below sea level. In this valley of desolation and hardship, associated with the suffering of forty-niners, with twenty-mule teams dragging ponderous borax wagons through the heat, the last thing we expected to encounter was too many people. Yet Furnace Creek Ranch swarmed with visitors. Cars whizzed past. Cars milled about. Cars lined up at the filling station. There were even hitch-hikers beside the road. People were playing golf under the palms of the Furnace Creek oasis. Private planes took off and landed at the nearby airport.

There was swimming at the Furnace Creek Inn and there was dancing at Stovepipe Wells. In the intervening years since the Jayhawker Party escaped across the Panamints, Death Valley has become a winter resort. We had arrived on New Year's week-end. The cabin we obtained at Stovepipe Wells was the last one left in the whole valley.

Among these vacationers we proved something of a curiosity. When we stopped for gasoline they strolled over to look at our rear wheels. Ours was the only passenger car equipped with snow tires. In the open winters of southern California, such tires are unneeded and largely unknown. But, for us, the roads of other winters lay ahead.

Once we were away from a few points of congestion, we found ourselves almost alone for great stretches of the valley. Running generally north and south, it extends for 140 miles. Its greatest width is sixteen miles. Wandering along its uneven floor, we encountered successive signs marking sea level. Now we were above sea level, now below, now above again. We seemed to be making porpoise leaps, miles long, down the valley. More than 500 of the nearly 3,000 square miles of this national monument lie below sea level.

Under our wheels, salty mud from prehistoric lakes and eroded rocks from the mountainsides filled the bottom of the valley with debris to a depth of as much as 7,500 feet. We moved about in a natural museum of geology. In Death Valley, the rocks of the earth take on the fascination that shells of the sea assume on the shores of Sanibel and Marco islands off the coast of Florida. Their colors are everywhere. Here they are garish and flaunting, there subdued with pastel shadings that resemble the delicate tinting of a moth's wing.

When we looked up the length of the valley from Dante's View, we stood on black Archaean rock, the oldest building material of our planet. Where the sweeping skirt of one alluvial fan extended out onto the valley floor, we found ourselves among small, squared-off reddish rocks. We seemed

HIBERNATING PLACE, where the first sleeping poorwill was found, is pointed out by its discoverer, Dr. Edmund C. Jaeger.

DEVIL'S CORNFIELD in Death Valley. Wind, cutting the dirt from around arrowweed, produces these shock-like clumps.

in a dump yard of discarded and broken bricks. At times we were in boulder fields white with desert dust, at other times among wind-rippled dunes of quartz or amid jagged pinnacles of salt or where yellow-tan deposits looked in the distance like wheat fields ready for harvest.

Among all these colored rocks, the ones that interested us most were dark brown or black. Seen against the sun, they shone as though greasy or coated with wax. When I ran a finger over one, I found its surface was smooth and hard and polished like porcelain. At times we wandered among acres of such stones. Where they were black, we seemed surrounded by chunks of shiny anthracite coal. I picked up one of the stones and examined it curiously. It suggested a meteorite. But it lacked a meteorite's weight. I held in my hand only an earthbound stone. But that stone was almost as exciting and mysterious as though it had fallen from outer space.

For the thin, glossy coating of its exterior was desert varnish. This is sometimes called desert gloss or desert glaze or desert rind. Its distribution is world-wide, and its mystery has occupied many minds. Darwin observed it in Brazil. Von Humboldt found it along the Congo and the Nile. It is not confined to deserts, although there it is most conspicuous. Chemical analysis has shown that it is formed of manganese and iron oxides. It is insoluble in water but dissolves in hot hydrochloric acid. The riddle that has occupied generations of scientists is: What brings desert varnish into being and how is it deposited?

Numerous have been the theories advanced. One scientist suggested that the coating was produced from the wind-blown pollen of desert plants. This, he thought, adhered to the rocks where its organic matter decomposed and left a mineral residue behind. According to another theory, the glaze was deposited by the receding waters of prehistoric seas. Rainwater, dust and underground water—rising, evaporating and leaving its mineral content on the surface of exposed rocks—all have been brought forward as solutions to the mystery of this dense and shiny coating. It is now believed that at least an important part of the explanation lies in the great heat of the sun. It draws or cooks moisture from the pore spaces of the rock, evaporates it on the surface and thus, bit by bit, over long periods of time, deposits the oxides that form the desert varnish.

In recent decades, lichens, those primitive, universal plants that are found in desert and jungle, on mountain tops and below sea level, have been shown to assume an active role in the development of the oxides. No climate seems too dry or wet, too hot or cold to support those "impossible plants," the lichens. Scientists working as far apart as California and Queensland, Australia, have reported corroborative evidence in connection with their role in producing the varnish. In the Mojave Desert, near Stoddard's Well, Dr. J. D. Laudermilk, of Pomona College, made hundreds of microscopic studies of a lichen so minute that, except in the mass, it is invisible to human eyes. Pioneers in breaking down rock surfaces and preparing the way for higher plants, all lichens produce acids that eat into stone. During their growth in the Mojave Desert, Dr. Laudermilk found, the plants take up iron and magnesium which is deposited again as oxides when the lichens die.

Only rocks that contain these two elements are coated with desert varnish. How long does the process take? Nobody can give a precise answer to that question. All that scientists can say is that the glaze is accumulated slowly, perhaps over a period of a century or more. If the rate of deposition could be determined exactly, Dr. Jaeger has pointed out, archaeologists would possess a valuable aid in dating ancient artifacts such as Stone Age implements found heavily coated with varnish on the dry mesas of the Southwest.

One of the old songs of the Paiute Indians of the Death Valley region contains the words: "The edge of the sky is the home of the river." Abundant water is far away. Rainfall is so rare an event that, in the course of a year, the average number of clear days in the valley is 283. The record is 351. It would require almost a century of Death Valley rain to equal the amount that falls in one year on parts of the Olympic Peninsula. Even in winter, the season of rain, the showers are infrequent. One had occurred not long before we arrived.

"Another rain like that," a park employee said with a grin, "and we will be hacking our way through the vegetation!"

In the course of an hour, on some occasions, a year's supply of water will be dumped on one part of the valley while the rest remains parched. Wherever we went across the gravelly outer edges of the alluvial fans, we stooped to examine the dry and yellow forms of minute plants rising among the pebbles. Those pebbles, under the full summer sun, may reach a temperature of 190 degrees F., providing a sound basis for the old Indian name for Death Valley—Ground Afire. But in the more moderate days of spring, on years when the rainfall has reached or exceeded two inches, a host of desert flowers spring up and burst into bloom across the floor of the valley.

Life, for these plants, is often telescoped. Many grow to a height of only an inch or two. Some reproduce through flowers that unfold, bloom and disappear in a single day. So specialized are the seeds of a number of desert plants that they not only require for germination a certain amount of rainfall but they need that amount in a certain number of days or hours. Even when conditions are favorable, only a small proportion of the seeds sprout. Thus, competition for moisture is reduced and the plants are spaced well apart in the arid soil.

It was after sunset when we first came to America's lowest point, Bad Water. The pool, bitter with chemical leachings, mirrored the reds and purples of the western sky, with the white summit of Telescope Peak rising against them. Behind us, far up the sheer face of a cliff, a small white sign read: "Sea Level." A few hundred feet to the northwest, a slight depression dipped to 282 feet below the level of the sea, and the earth's surface reached its lowest point on the North American continent.

As we walked about the edge of the pool, where low clumps of green and fleshy pickleweed grew, we noticed masses of tiny aquatic crustaceans sweeping outward over the bottom like reddish, wind-blown dust. One species of diminutive snail lives nowhere else in the world except in the bitter pool at Bad Water. Across the glowing surface of this pool, the water was speckled by the dabbing of dark little dipterous insects. At one time, the fly larvae of Bad Water and other salt pools of the valley formed a staple food of the Paiute Indians. As a kind of dessert, these Indians also ate the froth of the spittlebugs, or froghoppers, which is slightly sweet when made on certain plants.

Of all the more than 600 kinds of plants that grow within the boundaries of the Death Valley National Monument, the largest was introduced about half a century ago—the date palms of the Furnace Creek Ranch. Watered by springs, this 900-acre oasis attracts avian as well as human tourists. During our days of wandering up and down the valley, from the volcanic crater of Ubehebe, on the north, to Jubilee Pass, on the south, over the Panamints and up the valley beyond, we saw relatively few birds away from Furnace Creek. But here robins ran, with starts and stops, over the grass of the golf course. Say's phoebes fluttered under the swinging sprinklers. Red-shafted flickers flew above water pipits walking on the ground. Audubon's warblers flashed their yellow rump patches among the palms. Killdeer called and a black, red-faced Lewis' woodpecker hovered like a flycatcher to snap an insect from the air. For several weeks a Canada goose had been feeding near the ninth green of the golf course. The number of birds we saw was almost as surprising as the number of people who

had converged on Death Valley on this last week-end of
the year.

It was in 1917 that house sparrows first appeared at Furnace Creek Ranch. They have been thriving ever since. We
saw them darting in and out among the palm fronds. In 1951
the starlings arrived. A decade later their numbers had risen
to 800. We saw one flock perching on telephone wires, forming solid lines from pole to pole.

In the month of June, in 1893, when the temperature rose
to 116 degrees F. at midday, Dr. A. K. Fisher compiled the
first scientific list of the birds of Death Valley. He recorded
sixty-nine species seen below sea level. Thirty years later, Dr.
Joseph Grinnell raised the list to 124. By 1933 it had reached
131. Today, according to "A Survey of the Birds of Death
Valley," by Roland H. Wauer, published in *The Condor* for
May–June, 1962, the number of species recorded below sea
level in the valley totals 232. Most of these, of course, have
appeared during migration. But they include such unlikely
visitors to this desert fastness as pelicans, loons, kingfishers,
avocets, rails, snipe, ducks and geese. Once, for a period of
half a dozen years, a great horned owl nested in the date grove.

High on the list of things we had always wanted to see and
hoped to see on our winter trip were the kit fox and the desert
sardine. Both are inhabitants of Death Valley. The little fish
of the desert, also known as pupfish, are members of an ancient group, the *Cyprinodons*. Twenty million years ago, their
ancestors swam in the fresh-water lake that filled the valley.
As the climate changed and the prehistoric lake disappeared,
the fish retreated to pools that became more and more filled
with minerals and salt. From fresh-water dwellers they evolved
into the species of today that live in water saltier than the sea.

So long have these fish been isolated in their separate pools
and streams that they have developed the characteristics of
different species. Salt Creek, in the northern part of the
valley, contains *Cyprinodon salinus*; Saratoga Springs, close

to the southern boundary, *Cyprinodon nevadensis nevadensis.*
Related species live hundreds of miles away, in the Colorado
River Basin and elsewhere, offering biological evidence that,
in ancient times, water linked the widely separated present
homes of the pupfish.

Why pupfish? When we watched one of these plump, dark,
inch-long desert minnows swimming about in an aquarium
at the excellent museum in the new monument headquarters,
Nellie noticed the way its pectoral fins moved alternately
like the forepaws of a swimming dog. That seemed as good
an explanation as any for the name. To watch pupfish in
their natural home, we drove again and again down a dusty
side road and searched along Salt Creek and the encrusted
pools of its headwaters. And time after time we searched
in vain.

Here we were in a "chemical desert." Water was plentiful.
But its salt content was greater than any but a few plants
could endure. In the flora of this dry country, different species of plants have different tolerances for salt. Mesquite, for
example, grows only where the water contains less than one-
half of one per cent dissolved salt. Arrowweed is found where
it is more than one-half of one but not more than three per
cent. Pickleweed flourishes where it is more than three but
not more than six per cent. A few of the seventeen kinds of
saltbush found in Death Valley also can survive where the
saline content of the water is as high as six per cent. Such
chemical deserts, largely barren salt flats, comprise more than
300 of the 500-odd square miles of Death Valley that lie
below the level of the sea.

Meandering and many-threaded, Salt Creek wandered in
a shallow flow over a rippled bottom of yellow-brown sand.
It sparkled in the sun. Its water was as clear as though it
gushed from some sweet spring. I dipped a forefinger in the
current, touched it to the tip of my tongue and felt the bite
of brine.

Around the separated pools upstream, the pickleweed was heavily encrusted with salt. When I swept my foot through the vegetation, a cloud of fine white dust arose. On successive visits we worked our way from pool to pool. But it was only on our final trip that we discovered what we shall always remember as Pupfish Pool.

It was one of the topmost of these saline puddles, ten or twelve feet long and three or four feet wide. Masses of heavily encrusted, apparently lifeless, vegetation overhung the edge. I poked one such mass. Out shot a cloud of minute crustacea. Cutting through it were flashes and streaks of larger movement. Then our eyes began to focus on tiny, almost colorless fish and slightly bigger, more pigmented ones. They streaked ahead in swift and sudden rushes, then came to rest, then shot away again among the smaller creatures. At this time of year, the Death Valley pupfish are raising their families. They spend most of their time lurking in the shelter of the poolside vegetation. I had disturbed their hiding place, and young and old alike had rushed into the open water.

At one time it was thought that these little fish estivate during the hottest months of summer. Now it is known they are active the year around. For even more remarkable than the desert sardine's ability to endure salt is its ability to endure heat. William Bullard, naturalist at the monument, told me that in summer he has seen pupfish using as umbrellas the sheets of chemicals that form on the surface of the pools. Perhaps, like white suits in the tropics, such chemical deposits on and around the pools may reflect away some of the heat. In several places we came upon salt pools that were covered solidly, as with ice, by a floating layer of chemicals. They seemed frozen in for the winter. Bullard, on more than one occasion, has watched the little fish wriggle up through a hole in one of these sheets, slither across it and disappear down another hole. The ways of the pupfish are still mysterious. It is easier to measure the scales and count the fin-rays of collected specimens than to observe the living creatures in the hot griddle that Death Valley becomes in summer.

Over and over, each time I stirred the vegetation, families of pupfish shot into view. We were amazed at the speed of these diminutive swimmers. They streaked like little rockets, cut curlicues in the water, whirled like pinwheels. Occasionally one would plunge toward the bottom. We would see a tiny burst of sediment. A Lilliputian cloud would lift and hang in the water, marking the spot where the swimmer had vanished. Not infrequently, when alarmed, these desert fish dive and burrow out of sight in the soft material of the pool bottom.

As I stood there, contemplating the swift, exuberant rushes of the little fish, my mind somehow went back to an Oriental story of the two friends who stood on a bridge watching fish swim in the stream below. Thus ran their conversation:

"How happy the fishes are!"

"You are not a fish. How can you know whether fish are happy or not?"

"You are not me. How can you know whether I know whether fish are happy or not?"

On the evening of the last day of the year, we celebrated with a dinner at the Stovepipe Wells Hotel, then drove out into the desert night. The moon, in its last quarter, was late in rising. No other human being seemed abroad. The valley lay still, aloof, wrapped in darkness as New Year's Eve advanced.

We drove slowly. We stopped often. Nellie played the beam of a powerful flashlight over the land around us. Bright pebbles shot back quick stabs of reflected light. Saltbushes leaped suddenly from the darkness. We crossed dark mesquite flats. We paused beside silvery-green clumps of the beautiful desert holly, its leaves thick and soft as though cut from chamois skin or fine felt. Skirting the edge of flowing dunes, we came to the place where, in early days, a stovepipe is said to have marked the position of a well amid the shifting sand. Near here we stopped to examine a broken and weathered iron pump. It bore the still-legible words: "F & W, Kendallville, Indiana, USA. Hoosier." Later that night, for a long time, under the ceiling of the stars, we threaded our way on foot among strange, almost eerie shapes that rose all around us in the Devil's Cornfield.

Like the tepees of a great Indian encampment or like hundreds of acres of cornshocks, mounds of earth crowned with clumps of arrowweed lifted higher than our heads. This dry-country plant, *Pluchea sericea*, is a member of the sunflower family. The wands of its stiff stems provided Indians of the valley with arrow shafts and with material for the construction of primitive shelters. To pioneers, the sight of arrowweed meant water near the surface. In the Devil's Cornfield, the alkaline soil begins to be moist at the depth of only a few inches. It was among these cornshock-like clumps of the arrowweed that the long-suffering Jayhawker Party made its last Death Valley camp in 1849.

In only one other place, nearby Saline Valley, are such mounds known to exist. They all are the product of the sculpturing of the wind. Over the years, gales have eroded soil from around the clumps until they have been left growing at the top of pedestals of earth, each pedestal held together by the intertwining of the roots.

Strange by day, these upthrust masses are stranger still by night. As we walked among them, they appeared and disappeared, ghostly in the white beams of our moving flashlights. So intense was the silence that our ears caught the tiny chirping sounds of mineral fragments rubbing together beneath our feet. At each step, motes of alkali dust swarmed upward into the light. For minutes at a time we stood, torches switched off, enveloped in the dark. It was amid such memorable surroundings, on this New Year's Eve, that the second of our Death Valley wishes came true.

We had come back to the car. For a time, we sat with the motor idling. As I pulled out from the roadside, our headlights raked across a different stretch of mounds. Two shining eyes leaped into brilliance. Then, as the swing of the headlights passed the spot, they disappeared. I halted. Nellie's powerful dry-cell flashlight snapped on. Its beam probed between the mounds. The eyes shone again. They were set in a face silvery-white, with a pointed, black-tipped nose and great uplifted ears. We were seeing, at last, that most beautiful and charming of desert mammals, the little kit fox.

Hardly larger than a house cat, weighing only about three pounds, it is the least cunning, the most confiding and inquisitive of the foxes. One camper, sleeping on the desert floor, awoke in the night to find a kit fox exploring under his pillow. As he lifted his head, it whirled so suddenly it kicked a shower of sand into his face. Sometimes, at the Death Valley campground, these playful animals have been known to slide down the canvas of tents and then race back to do it over again. So fleet of foot is the kit fox that its alternate name is the swift. Most of the moisture it obtains is believed to come from the desert rodents that form the major part of its diet. Harmless to man, the small kit fox has long been a victim of man's persecution. Guns, poisons, traps have reduced its numbers until today it is one of our vanishing species, a beautiful and trusting creature that is nearing extinction.

For a minute or more, the fox remained in sight, looking intently in our direction. Then with a graceful turn, it whirled into the shadow of the nearest mound. We saw it side-view for an instant—its pale-gray flank, its fox-face, its bushy tail. Then it was gone. With the image of that buoyant creature vivid in our minds, we drove back to our cabin. Midnight came and, in the stillness of the desert night, the old year slipped away.

New Year's week-end was over when we left Death Valley.

Strengthened by stacks of "flannel" pancakes for breakfast, we headed south on desert roads where ravens were starting their own new year, south through the country of the Shadow Mountains and the Silurian Hills, through Shoshone and Baker and back to Barstow. All over the valley, that day, an exodus was in progress. Tents came down, motors started, machines rolled. Along the way, cars continually passed us. Drivers were speeding back to the city, back to school or office or factory. For them, the short vacation was over. For us, our season of freedom had hardly begun. Vacation, for us, stretched on and on, across the land, to the end of winter.

SIX

ROCK RAINBOWS

"TODAY you may write a chapter on the advantages of traveling; and tomorrow you may write a chapter on the advantages of not traveling." So Thoreau noted in his journal. For one day at Barstow, Nellie and I enjoyed the advantages of not traveling. We returned to the sedentary life. We slept late. We repacked the car. We went to bed early. We burned the candle at neither end. By the following morning, we were eager to return once more to the advantages of traveling.

A long, dry road, U.S. 66, carried us east down the tilted quadrangle of the Mojave Desert. We had descended 1,600 feet by the time we came to Needles, outspread on its floodplain beside the Colorado. In midstream on the bridge we lost an hour and left California behind. We climbed the farther side of the valley in Rocky Mountain Time and in the state of Arizona. During two seasons of the year, fall and winter, we had wandered through California, that state unrivaled in the variety of its natural-history interest. Now it all lay behind us, beyond reach of our eyes. But it still remained, as it always would, vividly alive to the eyes of remembrance.

Next day, a hundred miles upstream, we once more crossed the Colorado and crossed back again. This time our bridge was Hoover Dam. Rising as high as a sixty-story skyscraper, it blocks the river's gorge with 400,000,000 cubic yards of concrete and backs up a lake with a shore line of 500 miles. It also provides a playground for ravens. Winds rush up the 726 feet of the dam's slanted, curving downstream face, as at the head of a draw. Hour after hour, the somber, heavy-billed birds ride, with wings swept back, first one way, then the other, along the lip of the curve. We watched them sporting in the wild turbulence of the deflected wind.

Up to now, our travels had carried us beside the mild Pacific, through the warm sunshine of the California deserts. We had been west of winter. We had been traversing the fringes of the season. Now we turned east again, through Kingman and Peach Springs and Seligman and Ash Fork. As we climbed among slopes dark with piñon and juniper, then among tall ponderosa pines, we mounted to the top of the lofty San Francisco Plateau that extends across upper Arizona. At Kingman we were at an elevation of 3,336 feet; at Ash Fork, 5,144; at Williams, 6,762. And as we climbed, the temperature dropped. At the top of our ascent, the winter of the north, the white winter, lay all about us.

Across a snow-covered landscape, the following day, we headed north from Williams. For miles along the road, the dry stalks of a familiar plant rose above the blanket of snow. They were the stalks of that amazingly successful immigrant and colonizer, the mullein. Unknown to America before the coming of Europeans, it has spread across the land. Early colonists are believed to have introduced it as a medicinal plant. Its multitudinous seeds, carried by accident or design along the westward trails of the pioneers, have extended its range from coast to coast. In a thousand unexpected places, from Cape Cod to Sutter's Mill, we had encountered the great mullein.

It is a plant of romantic history and many names—blanket leaf, hedge torch, velvet leaf, Adam's flannel. Twenty centuries ago, the Greeks used the dried leaves of the great mullein for lamp wicks. Romans dipped the stems in tallow to make torches for their funeral processions. From the Middle Ages to modern times, the plant has been considered a remedy for innumerable ailments. Mullein tea was long employed for the treatment of pulmonary diseases in both men and cattle. An infusion produced by boiling the flowers was recommended for catarrh. On the American frontier, the thick, gray-green, woolly leaves of the mullein provided a substitute for flannel in binding up sore throats. They were also rubbed on as an irritant in place of mustard plasters. In the Ozarks, asthma sufferers smoked dried mullein leaves in search of relief. The juice of the plant, at one time, was believed to be a cure for deafness of the middle ear, and a decoction made from the leaves was used in the treatment of rheumatism. A century ago, New England farmers relieved chafed feet by placing the soft cushion of mullein leaves inside their shoes.

Of all the thousands of mullein stalks we saw as we drove north that day, one stands out in retrospect. As we came near it, I braked to a sudden stop. Balancing at the tip, nearly four feet above the ground, perched a gray-brown little bird, plump and round-headed. Its large eyes were yellow. Thirty miles south of the Grand Canyon, we were looking at our first Rocky Mountain pygmy owl, an owl no larger than a bluebird. So tiny a predator, so innocent in appearance, so toylike in form, it nevertheless is as courageous and as rapacious as the largest of its night-flying relatives. It pounces on birds as big as robins. It attacks and overcomes ground squirrels twice its own size. It is hardy, enduring the high-country winters and nesting, usually in abandoned woodpecker holes, at elevations as great as 10,000 feet.

Through our field glasses, we watched it turning its head in the sunshine, constantly alert to movement around it. When it darted into the air from its lookout, it exhibited none of the buoyancy usually associated with the flight of owls. It buzzed along close to the ground and then rose sharply to alight on another perch. Nor is the wingbeat of this diurnal owl completely silent, as is the wingbeat of the night hunters. Close at hand, its feathers produce a faint whistling sound as they move rapidly through the air.

Once, after it had zoomed up and alighted in a nearby pine, we caught a low, musical note. It was far removed from the loud hooting of the larger owls. It suggested the call of a gentle bird. Rather sweet in tone, it has been compared by some listeners to the cooing of a dove. John Burroughs, who heard it during his Yellowstone trip with Theodore Roosevelt, thought it resembled the sound "a boy might make by blowing into the neck of an empty bottle." As we rode on that morning, we scanned the tip of each mullein stalk beside the road. But nowhere else did one form the perch of a pygmy owl.

To come upon the Grand Canyon completely without warning, as the first Spanish explorers did 400 years ago, is, of course, impossible in this twentieth century. But even now, the overwhelming effect of the chasm is heightened by the suddenness of its appearance. There is no gradual preparation. It remains unperceived until the rim is almost at your feet. You see nothing until you see all.

It was thus that the canyon, a mile deep and miles wide, opened up below us. It descended through layers of colored rock laid down over a period of more than a billion years. Like a titanic band saw, running day and night for aeons, the grit-filled flow of the Colorado River has cut through the stone pressed against it by the slow rise of the plateau. The result is a ragged abyss more than 200 miles long. As we looked into the chasm, lighted by the brilliance of the winter sunshine, all its walls seemed formed of rainbows solidified, rainbows of rock.

For two days and part of a third, we watched the changing light on the colors of the canyon. A whole season, a year of seasons, could be spent in this pursuit. Each shift in the angle of the sun's rays subtly alters the effect. Each hour of the day, the picture varies. Now, in January, a wash of white, a bloom of snow, added its delicate touch to the canyon's beauty. It dusted the tops and descended the slopes of all the pinnacles and buttes of that lower landscape.

On the south rim where we stood, snow comes before winter. The ground is often white in November. Here the elevation is more than 7,000 feet and the climate is comparable to that of southern Canada. At the bottom of the canyon, a mile below, it is like that of northern Mexico. While snowstorms rage along the rim, the temperature beside the river may be no lower than fifty degrees F.

On the second morning, when we awoke in our log cabin close to the head of Bright Angel Trail, the mercury stood at eleven degrees above zero. All the windows of our car were spangled with stars of frost. Rarely have I seen ice crystals so beautiful. They formed galaxies and streamers that curved inward like the arms of a spiral nebula. The paths of invisible airstreams swirling about a speeding car seemed recorded by the lines and curves of the shining crystals. In the dawn light, under the ponderosa pines, I looked from the fragile beauty of the frost to the colorful immensity of the canyon—the canyon so vast, fashioned from rock, shaped by millions of years of slow erosion; the frost, so swiftly formed, so swiftly fading, its life measured by the fraction of a day. Here were the opposite extremes of natural beauty. The canyon would remain for other generations to enjoy; we alone had seen the beauty of this frost. Its brilliance already was dimming when we returned from breakfast.

That breakfast—fried mush and maple syrup—was the perfect beginning for a carefree day of wandering in sparkling mountain air, on sparkling high-country snow. Along the lip of the canyon we made the acquaintance of the wavy-leaf oak and the red-backed junco, the cliff rose and the Abert squirrel. Mountain chickadees kept us company and, on more than one occasion, we rounded a turn in the trail and came upon mule deer browsing among the juniper.

At frequent intervals, as though peering into the interior of the earth, we gazed down into the depths of the canyon. Through our glasses we explored the jumble of chasms, the snowfields white amid the rainbow of rocks, the tiny junipers so far below that they appeared to be a kind of moss. We imagined the scene before us on a night of the full moon and envied those who had experienced it. We repeated the dizzying sensation of sweeping our binoculars downward in long eagle plunges into the depths.

Once they came to rest on a short string of mules, Lilliputian even in our powerful glasses. They were crossing the Tonto Plateau on a descent to the bottom. Since 1906, hundreds of thousands of visitors have ridden these specially trained animals down the Bright Angel Trail. Some have been in their eighties. Probably ninety-five per cent of them have never been in a saddle before. They are used to steering automobiles and their commonest misconception is that they have to steer the mules. These animals, in fact, know every step of the way. Some of them have been descending the Bright Angel Trail and climbing up again for as long as twenty years. Before they carry their first riders, new mules serve an apprenticeship in the pack trains that transport supplies five times a week to Phantom Ranch, at the bottom of the canyon. Then they are ridden and trained by guides before they are put into service. Mules are used in preference to horses because they are more steady, less high-strung.

While working the canyon trails, these animals feed not only on a plentiful supply of hay but on a grain mixture including crimped oats, rolled barley, cracked corn, alfalfa meal, molasses, linseed oil meal and iodized salt. Little do riders realize what is inside the mules they ride! When their canyon days are over, the animals are retired to a kind of old mules' home established in—of all surprising places—Death Valley. We remembered seeing several in a corral back of the golf course at Furnace Creek. There they have ample food and little work to do. The high temperatures disturb them but slightly. They are used to heat. At the bottom of the Grand Canyon, during July and August, the thermometer often stands at 115 or even 120 degrees in the shade.

Death Valley and the Tonto Plateau are also linked, for us, by recollections of another beast of burden. On one of our side trips across the Panamints, we saw, far off on a wide gray slope, a wild burro and its colt. They stood unmoving in the manner of patient burros everywhere, as gray as their gray surroundings. We had been looking at them for five minutes or so when I became aware of something unsatisfied in the back of my mind. I had been scanning their surroundings for the sign of a campfire or the figure of a prospector. Without thinking about it, I had assumed the animals must be dependent on a human being. As we drove on, Nellie recalled Joseph Wood Krutch's story of the visitor to the Grand Canyon. After looking into the depths for a long time, he commented: "You can't tell me that this was made without human aid!"

Down there, on the Tonto Plateau, wild burros live also. Descended from animals deserted by prospectors, they have multiplied. Mountain lions, which would have kept them in check, had been eliminated by stockmen. Before their numbers were reduced, the wild burros ate the plateau almost bare, reducing the food needed by bighorn sheep. In two round-ups, in 1957 and 1958, Jim Wescogame, a Havasupi Indian, herded 102 of the animals up the Kaibab Trail. Starting at one end of the fifteen-mile-long plateau with horses, he combed its thirty square miles, driving the feral burros before him. The few that still remain made their escape into side canyons during the drives.

For the little burros, abandoned in the desert in pioneer times, hardships multiplied. Those that survived the hazards of climate and terrain often fell prey to Indians, who sought

them for food, or to big-game hunters who, just to kill something, shot them and left them where they fell. During
World War II, pilots training in New Mexico virtually wiped
out the wild burros of the White Sands region. Diving on the
helpless animals, using them as slow-moving targets, they
fired with machine guns and rockets. A brighter page is now
being written in the story of the long abuse of the burro. In
several places in the West, desert sanctuaries have been set
aside. There the wild burros can live in peace.

Late that afternoon we were near an ancient juniper,
thought to be ten centuries old, when a raven flew low above
us. Out over the abyss, where a little cove indented the rock
wall, it joined half a dozen other ravens in a wild aerial dog-
fight. Here, as at Hoover Dam, the canyon winds were providing the dark birds with a playground. They plunged,
twisted, tumbled, flew upside down, reveling in the violence
of the updrafts. Like a waterfall reversed, a wind from the
northwest rushed in a torrent of air up and over the rim. We
heard the croaking of the birds faintly. The sound was partially swallowed up in the immensity of the canyon, partially
whirled away by the wind. One raven flew through all its
aerobatics and power plunges with its legs hanging down.
Another seemed inconvenienced not at all by a feather missing from its right wing.

Toward the end of the day, the Grand Canyon ravens often
gather into such flocks for a social frolic before going to roost.
During the summer, they sometimes ride high on thermal
currents carrying bits of knotty wood or the shiny caps from
soft-drink bottles. Letting these fall, they plunge and catch
them in mid-air. In winter months they have been seen going
aloft with chunks of snow, breaking them up while on the
wing and diving after the falling fragments. The light had
begun to fade, at the close of that short January day, before
the ravens ceased their sport. Chilled from standing, we hur-
ried home. That night, coyotes howled around the village.

The Mexicans have a saying: *Como Arizona no hay dos*—"Like Arizona there are no two!" In succeeding days, from top to bottom, we sampled the ever-changing variety of this state of vivid colors. In other places besides the Grand Canyon, its rainbows of rock are evident. We saw the colors imprisoned within the chalcedony trees of the Petrified Forest. We came to the Painted Desert with the blue haze of evening overlying the richness of its hues. And, one morning at dawn, on a road banded with frost wherever tree shadows crossed it, we rode through the chromatic beauty of Oak Creek Canyon. Wisely, in a state where stone is so important a part of its heritage, wayside signs read: "Defacing or Writing on Rocks Prohibited by Law."

At the end of the autumn trip, we had returned home through Arizona. At the end of the summer trip, we had swung south through its northeastern corner. Now, in winter, we were traversing its length. Thus three of the four seasons were linked together by memories of Arizona. Our memories live in a world without time. Clocks and calendars mean nothing to them. As we wound southward during these winter days, fragments of other trips revived in random recollections. We saw again, sharply defined, a hundred piñon jays streaming overhead between Show Low and the Salt River Canyon, their soft, musical calling—which close at hand resembles "piñone-piñone"—mingling like the clamor of far-away Canada geese. We recalled the high, twin plumes of chemical smoke from the copper smelter at Douglas, with little "cottontops," scaled quail, feeding beneath them at sunset. We remembered an isolated mesquite at the mouth of Carr Canyon, its branches aflame with the darting red of thirty pyrrhuloxias.

Such things we remembered as we followed our zigzag trail down the length of the state. We climbed switch-backs to the mile-high copper town of Jerome—named for the father of Sir Winston Churchill's mother. We counted fifteen bulky oriole nests in a single cottonwood where trees grew far apart on the open rangeland of the Chino Valley. We pulled up short, not far from Wickenburg, to watch a sparrowhawk dart down, miss a lizard, and then pursue it on foot over the dusty ground.

And all the while, as we moved southward, we descended toward a warmer, dryer land. Mountain forests receded; ocotillo and paloverde reappeared. Here and there we saw scattered flowers, a few red spikes of crinkly-leaved desert mallow, a sprinkling of yellow blooms on brittlebush. We crossed the Gila River which, before the Gadsden Purchase of 1853, formed the boundary between the United States and Mexico. Everywhere now, we followed old Spanish trails. When we settled down at Ajo, on the Sonoran Desert, we were the length of the state away from the Grand Canyon. Ice and snow were far behind. Once more we were on the warm fringes of the season.

SEVEN

DRIPPING SPRINGS

IF, LIKE some Rip Van Winkle in reverse, we could fall
asleep and awaken in a prior time, in what other period
of history would we rather be making our trip through winter? In Coronado's day? At the time of Lewis and Clark?
When the forty-niners were moving west? At the turn of the
present century?

As we ate breakfast in an Ajo restaurant, Nellie and I ran
over the possibilities. We considered each in turn. We regretted the lost herds of bison we would not see. We regretted
the miles of prairie-dog towns, now gone. We regretted the
drained swamps and felled forests and all the wildlife we
would miss. But, we decided, it was now, in the present
period, that the greatest variety of winter was accessible to
us. Only now did the modern automobile and roads leading
into remote areas permit, in a single season, such a continent-
wide survey as we had undertaken. As we climbed into our
car and headed south into the great cactus forests of the
Mexican border, we knew the mood of the Roman poet,
Ovid, who, in the first century A.D., wrote:

"Let others revel in the past, but for me I rejoice in my
own age. These are the times for me."

Two hours later and forty miles to the south, we looked
up from the delicate lacework of tracks left by a gray lizard
skittering across a drift of dust and our eyes worked up and
up along the fluted green column of a saguaro cactus. It

towered to a height of nearly three stories above us. The saguaro is the botanical giant of its range. It may weigh as much as ten tons. It may rise to a height of fifty feet. It may live as long as 200 years—an age exceeding that of the American Republic. Its large blossom, with golden center and cream-white petals, is the state flower of Arizona. Its form is the symbol of the Sonoran Desert.

It is easy to imagine the amazement of Coronado and his Conquistadors when, nearly a century before the Pilgrims landed at Plymouth, they rode north from Mexico City and entered the forests of the saguaro. They were the first white men to see the giant cactus. They gave it its name. The branching, fluted columns, with bizarre and often grotesque forms, are native only to a relatively small area in northern Mexico and the Southwestern United States. All the saguaros in the world are confined to a range roughly 200 miles wide and 250 miles long.

That day and on succeeding days, as we rode down the Ajo Valley, along the edge of the Mexican line and in the Organ Pipe Cactus National Monument, we moved through a landscape dominated by saguaros. We walked around them. We looked up at them. We ran our hands carefully between the spines over the tough, waxy skin. It is these giant cacti that come first to mind when we remember southern Arizona.

Each column that towered above us was, in effect, an expandable storage tank. The accordionlike pleats that run vertically up the side of a saguaro enable it to expand or contract, to increase or decrease its circumference. The cactus becomes more slender in times of drought, more plump when rain has fallen. Its spongelike tissues have enormous capacity for holding liquids. A large saguaro may collect as much as a ton of water from a single rain.

Each of these green, living water towers of the desert, we discovered, represents a marvel of evolutionary engineering. Running inside the length of the column is a ring of from twelve to thirty strong, slender vertical rods. They form the skeleton of the plant and support its mass of spongy tissue. In a number of places along the Forty-Mile Loop and the Ajo Mountain Drive, and later at the Arizona-Sonora Desert Museum at Tucson, and at the Saguaro National Monument east of that city, we came upon dead cacti with all their tissues fallen away and only the long-enduring rods, like bleached bones, remaining in place. The saguaro is spectacular in death, as it is in life.

At the bottom of each plant, the woody rods of the skeleton are fused together to form a sturdy base. This is anchored to the earth by a taproot that plunges deeply into the ground and by a network of strong lateral roots that may have a spread of fifty or even seventy feet. They run close to the surface and their maze of branching rootlets absorbs moisture with astonishing speed. Desert rains are infrequent and often short-lived. Collection and absorption must be swift. During abnormal periods of rainfall, instances have been recorded of saguaros storing water beyond their capacity and splitting open down the sides.

In addition to collecting moisture, these lateral roots grip the earth and prevent the vertical columns from being overturned by the wind. A saguaro may sway as much as two feet from vertical when hit by a heavy gust. But, until it is near the end of its life, it is rarely blown down. Occasionally, a column will snap off a few feet above the ground. We came to the scene of one such accident soon after we left a curious stretch of "desert pavement" where the action of wind and water had paved the ground with an almost solid mosaic of small, flat brown stones. In a sheer break, the stem of this saguaro had parted, revealing a cross section that suggested a cogwheel. We examined it carefully. Unlike most trees, the saguaro has no annual growth rings. The broken stem offered no clue to its age.

But it may well have been more than a century old. For

the development of the saguaro is protracted over many decades. The drama of its life unfolds slowly. Two years after the seed has sprouted, I was told, the little button of the baby cactus may be no more than a quarter of an inch high. At the end of a decade, a saguaro that is destined to grow as high as a forest tree may be four inches tall. As the years advance, its rate of growth speeds up. By the end of three decades, it may be three or four feet high. Around the half-century mark, when it has reached a height of eight or ten feet, its first flowers open in a circle at the tip of the growing column.

Only a few months after our visit, with the coming of May and June, all the high saguaros around us would be decked with striking white-and-gold blooms that often have a diameter of as much as three inches. They cluster at the tops of the columns and on the tips of the branches. Opening a few at a time, they unfold in the spring night and wither away before the next night falls.

During this short life, the showy blossoms are surrounded by clouds of insects, including wild honeybees that have descended from colonies first introduced into the Southwest in the eighteen-seventies. But, scientists have discovered, insects are not the only pollenizers of the saguaro blooms. Both white-winged doves and nectar-feeding bats are sometimes instrumental in transferring pollen from flower to flower. The result of this fertilization is the scarlet fruit that ripens in midsummer. For centuries the juice, the pulp, the seeds of this fruit have been staple items in the diet of the Pima and Papago Indians of Arizona.

In a favorable year, a large saguaro will produce as many as 200 fruits, containing between a quarter of a million and a half million black, shiny seeds. Under the harsh conditions of the desert, the odds are always against the seed and the seedling. One scientist has estimated that not more than one out of every 275,000 saguaro seeds that reach the ground produces a plant. We saw few seedlings. Virtually all the small saguaros we noticed were growing under paloverde trees. There they found shade and protection. Occasionally we came upon cacti that had ascended among the branches of such nurse trees until their tops projected above the crowns of the paloverdes that they would long outlive. I remember once, at night, we halted where the silhouette of a double-branched saguaro rose above the dark mass of a paloverde, lifting like the two ears of some immense deer peering at us over the treetop.

A paragraph or so back, I mentioned the wild honeybees of the desert. We had seen their exposed combs high on a cliff in Sandstone Canyon, at Anza-Borrego. Here, among the saguaros of the Sonoran Desert, we met honeybees again, this time under even more unusual and dramatic circumstances.

We were climbing up from the desert floor on a rocky trail of switchbacks. The path wound among yellowish boulders gaudy with lichens—green and russet and pastel-hued. Goatnut and cat's-claw and brittlebush clung to the steeply tilted ground. Our ears caught a faint humming sound. It grew louder as we advanced. It rose almost to a roar when we came to the mouth of a small cavern in the rock. Cool, moist air flowed from the opening. Inside, the little cave was wet and dripping, green with moss. Water continually oozed from fissures above and splashed in large drops into a gray-green pool, about six feet across, that filled the rock basin of the sunken floor. We were looking into the grotto of the famous Dripping Springs of the Ajo Valley.

Honeybees, going and coming, streamed past us. We saw them crawling over the shining rock, lined up at the water's edge, obtaining moisture. The sound of their wings was gathered and magnified and projected outward by the curved rock walls of the shallow cave. On the surface of the pool floated a small raft of drowned bees. Each day thousands of

these insects come to the cavern for water. So regular are
the trips of wild honeybees to sources of moisture that, on
more than one occasion, Dr. Jaeger told me, he has discovered small "coyote wells" in the desert by following the con-
verging lines of these thirsty insects.

In all the Ajo Valley, in all the nearly 520 square miles of
the Organ Pipe Cactus National Monument, there is not one
permanent stream of flowing water. The wildlife of this region depends mainly on a handful of springs and seeps. To
drink at the Dripping Springs pool come javelinas and coyotes, antelope and mule deer and desert bighorn sheep. Birds
of many kinds enter the cavern for water. When I dipped
up a handful, I found the liquid was clear and cool and sweet.
With its damp walls and fissures, its falling drops and collected water, with ferns growing here in the midst of the
desert, this moist cave on the slope of the Puerto Blanco
Mountains is a center of life for the region. As we came up
the trail we had seen rufous-crowned and desert sparrows dart
from the doorway. Now, as we moved away down the slope,
the birds came flying back.

A dozen dry, cactus-studded miles to the south, we came
to another life-giving source of water, the historic spring of
Quito Baquito. The dusty road that carried us in its direction wound among saguaros that rose in an infinite variety
of forms. Of all the tens of thousands of these giant cacti
we saw on the Sonoran Desert, no two seemed exactly alike.
Often their distinctive shapes became landmarks. We grew
to recognize, from a long distance, one particular saguaro
that towered up with two branches, each curving downward
and sweeping low like the trunk of an elephant.

Most commonly, branching begins about half way up the
stem of the cactus. It commences when the plant is around
three-quarters of a century old. Each branch starts as a bud
or nubbin. Elongating outward and frequently turning up or
down, it may attain a length of as much as ten or fifteen feet.

The cause of branching is still another of the many mysteries of botany. Some columns develop no branches at all. Others produce as many as half a hundred. Some are straight, some curved, some twisted into grotesque forms. There is one recorded instance of a saguaro with branches formed of chains of globular growths. The top of this cactus resembled a mass of toy balloons. I recall one of these cacti with a column that was twisted like a rope of taffy. Several we saw had curious convoluted growths at their tops. This cristate form of the saguaro, like the cause of branching, is a botanical riddle. Variously it has been attributed to early injury, to a virus, to lightning and to radioactivity in the soil.

It was well along in the afternoon when we first sighted Quito Baquito's little oasis of cottonwoods and tule, mesquite and mistletoe. More than two and a half centuries had passed since the eyes of the first European had beheld it. Then, the famed Spanish explorer-priest, Father Eusebio Francisco Kino, had camped here on his way to Casa Grande, the prehistoric pueblo on the Gila River. Here again, in a later year, he replenished his water supply before blazing his short-cut trail to Yuma across more than 100 miles of parched land, a trail known to the pioneer Spaniards as *El Camino del Diablo*, The Devil's Highway. Three thousand persons, one historian estimates, lost their lives along this deadly road. In the days of the California gold rush, parties taking the southern route camped as long as possible at Quito Baquito. It was the jumping-off place, the last good source of water before the dreaded passage of the Devil's Highway.

We walked about this oasis, so celebrated in the romantic history of the Southwest. Here had slept missionaries and desperadoes, gold-seekers and Indians. We thought of all the dreams that had passed through the heads of slumbering men, dreams of unearthing nuggets and saving souls, of riches on earth and in the hereafter. Each square foot of soil was dramatic ground. Standing there with the calling of birds around us, with the fresh smell of water in the air, with the musical clash of breeze-stirred leaves like the lapping of little waves in our ears, it was easy to appreciate how great a miracle this island of life must have appeared to early travelers entering its shade from the mirage-heat of the summer desert.

The almost prostrate form of an ancient cottonwood extended out over the spring-fed pond. So long had it been tilted in this position that all its topmost branches had turned upward toward the sun. We walked out on the deeply grooved, silvery bark of the trunk. It had been scuffed and worn by innumerable feet before us. Among the outer branches, screened by a luminous curtain of tans and greens and golds where sunshine played on leaves still clinging to the twigs, we looked directly down into the transparent water of the pool. There, once more, we saw the darting rush of tiny desert pupfish. They streaked from the bordering sedges and shot in and out among drifting leaves. The species here, inhabiting fresh water instead of salt, is known as Pursey's minnow.

Over the pupfish in short rushes a dragonfly, spotted with red, ripped through clouds of pale gnats dancing beside the sedges. A dark little spider, carrying a white egg case, ran across the surface film. All around us there was the sound of birds—Gila woodpeckers in the cottonwoods, robins and verdins and Audubon's warblers in the mesquites, a cactus wren in a crucifixion thorn, phainopeplas among the mistletoe, marsh wrens in the tule. Virtually every species of bird found in the Organ Pipe Cactus National Monument comes to the green oasis of Quito Baquito.

Only a few acres in extent, it is situated almost exactly on the International Boundary. Across its southern edge runs a high fence of woven wire. Beyond lies Mexico. Only a few hundred yards or so in that direction, we saw the concrete of a superhighway paralleling the fence. It linked the Mexican towns of Tijuana and Sonoita. At long intervals cars passed, traveling a mile a minute across land where horsemen once plodded in peril on the Devil's Highway. But as the whine of each car faded away, we seemed isolated as though living in a remote time.

I had skimmed through the headlines of a Tucson paper that morning. They featured blocked roads, record freezes, cold waves and blizzards in the north. People congratulated themselves on what they were escaping. As is the way of the world in winter resort regions, the impression grew that northern states were in the grip of a new Ice Age, that people there soon would be living in igloos. In truth, this was January. This was the Snow Moon of the Iroquois. But here, at the end of this winter day, the air was warm and still. The sun set over the Mexican mountains a little south of west, a slender new moon hung above the western glow and small bats hunted with staggering flight over the open spaces. We seemed in a late-summer, a September, evening.

Again and again we returned to Quito Baquito. We saw it at night, at dawn, at midday. We wandered along remnants of little irrigation ditches dug by Papago Indians. We came upon fig and pomegranate trees run wild. And when we left in darkness, all around, beyond the confines of the oasis, the high columns and contorted arms of the saguaros rose, massive and black, against the glittering expanse of the desert stars.

Once, as we were driving the dusty miles out to the highway, often within yards of the Mexican line, we ascended from a dry wash and our headlights swept upward along the tall saguaros. For an instant, they caught and spotlighted the form of a great horned owl silently winging its way among the cacti. Altogether, twenty-one species of birds are known to nest in saguaros. They range from the great horned owls and red-tailed hawks that construct stick nests among the spine-covered branches to numerous species that occupy holes after they have been abandoned by woodpeckers.

The gilded flicker, a bird with exactly the same range as the saguaro, is responsible for most of these excavations. The others are produced by Gila woodpeckers. Fortunately, all these cavities are hollowed out in a dry time of the year when the menace of bacterial disease is reduced. For the greatest threat to the saguaros is the insect-transmitted necrosis bacteria that sweep through the body of the cactus and destroy its tissue in as short a time as three weeks. Over large areas in Arizona, this disease has reached epidemic proportions.

Within a few days after the woodpecker's nesting hole is excavated, the sap of the saguaro hardens around it into a dense, varnish-like wall that seals it off from the rest of the plant. Long after a cactus has died, these retort-shaped objects remain intact. Indians collected them and used them for dippers and storage jars. Birds hatching within these cavities are not only sheltered from the harsh desert sun, but they live in a water-cooled nest, surrounded by the moist, spongy pulp of the saguaro's interior.

Once, at a turn in the road, we were standing directly beneath one hole when a Gila woodpecker poked out its head, spotted us, and bounded away with strident calling. Several times we counted as many as a dozen holes in the upper trunk and branches of a single saguaro. When their builders have deserted them, they are taken over by such birds as desert sparrowhawks and elf owls. No larger than a house sparrow, this latter bird is the most diminutive of the world's owls. It is a hunter of moths. The largest of our cacti shelters the smallest of our owls.

Although nesting holes are numerous in saguaros, only once did we see one excavated in an organ-pipe cactus. This species, from which the national monument derives its name, is confined to south-central Arizona and northwestern Mexico. Ranking next to the saguaro in size, with unbranched stems that sometimes rise to a height of twenty feet, it appears in clusters like the tubes of a pipe organ.

This whole Ajo Valley seemed a vast natural cactus garden just as Death Valley had appeared an outdoor museum of geology. Wherever we went, here along the Mexican border as well as in a number of other desert areas of the Southwest, we encountered what looked like young saguaros. But they invariably leaned to the south, growing faster on the shaded northern side. These were the barrel cacti, the compass plants of the desert. It is this species that is celebrated in western stories as a source of fluid for thirsty travelers. However, the thirsty traveler who lops the top from a barrel cactus and expects to find a kind of vacuum bottle filled with water is in for a disappointment. What he will find is pulpy material containing a thick juice that can be extracted by chewing.

Of the more than thirty species of cacti native to the Organ Pipe Monument, the rarest of all, growing nowhere else in the United States, is the senita, the "old one." A valley cactus, it inhabits the sandy washes that drain away into Mexico. Like the organ-pipe cactus, it grows in clusters. But the tips of all the larger stems are tufted with masses of fine gray, whisker-like spines.

One midmorning we had left a wash where the "old ones" grew and had stopped among saguaros a mile or so beyond. Out from among these giant cacti came wandering a small burro, beautifully gray with tinges of silver. It greeted me like a long-lost benefactor. It followed me to the car. It thrust its head in the open window. Nellie remembered a box of dry, discarded cookies. The burro ate and ate until they all were gone. Then—toward what destination we could not imagine— it wandered off again and disappeared among the saguaros.

It was past whole mountain slopes forested with these tree-like cacti that we approached Tucson next day. For us, the attraction of this city is always one of our infrequent reunions with Marcelle and Joseph Wood Krutch. The pleasures of our visit ranged from an ascent of nearby Mt. Lemmon to

MULE DEER, with huge ears uplifted, sniffs the air amid
junipers in the snowy highlands of northeastern Arizona.

TAPESTRY OF FROST on glass reveals the variety of delicate shapes that are produced by the ice crystals.

eating candied strawberries imported from France and watching for hours the desert birds that fed beyond a picture window. The first to appear at dawn was the Gambel's white-crowned sparrow. Then came the jays. Then the verdins. About breakfast time, thirty or more brightly colored Gambel's quail emerged from among the creosote bushes. They gave the impression of running with a slightly off-balance gait, as though falling forward as they advanced. For half an hour they fed. Then, in little coveys, they wandered off. But the white-crowns stayed on.

These two birds, the beautiful sparrow and the beautiful quail, honor the memory of a pioneer naturalist who compressed into his tragically short life an amazing amount of achievement and adventure. One-time assistant to Thomas Nuttall, one-time assistant curator of the Academy of Natural Sciences of Philadelphia, William Gambel (1821–1849) was the first ornithologist to spend any length of time studying the birds of California. To collect ornithological and botanical specimens in the Southwest, he joined a party of trappers. To explore the California coast for specimens, he worked on a vessel that put into small mission ports along the way. He was the first to describe the wren-tit, the mountain chickadee, the plain titmouse, the California thrasher and the green-tailed towhee. In 1849, the year of the Gold Rush, Gambel followed the northern route to California. Cold weather set in before he crossed the Humboldt Sink. He climbed the Sierra Nevada in snow. Ill with dread typhoid fever, he reached a gold camp on the Feather River, in California. There he died, on December 13, 1849, at the age of twenty-eight.

On our last night in Tucson, before we went to bed, we noticed a brilliant light low in the southern sky. A star of the first magnitude shone just above the horizon. Only south of thirty-seven degrees latitude does this star, Canopus, become visible. The next day we planned to ride east, to leave the

Sonoran Desert behind, to climb to the Continental Divide and cross into the high country of New Mexico. Why we did none of these things, why our plans suddenly changed, will be recounted in the following chapter.

EIGHT

OUR IDLE DAYS IN PATAGONIA

SOMETIMES when I have long known some magic place, I have envied those who might come upon it unprepared, suddenly, in a moment of surprise and delight. This is the way we came to Patagonia.

It happened in this manner. We left Tucson that morning on the superhighway, U.S. 80. A dozen miles southeast of the city, we pulled to the shoulder of the road and sat enjoying the vast sweep of the desert that stretched away, miles on miles of cholla and creosote bush, until the land tilted abruptly upward into a jagged horizon-line of peaks. Cars zipped past, some with a silky swish, some with a rising whine like wasps. Trucks tore by—red trucks, white trucks, blue trucks, varicolored trucks, a rainbow parade of traffic. Each thundering machine trailed a tornado of wind that struck and shook our car in passing.

We had been sitting there no more than three minutes when a trailer truck as long as a flatcar, loaded with a factory boiler, slowed to a stop beside us. Were we in trouble? Did we need any help? No. No—thanks. With a blast of power from its Diesel engine, the leviathan gained momentum and joined the rush of traffic. It occurred to us that everyone in all that stream of hurtling machines probably assumed that because we had paused we *must* be in trouble. The only comprehensible reason for halting was a car that would run no farther.

All at once we were overwhelmed by a distaste for super-highways, for miracle miles, for the thunder of traffic and the thousand whirlwinds blasting down wide ribbons of concrete. We longed for some side road, slower-paced, where we could see and enjoy our surroundings. To those whose sole need is to get from here to there, superhighways are a boon. In truth, without their aid it is doubtful that we could have seen, in a single season, all the varied aspects of winter across the continent. Yet they are part of a present paradox: the more the land is traversed, the less it is seen. Year by year, jet airliners fly higher, passenger cars on superhighways go faster. One shows the land as a distant map unrolling, the other as a landscape blurring by. Both remove us from con-tact. I remember Wilbur Shaw, three times winner of the Indianapolis 500-mile race, once saying to me: "The faster you go, the farther you have to look ahead." I remembered John Muir, in the California mountains, protesting that noth-ing could be seen traveling in a stagecoach at the rate of *forty miles a day*. Modern cars multiply that distance ten times or more. The unseen country is the land traversed at rocketing speed.

We sat there for a short time longer, thinking of leisurely roads, praising back roads, remembering the silent appeal of all the little roads whose invitation we had turned down. And as we talked, our discontent grew. We determined to turn off on the first good side road we came to, no matter where it led. While I pulled out and rejoined the torrent of traffic, Nellie studied the map.

The road we chose turned south. A name had caught our attention. It was Patagonia. Years before we had read W. H. Hudson's *Idle Days in Patagonia*. The charm of that book lingered about the name. Hudson's Patagonia extended to the southern tip of South America. Ours, a hemisphere away, lay about a dozen miles north of the Mexican border. What we would find there, we had no idea. We imagined a region of illimitable plains stretching away to the horizon.

Once, in our autumn travels, we had cut down across the Dakotas on a highway numbered 83. We always remembered that road as "wonderful 83." Now, far to the south, we were on another highway of the same number. Even under low clouds, dragging rain veils across the slopes around us, it, too, was a "wonderful 83." Neither rain nor wind nor a sky clamped tightly shut reduced its appeal or lessened our sense of adventure.

The road climbed steadily. And as it climbed, wands of the ocotillo multiplied around us. They ranged across whole mountainsides and ran in a fringe or mane along the high horizon. Nowhere else had we observed so wide and dense a stand of ocotillo. We pictured, in our mind's eye, all those slopes at blooming time, those hundreds of thousands of wands, each tipped with the red flame of the flowers.

Along this highway we encountered hardly another car. Gone were the trailer trucks and moving vans, gone the torrent of speeding traffic. We felt elated, set free, as free as the ravens that soared on the wind beneath the scudding rain clouds. We left the ocotillo and ascended through a kind of luxurious badlands, a country cut and scarred by erosion but now richly clothed in grass. We crossed a rolling plateau, more than 4,000 feet high, where live oaks grew in the hollows. Ours was a road of superlatives. For here the beargrass, *Nolina*, grew in unparalleled profusion. All across this widespread land, where Cochise had led his Apache braves in raids on the early settlers, the range was dotted with fountainlike clusters of this fine-leaved plant.

Sonoita Creek led us south to Patagonia. Rain was falling when we came to the edge of this small town, set in a narrow valley under the height of white-robed mountains to the east. Its elevation is 4,050 feet. Both here and in South America, the name, Patagonia, is derived—presumably from the tracks of the aborigines—from the Spanish word for "large foot." The Indians themselves had a better name. To them, because of the abundance of wood and game, the area was known as "The Enchanted Land."

It was almost noon when we splashed up to the white wooden building that housed the Patagonia Post Office. Half a dozen high school sophomores were inside selling cakes and coffee and homemade candy to raise money for a trip, in their senior year, to see Los Angeles and Hollywood. This is the way of human nature. If we live in a Los Angeles, we dream of some quiet Patagonia. If we live in a Patagonia, it is the exciting Los Angeles that we long to see. Exerted in both directions is the pull of the different and far-away.

While Nellie and I drove out the chill with a hot drink and a piece of homemade cake, we learned that the whole creek bottom here is a nature sanctuary. Rare birds seek the protection of its cottonwoods. Following directions, we turned down a side street where a raven walked, with swinging body, along the edge of a sodden baseball field. We crossed a pebbly wash and turned onto a dirt road that, keeping its distance, followed the other side of the stream. It carried us into a wild park, a place of special magic, that extended for several miles along the creek bottom, open and level, with immense and ancient cottonwoods scattered down its length. A weathered sign, nailed to a tree, carried the almost illegible words: "The San Jose de Sonoita Wildlife Sanctuary." Nearby, a newer notice read: "BIRD REFUGE. No shooting. No molesting or collecting birds or eggs. *Se prohibe cazar.* Tucson Audubon Society."

The rain halted. It started up again. Then it stopped entirely. Along the creek and among the cottonwoods and under eroding cliffs, we drifted down this valley of birds. All that afternoon, experiences unfolded, piled on each other, grew better hour by hour. Birds were everywhere after the rain. Northern and southern species met and fed together. Eastern and western birds alighted in the same trees.

Over robins, running across the wet ground, Mexican jays streamed in a screaming flock. Almost side by side, a bird of the dark northern forest, a hermit thrush, and a bird of the open plains, a lark sparrow, hunted for food. We saw an eastern phoebe and its western relative, a Say's phoebe, tipping their tails on adjoining branches. Birds of the desert— phainopeplas and curve-billed thrashers—and birds familiar to New England pastures—vesper sparrows, flashing their white tail feathers, and field sparrows, with their light bills and reddish caps—all had found sanctuary in this protected valley. And where, at a turn in the road, hackberries and ash trees grew at the foot of a cliff, half a dozen black and yellow and white evening grosbeaks hopped from limb to limb with the brilliant red of a male cardinal in their midst.

We had been here no more than five minutes when our minds were made up. For the time being, our travels through winter had come to a stop. In this small valley, we would spend our own idle days in Patagonia.

We sat on a log beside the stream and ate our lunch. A great blue heron, fishing in the shallow flow of the creek, moved away upstream with slow and stately wingbeats, and a red-shafted flicker, which we had surprised in its ant-hunting, bounded into the air and disappeared among the cotton-woods. But other birds remained all around us. Close by, a rock wren trilled again and again. Here the birds appeared to have everything—protection, shelter, food, cover, water. There were great trees, side canyons, fallen trunks, stream banks, running water. There were berries for thrushes, grass seeds for sparrows, open ground for robins. If we were winged creatures, we decided, we too would head for Patagonia. For birds also, this is The Enchanted Land.

We had drifted the length of the road and back again when we stopped near a neat cottage beside the stream. Birds darted among feeders set out in the yard. For a dozen years, we had learned, a couple from Lebanon, Ohio, the

Hal Sorters, had spent their winters here. To their feeders come an amazing variety of species. Standing in one place that afternoon, Sorter pointed out two birds in succession that we never in our lives had encountered before—a bridled titmouse and an hepatic tanager.

While we were there, two cars turned into the drive. They contained four bird enthusiasts, Bill Harrison and Warren Winslow, of Nogales, and Mr. and Mrs. Frederick Hatch, who had come south for the winter from Massachusetts. Time passed swiftly as we all watched the colorful parade of birds that came and went in the yard. For us they presented a mixture of the familiar and the bizarre—chipping sparrows and ladder-backed woodpeckers, white-breasted nuthatches and Audubon's warblers, rufous-sided towhees and Lincoln's sparrows, phainopeplas and Bewick's wrens.

A few days before, more than 100 meadowlarks had alighted around the house. On dark and rainy days, Sorter has the most bird visitors. Chilled and hungry, they seek out his feeders. On this day, white-crowned sparrows were numerous. But among all the species we saw, so many rare to us, the bird that caused the most excitement, a species that had not been seen in Sorter's yard before, a bird that Harrison had never set eyes on before, was that familiar minstrel of the north woods, the little white-throated sparrow.

Following the other cars, we traversed the windings of the dirt road once more. At the foot of the cliff where we had observed the cardinal among the grosbeaks, a new surprise awaited us. In a little flock, a dozen or more Cassin's finches, the first of these high-mountain birds we had seen, flitted among the bushes, the females striped and sparrowlike, the males tinted with pale rose.

The cliff above us, the twisting dirt road, the great cotton-woods, the narrow side canyons, all the picturesque features of this little valley, we were told, had been seen by millions of people in many parts of the world. Hollywood had dis-

covered Patagonia before us. More than one western movie
had been filmed on location in this creek-bottom valley. The
cliff top, in fact, was a favored place for Indians to launch
their attack on covered wagons and, more than once, bandits
had ridden out of the side canyon to waylay a stagecoach as
it came thundering around the bend.

The next morning, after a night at Nogales, when we returned for another of our idle days in Patagonia, we wondered if the magic of the valley had sprung from our surprise,
from the unexpectedness of our discovery, or from the dark,
closed-in character of the day of rain and lowering clouds.
Not so. The charm of the place seemed augmented in sunshine. We walked along the creek where the clear stream
wound in innumerable skeins of flowing water that joined
and parted, glinting and sparkling in the sun. The wind and
the rain were gone. The air grew warmer as the day advanced.

Once, for a long time, while Nellie followed an elusive
bird call among the cottonwoods, I sat with my back against
the rough bark of an ancient tree. Above me, and off down
the valley, Gila woodpeckers and red-shafted flickers called
and drummed on the dry wood of dead limbs. I could smell
the moist ground after the rain. I could catch, from somewhere beyond a sycamore, the scent of willow leaves. The
damp earth and the ringing call of the flickers carried me
back to early spring in Indiana.

As I sat there, relaxed, thinking of nothing, warmed by the
sun, aware—with animal senses—of all the world around me,
my outlook, too, shifted back to an earlier, simpler time. At
such a time, with awakening childhood perceptions, we walk
through the out-of-doors accompanied by wonder and delight.
In later years we learn the names of the things that long ago
we saw and wondered at. We catalogue them in our minds.
And some of the freshness fades away. Deservedly, the pursuit of factual knowledge holds a high place. Knowing the
wildflowers, naming all the birds without a gun, these are

admirable attainments. But there is always a residue of sadness when we learn the name and lose the wonder of the living thing itself.

We become specialists and our interests shrink. I know one woman who is interested *only* in warblers, another who is interested only in *female* ducks. There is more to the out-of-doors than a schoolroom and much has been lost when the sight of a hermit thrush stirs in our consciousness merely the scientific name *Hylocichla guttata*. The simple enjoyment of universal nature, with no other end in mind—this, too, has its importance. And fortunate indeed are those who know this enjoyment to the end of their days. Richard Jefferies, the English author of *The Story of My Heart* and *The Life of the Fields*, was one of these. Few men have ever lived whose delight in all-embracing nature was so intense. Ten years after visiting a beach on the seashore, Jefferies declared he could remember every drift of sand grains, every fragment of a shell, every pebble, and find a joy in each.

Yet, in all ages, this simple enjoyment of nature has felt the need of a disguise. Unless some trophy resulted, unless some pressed plant or dead bird or cyanided butterfly accompanied the wanderer home, he was considered an idler who had wasted his day. Never the pure enjoyment! Never the delight in nature for its own sake! To appreciate nature with singleness of heart, as the child loves it—this was felt to be a weakness, an inferior employment of time, not readily to be confessed. Only those who stuffed birds or robbed nests could claim the title of true naturalist. The simple-hearted appreciator and enjoyer of nature was considered at best a trifler. Picking flowers, collecting butterflies, stuffing birds—all these indicate a love, or at least an interest in nature. But on a plane far higher lives the one who leaves the flower blooming and the butterfly and bird flying.

One of the volumes in my library, more than a century old, is a duplicate of the entomology textbook Thoreau owned.

It is *The Life of North American Insects*, by B. Jaeger, "late professor of Zoology and Botany in the College of New Jersey." To the author—as to most of his contemporaries, but not to Thoreau—a simple enjoyment of nature needed an apology. The apology most readily accepted in his time was a search for moral lessons. They were the conventional trophies required from days afield. "To every thoughtful person," the author writes in discussing the katydid, "all nature conveys some important moral lesson. The busy bee, that improves each shining hour, cannot fail of favorably impressing us with the contentment and the sure success that follows patient and persevering industry. The ever constant and faithful dog that bears us company is ever silently but surely impressing upon us the great lesson of fidelity." And so on—a thread of self-conscious moralizing ran through the nature books of a hundred years ago. In all times, the appreciator has had to have his excuses ready. Different times, different excuses. A century ago, it was looking for a moral lesson. Today, it may be a hunt for ecological significance. But, in this speeding modern world, an increasing number of people are realizing that just to stop, just to enjoy nature, has its own significance.

On this day we had the valley all to ourselves. We saw no other person as we loitered along the way, pausing often at the call of a bird or the sight of a squirrel. Again we ate our lunch beside the Sonoita. And again we wandered through a world of colorful birds. In our glasses appeared varied birds, unfamiliar birds, never-before-seen birds. And often, for surprising stretches of time, no two were alike. We saw a cardinal and a pyrrhuloxia in the same bush. We saw gray-headed juncos and Oregon juncos with black heads. We saw canyon wrens in a canyon and house finches among the cottonwoods. In a clump of mistletoe, phainopeplas and western bluebirds fed together.

Special moments of pleasure come back from those idling

days in a valley of birds. Once, where bushes ascended a cliff, clinging to cracks in rocks that were mottled with lichens, a male vermilion flycatcher mounted up from bush to bush in the sunshine. It resembled a running spark or flame leaping in a zigzag path up the face of the cliff. In glimpses we followed the restless darting among twigs and branches of gray, golden-headed little verdins. And at the foot of the same cliff where we had seen the Cassin's finches and the cardinal with the evening grosbeaks, we watched a pair of brown towhees engage in what appeared to be a kind of mating performance. They fluffed their feathers, gave odd little cries, and followed one another about, ascending higher and higher among the rocks.

Before our stay in Patagonia came to an end—and we rode north again over rolling yellow-grass country where rarely a windmill or the smoke of a ranch house peeps above a hollow—we had seen among the varied birds of this small overwintering valley three kinds of thrushes, three kinds of flycatchers, three kinds of wrens, three kinds of towhees and three kinds of woodpeckers. So far, the enlightenment of successive owners has kept the area a sanctuary. But plans have been advanced for flooding the valley to provide a resort lake. This "Enchanted Land" needs permanent provision for its protection as an endowed sanctuary, a Federal refuge or a national monument. In all America, such magic places are few.

Coming upon it by accident, as we did, emphasized the impression it made. The thoughts, the memories, the delights of this valley interlude remain with us. One of the entries in Richard Jefferies' *Nature Diaries and Notebooks* concerns a beautiful gull he once had seen. Remembering it long years after, he observed: "The gull is dead but I think of my thoughts of the gull as living on." So, for us, the valley lives on. As long as memory is with us, we shall see it vividly as we saw it then, in sunshine and in rain.

NINE

WHITE DUNES

A HUNDRED miles beyond the Continental Divide and 400 miles east of Patagonia, we dropped in a long descent down the arid eastern slope of the Organ Mountains of New Mexico. Before us, across the level floor of the Tularosa Basin, spinning funnels of brown rose hundreds of feet into the air. As many as fifty at a time, the dust devils whirled around us as we advanced. One raced along the roadside for a quarter of a mile. I kept pace with it. It was traveling at a speed of almost exactly forty miles an hour. Away from the foot of the mountains, the turbulence of the air grew less. But the strength of the wind increased. Long, trailing yellow-brown clouds of dust, like smoke from a grass fire, extended for miles across the desert.

Beside the highway, tumbleweeds tugged at their stems. When one snapped, we saw the released globe bound away, its stiff, curving, resilient branches bouncing it like a rubber ball. Several times, instead of tumbling haphazardly, a globe would momentarily strike a balance in the wind. With the heavier stem end holding a position against the pressure of a long gust, it would spin as though revolving on an axle and go wheeling away in a long, angling run across the level surface of the roadway.

When we opened the car window for a moment to listen to the surf-sound of wind among the yuccas, a thin film of grit formed on our faces. Above the land that smoked with the swirling dust of the storm, the blanket of haze became denser. It rose higher, glowing with a dim and tinted light, a brownish shine that filtered down through the clouds of airborne soil. All living things were lying low. Once we passed a little flock of horned larks hugging the ground in the lee of a bush. They took alarm, scudded away downwind and, dim shapes in the haze, dropped into the shelter of a yucca. It was thus, whipped by the wind, abraded by the dust, riding with headlights on through the eerie midday twilight of the storm, that we first glimpsed White Sands and its miles of wind-formed gypsum dunes.

Ever since my childhood among the sand dunes of northern Indiana, I have been fascinated by the beauty and mystery of these hills that move. Often in our travels with the seasons we had turned aside to visit some lonely stretch of duneland. We had seen the dunes of Cape Cod and the Oregon coast, of Death Valley and the Hiawatha country on the shores of Lake Superior. We had visited the Great Sand Dunes of the San Luis Valley of Colorado and Kitty Hawk on the Carolina coast, where the Wright brothers first flew. Near Moses Lake, in Washington, we had wandered over black dunes, and now we were seeing white dunes—night and day represented in hills of wind-moved mineral fragments.

When we returned next morning, the air was clear, the sun shining, the rolling sea of dunes around us gleaming white like hills of salt. Where these gypsum mounds were crescent-shaped, they curved like drawn bows aimed toward the southwest, the source of the prevailing winds. Unlike the Indiana dunes of my boyhood, those hills of quartz on the Lake Michigan shore, the slopes and ridges here had no gritty quality. We seemed to be walking on granules of soap. Gypsum, the mineral that forms alabaster, that creates the shining plates of the Glass Mountains of Oklahoma, that—when ground—makes plaster of Paris, the mineral of schoolroom chalk and casts for broken limbs and plasterboard for the builders, this material is one of the softest of the minerals. A fingernail will scratch it. Only talc is softer.

Deposits of gypsum are found around the world. But deposits of gypsum sand are rare. Dunes of this material are known in only two other places on earth besides White Sands. One is in Utah, the other in South Australia. Neither approaches in magnitude the miles of shining hills held within the Tularosa Basin. More than 200,000,000 years have passed since, at the bottom of inland seas, the gypsum of the valley was laid down. Bounded by mountains of limestone, shale and sandstone, the windswept basin has no outlet for running streams. Eroded gypsum remains within it. In the course of time, the particles have been transported and shaped into dunes by the prevailing wind from the southwest.

Although nearly half a million visitors a year come to White Sands, during the winter days we were there we often found ourselves entirely alone. How far we walked along the ridges and in the hollows I do not know, any more than I know how many hundreds, or even thousands, of miles we have wandered on foot during our travels through all the four seasons. Often we had the impression of crossing mountainous seas, miraculously stilled and solidified under our feet. For these white ridges, in the main, belong to the "sand-sea" type of dunes. From the air, they have the appearance of ocean billows. The crests of some are as much as sixty feet above their troughs.

Here, as in other dunes we had seen, a few had become stabilized, overgrown with a covering of vegetation. But most are active, on the move, advancing with the wind year after year. The rate of movement of sand dunes varies considerably in different parts of the world. On the coast of Denmark, the average advance is twenty-nine feet a year. In East Prussia, it is forty-three feet. In the Sahara, it is forty-nine feet and on France's Bay of Biscay, 105 feet. At White Sands, something of a world's speed record has been set among some of the marginal dunes. They have advanced as much as 264 feet in a year.

Always the forward movement of a dune occurs in the same way. The sandhill advances like the slow revolving of a wheel as the wind subtracts material from one side and adds it to the other. Component particles are blown up the longer slant of the windward slope and over the summit to drop down the more abrupt descent of the lee side. Nowhere else had we seen these latter advancing faces of the moving dunes so steeply formed as at White Sands. Quartz sand is more rounded, more likely to roll. Gypsum sand is more angular, more able to sustain itself in steeper banks. But, in either case, this abrupt descent of the face of a dune represents a temporary stalemate. At this extreme angle, the opposing forces of friction and gravity come to a balance.

The second unique feature of these gypsum hills that impressed itself on us was their stillness. These are the silent dunes. Here there was no squeaking of quartz grains under our feet, no lisp of running sand drifting along the surface. Even when the wind rose—and there is almost always a wind in the valley in the afternoon—all this sea of rolling dunes remained hushed. I strained to catch the slightest sound. I strained in vain. As I stood there, my head cocked on one side, concentrating on a search for even the tiniest sounds, I recalled a rather famous American ornithologist of an earlier time. In his later years, not realizing he was growing deaf, he wrote a paper on "The Alarming Decrease in Small Singing Birds." Hastily I put my wrist watch to my ear and was reassured by the small but steady sound of its ticking. The silent dunes were really silent.

Across their rippled surface the pawprints of varied animals had written, as on gypsum pages, a record of nocturnal wanderings. We saw the trail of a coyote ascending a steep duneside to a clump of rabbitbrush and then slanting away down again. When we followed the looping, zigzagging course of one rabbit, we came to a place where its tracks formed a jumble in the sand a foot or two in diameter. It seemed to have stopped and danced a jig. Not infrequently, where the top of some yucca or other plant thrust above the drift of gypsum, the sand around was embroidered with a lacework of delicate tracks left by the feet of pocket mice and kangaroo rats.

Among the rodents of the Tularosa Basin you find a dramatic instance of evolution providing inconspicuousness for creatures living in special environments. Amid the dunes themselves there lives the very pale, almost white, race of the Apache pocket mouse, *Peroganthus apache gypsi*. Not many miles away, beyond the dunes, another race of the same species lives among hills of reddish earth. There mice are nearly red. To the north, in an outcropping of black lava, the same species is almost black.

Transfer the wild white mice of the gypsum dunes to the black lava and the black mice of the lava to the white dunes and you would make them more conspicuous to their enemies. Their chances of survival would be reduced. Originally, the mice that inhabited the dunes were darker than the light-colored sand. From time to time, paler-hued individuals were born of darker parents. In the case of such mutations, the characteristics are transmitted to the progeny. Better camouflaged, more often overlooked by enemies, these light-colored mice had increased chances of surviving and reproducing, and the lighter their hue the greater their chances. Thus, over vast stretches of time, through repeated mutations and the elimination of darker forms, evolution produced the famous White Sands mice.

In a similar way, other pale-hued forms of life came into being among these gypsum hills. Originally, the bleached earless lizard that is almost invisible on the dune sand was an ordinary brownish species inhabiting the basin. Insects have developed lighter forms in these surroundings. One robber fly of the area is so ashy gray it is almost white. But on this winter day, the only insect we saw, a tenebrionid beetle lying dead on the lower skirt of a bordering dune, was coal black. We recognized it as an old acquaintance, the "circus beetle" we had seen standing on its head among the Mud Hills of Anza-Borrego. Perhaps the fact that this insect can repel enemies by the discharge of a chemical fluid has made camouflage unnecessary. Without the evolutionary elimination of darker forms, it would retain its original color.

For a long time, the only living creatures we encountered were little bands of horned larks. Many of them were desert larks, pale in hue. Then, where a marginal dune rose like a high, breaking wave above a stretch of lowland vegetation, a red-tailed hawk swept to a landing. For a quarter of an hour it perched on the dune top, turning its head from time to time as it scanned the ground below.

Toward evening, on another day among these shifting hills, a white-crowned sparrow serenaded us with snatches of song from a mass of aromatic sumac clinging to the top of a sheer column of gypsum. This pedestal had a diameter of nearly four feet and ascended higher than my head. It rose from a hollow excavated by the same winds that had cut away the material from around it. Hundreds of thousands of minute root hairs of the sumac plant held the mass together. Its top marked the crest of a receding dune. Wherever a sumac grows among the gypsum sands, a potential column is formed by the intertwining roots that plumb deeply. In many places, we came upon these stark white columns, sometimes rising to a height of ten or a dozen feet. Always they were crowned by the tangled mass of the desert sumac, *Rhus trilobata*. Pioneers, in early days, made a kind of lemonade by crushing up the berries of this plant. We tasted a few. They were tart to the tongue and aromatic.

The dunes of the Lake Michigan shore, which I had known in my boyhood, are located in a moister climate and include several swampy areas. They support 755 kinds of flowering plants. In contrast, the entire flora of White Sands contains hardly more than sixty varieties of plants. Almost all of these grow at the edge of the marginal dunes. Seven species only can survive in the midst of the gypsum dunes where the sea of sand rises and falls as the hills move forward.

These seven are: the sumac, *Rhus trilobata*; the yucca, especially *Yucca elata*; the cottonwood tree, *Populus wislizeni*; the four-winged saltbush, *Atriplex canescens*—whose stems were eaten as greens by the Apaches; the yellow-flowered rabbitbrush, *Chrysothamus*; the Mormon tea, *Ephedra*; and the mint bush, *Poliomintha incana*, with its square stem, mint odor and silvery-gray leaves which Indians employed for seasoning meat.

All seven survive in the same manner. They originally take root in the soil of the desert floor in front of the advancing dunes. They remain anchored there and obtain their nourishment less from the gypsum in which they appear to be growing than from the ground beneath the dune. While other plants around them are being overwhelmed and buried by the movement of the hills, these seven are able to elongate their stems and keep their heads above the sand. Yuccas sometimes are found in the wake of a dune with their stems drawn out to a length of as much as forty-five feet. Well up on the slopes of the higher dunes, we came upon such plants lifting their dark-green, fountain-like masses of slender leaves above the ripple marks, those miniature dunes, that form on the surface of the gypsum.

Across such ripple marks, late on an afternoon, we followed a trail of dry, windblown leaves. They led us to a cottonwood. Only its upper branches remained unburied. Yet all across its top, the leaves of another year were rolled tightly into long brown buds. We ran them between thumb and forefinger. Each, as a protection against loss of moisture, was heavily coated with wax. Like the yucca and the other enduring plants that survive in this gypsum sea, the cottonwood is able to put forth extra roots along its stem. It is the giant of the White Sands flora. The name of the nearest town, Alamogordo, means Big Cottonwood Tree.

One of the largest of the other plants of the Tularosa Basin found its way into the region in a curious way. This is the honey mesquite. In the manner of other members of the pea family, its root system harbors bacteria able to convert nitrogen from the air into solid nitrates that form tiny nodules among the root hairs and enrich the soil. Not far from the white dunes, a line of these bushes runs across the desert. They mark the route of an ancient road used by oxcarts in Spanish times. Droppings from the oxen introduced the mesquite into this portion of the valley.

Sometimes when we descended into deep troughs between the dunes, we walked on a floor almost as hard as solidified plaster of Paris. The gypsum sand, unlike quartz sand, is soluble in water. In the hollows, where moisture tended to collect, the outer layers of the gypsum had dissolved, then hardened into a kind of pavement. Where drops of rain, driven by the wind, had struck at an angle on several slopes, we noticed how each had plowed out a little groove that was floored with hardened gypsum. Only in a country like this, a land of dry atmosphere, mainly a land of winds without rain, could gypsum dunes have come into being.

Walking here, in the rain shadow of the western mountains, we came over the brow of one dune and saw with surprise on the sheltered opposite slope a drift of snow. Later, in two other protected places, we came upon other small drifts. Across one, nearly as unexpected as Friday's famous footprint on Crusoe's island, ran the runner marks of a child's sled. We decided to add an element of surprise of our own. I opened the trunk of the car and rummaging around extracted my webbed snowshoes. When I walked the length of that thin drift, I left behind what may well have been the first snowshoe tracks on snow these white dunes had ever seen.

While I unbuckled the snowshoes, we looked away from the slender scarf of that transitory drift to the immense snowfields of the Sierra Blanca, the White Mountain. It rose in the northeast like a gleaming cumulus cloud, ascending to a height of more than 12,000 feet. This remarkable peak is the southernmost in the United States to exhibit evidences of glaciation. No other North American mountain represents so many life zones. It contains, stacked one on top of another, all the zones from Upper Sonoran to Arctic-Alpine.

Wherever we went among the white dunes, this white mountain remained in view. It stood out like Pikes Peak seen from the plains of Colorado, like Mt. Hood viewed from the valley of the Columbia. Yet only a few months away, on the summer side of the year, all that immense gleaming cloud would have faded away. The snowfields would then be gone. Alpine wildflowers would carpet the high tundras and thousands of hummingbirds, gay as the flowers, would sip nectar where now the mountain meadows were buried in drifts. For us, on that day in January, most of our trip through winter lay ahead. What would we see, what would we experience, before those snows were gone?

TEN

BITTER LAKE

THE most durable harvest of our lives, in all probability, is our harvest of memories. No depression, no bank failure, no material reverses can rob us of them. They form a mental bank account on which we draw in leaner times. To a friend who remonstrated with him that he could not afford an expensive concert ticket he had bought his daughter, a man once replied:

"I am buying her more than a ticket. I am buying her a memory."

Even the simplest of memories can bring to life again some pleasure of the past. Henry Thoreau tells us how, many a time, he lay awake at night thinking of the barking of a dog he heard long before, bathing his being once more in those waves of sound "as a frequenter of the opera might lie awake remembering the music he had heard." In that "immense, unfriendly wilderness of London," when Richard Jefferies lay dying of consumption, he turned for solace to memories of his windswept hours out-of-doors, recalling "the exceeding beauty of the earth, in the splendor of life."

Beauty to remember formed the winter harvest of the days that followed White Sands. We traced a long, lazy loop up the Rio Grande from El Paso to Albuquerque, on to Santa Fe and back again to Tularosa. Far horizons gave way to other far horizons. Our road rose and fell. The thermometer went up when we went down and down when we went up. Always in the distance, like jagged strips of the desert floor tilted on their sides, pale-tan, arid mountains rose into the radiance of a sky that comprised a major portion of the scenery. "Elsewhere," Willa Cather noted of this widespread New Mexican land, "the sky is the roof of the world; but here the earth was the floor of the sky."

When I recall the beauty of those days, I remember first of all the blue snowbank. We had headed south from Santa Fe and had left the city thirty miles behind when we came to a small coulee. A scarf of snow lay melting at its edge. From end to end it was richly, vividly blue. As we drew near, all its coloring suddenly broke away, took wing and filled the air. Half a hundred mountain bluebirds, quenching their thirst with snow water, had carpeted the drift with the color of their plumage, one of the world's most entrancing shades of blue.

Another time, soon after dawn, we stood beside a pool where mist curled up and froze into glittering needles of ice. In a continuous stream, the ice needles formed and drifted downward toward the ground, shining against the sunrise. They were the product of a moment when conditions were just right. Never before had we known this experience. It was as though we stood in the midst of a cirrus cloud forming in the stratosphere.

As Lord Grey pointed out long ago, our enjoyment of an outdoor adventure is threefold. We know the pleasures of anticipation, of realization, of memory. How many times in memory we have renewed the delight we felt in such small encounters beside the road!

The wind was with us much of the time as we traversed the country of Billy the Kid and followed ancient roads that had known the Conquistadors. At times the highway ahead was alive with the motion of tumbleweeds cartwheeling along. Dust clouds—"New Mexican rain"—swept in long tongues into the sky. One day we bought a morning paper to see what world events we were missing. We learned the Duke of Windsor was dancing the twist. We also discovered that the weather bureau at Albuquerque had taken special notice of the strong winds of recent days. They were a sign of approaching spring—or, as the official statement read, "an early beginning of the usual spring blowing" in this Southwestern state.

We had climbed over Apache Pass among Steller's jays and ponderosa pines and had followed the windings of the Hondo Valley when, not far from Roswell, we pulled to a stop behind a straggling line of bushes. Sandhill cranes, resembling at first glance a large flock of blue-tinted sheep, were feeding in a cut-over grain field. First one, then another, then all lifted high their heads to watch us. I counted 227. This flock was part of the immense concentration of these birds that overwinters at the Bitter Lake National Wildlife Refuge along the Pecos River northeast of Roswell, south of High Lonesome and west of Mescalero Sands.

This 24,000-acre sanctuary was established in 1937. It forms an important link in a chain of Government refuges that extends down the Central Flyway from Canada to Mexico. More than twenty different species of waterfowl stop here during the fall migration. But it is as the wintering place of the cranes that the sanctuary is most famous. While a few come down from their far-northern breeding grounds as early as during the latter part of September, normally the "peak-out," or maximum number of cranes, is reached toward the end of December. This may range from 10,000 to more than 30,000. The record, set in January 1957, is 35,000. The last of the northbound migrants leave the refuge about March 1.

Derived partly from Lost River, a stream that disappears and flows underground, the water of Bitter Lake is salty and alkaline, unfit for drinking or irrigation. South of it, a series of impounded pools extends down the ancient valley of the Pecos. They are filled by the flow of artesian wells and by seepage from the red, eroded bluffs of the Mescalero Escarpment beyond the river. One curious inhabitant of this inland salt water is *Batophora*, a marine alga common in tropical lagoons of the Gulf of Mexico. How did it reach these dry-country ponds more than 600 miles from the nearest coast? Probably on the legs of some swift-flying waterfowl arriving from the sea during the northward migration of spring.

We found ourselves, the following afternoon, wandering among these isolated ponds. Gadwall, pintail, mallard, shoveler, hooded merganser, and ruddy duck floated in the January sunshine. Greater yellowlegs called in the sky. From shelvings of ice and the fields beyond, blue geese, Canada geese and lesser snow geese took to the air with a wild clamor and flashing of wings. Wildlife abounded. But it included no cranes.

The thousands of stately birds, Robert Garrett, Bitter Lake Fish and Wildlife biologist, told us, were scattered across more than fifty miles of open country. Soon after sunrise they begin moving out to feed in cutover grain fields. Some apparently fly as far as the Clovis region, eighty miles away. Toward sunset, and in the twilight, the flocks come winging home.

While the afternoon waned and the time of the returning flocks drew closer, we talked to Garrett about another picturesque bird of the region. This is the running cuckoo, the unforgettable paisano, the subject of song and tale and legend in the dry Southwest, the state bird of New Mexico, *Geococcyx californianus*—the road runner. In early days, its habit of racing down roads ahead of teams gave rise to its name. Today it dashes from one side of a modern highway to the other at top speed. Not far from the Salton Sea we saw a road runner and a jackrabbit pass, streaking in opposite directions across the hardtop.

For several winters, one of these long-legged, long-tailed birds stayed in a bushy area close to the refuge headquarters.

On cold days when a visitor would drive up, park his car and go into the building, the road runner would race from its hiding place, leap onto the hood of the car, spread its feathers and bask in the warmth rising from the heated engine.

All along our zigzag path through the arid lands of California, Arizona, New Mexico and Texas, we frequently encountered these conspicuous giants of the cuckoo family. Their tails are a foot long and their over-all length is nearly two feet. We saw road runners in the snow; road runners in the sun. On the coldest mornings, we sometimes passed them perched on fence posts, tails hanging down, the plumage of their backs parted and revealing the bare skin, as they absorbed warmth from the rays of the ascending sun. Strong of limb and weak of wing, the road runner is essentially a bird of the open country. In making abrupt turns on the ground, it appears to use its long tail as a rudder. One road runner was clocked racing across level land at a speed of thirty-two kilometers—a shade under twenty miles—an hour.

Speed of movement aids this bird both in saving its life and in obtaining its food. Riley Kaufman told me of a coyote that was outwitted by the agility with which a "chaparral cock" dodged about a bush in the desert. With swift changes in position, it avoided each leap and rush. In the end, it was the coyote that gave up the game and trotted away. Dr. Jaeger once observed a somewhat similar contest taking place around a creosote bush. Two marsh hawks attacked a road runner. In spite of the odds, the speed and dodging ability of the cuckoo enabled it not only to escape but at times to become the aggressor.

At Bitter Lake, one year, a road runner used its speed in a novel way in obtaining food. On more than one occasion Garrett saw it draw close to a flock of scaled quail while they fed near a wire-mesh fence. With a sudden rush, it would dash toward the birds, race back and forth in front of them, and drive them toward the fence. The quail would panic.

Several always flew into the fence in trying to escape. Each time, the road runner darted upon them, striking with its bill. In this way, it always obtained one, and sometimes two, of the feeding "cotton-tops."

But even such an unaggressive bird as a quail will develop surprising stout-heartedness in defense of its young. Connie Hagar, famous for her observations of the birds of the Texas coast, once told me of seeing a bobwhite quail fly bang into a road runner time after time. It struck hard, then fluttered off to turn and come back for a fresh attack. The road runner was making off with a baby quail in its bill. This running attack, perhaps aided by the simultaneous appearance of a human being, caused it to drop its small prey which ran off little the worse for its adventure.

Near its own nest, the road runner sometimes employs a curious variation of the broken-wing performance by means of which many birds seek to lead intruders from the vicinity of their young. Instead of a broken wing, these running birds pretend to have a broken leg. A detailed account of this decoying stratagem was first published in 1916 by J. R. Pemberton in *The Condor*, the journal of the Cooper Ornithological Society, of California.

By nature, the road runner is aggressive and fearless. In the lower Rio Grande Valley, a few years ago, one tried to intimidate a light truck that had come to a halt in its territory. It circled around, dashed back and forth, several times seemed on the point of launching an attack. When it is excited, the paisano lifts its black crest, elevates its long, narrow tail and utters a rattling *brrrr*, apparently made by a rapid clicking of its mandibles. Held at various angles, its tail seems to express emotions all the way from alert awareness to dejection. Few other birds have such striking personalities. It is intensely curious. Oftentimes, when we stopped nearby, one would fly to a fence post, lift and drop its tail a hundred times, cock a canny eye in our direction, raise and lower its crest continually. When a friend of ours sat for a long time in his car watching a road runner, the bird grew so fearless it approached close enough to pick flies from the tires.

While it undoubtedly does some damage as a predator, the road runner also does a great deal of good by its consumption of injurious species of what is probably the main item on its bill of fare—insects. It sometimes leaps high off the ground to catch grasshoppers in flight. Almost anything that a road runner can swallow suits its taste. Horned toads, tarantulas, seeds, centipedes, fruits, snakes, rodents, lizards, snails—all are gobbled down.

Near the mouth of the Rio Grande, on a later day in our trip, we saw slender white tree snails on the bushes. These the road runners gather as a special delicacy. Sometimes stones or hard clods in this region are surrounded by a kitchen midden of shells. The birds bring the snails to such spots to break open the shells on these natural anvils.

The night we camped near the poorwill canyon of the Chuckwalla Mountains, Dr. Jaeger recalled the sagacity of a road runner he once watched near Mecca, above the Salton Sea. An extensive mud puddle had dried and cracked into plates with curled-up edges. Grasping with its bill the side of a plate, the bird would turn it over and then feed on the crickets hiding beneath.

On the edge of the Lucerne Valley, in the Mojave Desert, a road runner used to come close to the Kaufman home hunting for lizards. With a single exception, it paid no attention to vegetable food. That exception was long string beans. Several times, when Bonnie Kaufman tossed a few into the yard, it gobbled them down under what seemed to be the mistaken impression that it was eating slender lizards or small snakes. Occasionally, snakes are consumed too large to be digested all at once. I remember talking to a man in the Big Bend region of western Texas who had watched one of these birds walking about digesting the forward part of a snake while the tail still dangled from its bill.

Among the many superstitions and fanciful beliefs concerning the feeding habits of the road runner, one never seems to die. Father Ignaz Pfefferkorn, S.J., who came to the Southwest in 1756, includes it in his *Sonora, A Description of the Province*. This is the story of how the paisano builds a corral of cactus to imprison the sleeping rattlesnake. When a double ring of cholla fragments pens in the serpent, according to the tale, the bird attacks it and causes it to lash about, impaling itself on the spines. In another version, the rattlesnake bites itself and commits suicide. In either case, the road runner dines at leisure on its venomous prey. Thus the fact that these birds sometimes do kill and eat small rattlesnakes has been embroidered and handed down through credulous generations.

The facts concerning the life of the road runner are odd and dramatic enough. They need no embroidery. Almost everything about the bird is surprising. Robert Garrett told me that when he once held one in his hand he was amazed to discover it had "eyelashes." Many months later, and many miles farther east, on another winter day after our trip was over, I examined a dozen skins of road runners in the collection of the American Museum of Natural History, in New York City. Above each eye I found a line of curving, bristle-like feathers, for all the world like a row of eyelashes. In the dusty desert, among the scrubby vegetation, they may serve some useful purpose.

By now, the short winter day at Bitter Lake was drawing to its close. The cranes were heading home. We waited in silence beside the darkening lake. We strained our eyes and ears. It was from the west that the first fluttering *per-r-r-ump* of an approaching flock reached us. A hundred or more great birds, flying in a single line, came directly out of the sunset sky. They were almost on us before we saw them. In a wide circle they swung over the water, pulled into a tight spiral and, milling about, descended on the farther shore.

From then on, flock after flock came weaving across the sky, often in mile-long skeins, changing shape, flowing without a pause. The air, before and behind us, seemed filled with their moving forms, filled also with the clamor of their voices. The wild chorus rose and fell, changed continually. At one time it suggested brant in flight, at another the rough purring of a cat, but in the end it remained unique, the commingled calling of many cranes.

We noticed how the homecoming birds veered away from us. As soon as they sighted the white automobile and the two dark human shapes beside it, they altered course, curving widely to one side or the other. Cranes are among the wariest of birds. Only when they are flying very high will they pass over or in front of an automobile. Usually they turn away or circle around until the car passes by. At the sight of a man walking half a mile away, they take alarm. But these cautious birds have a weak spot in their psychology. They come readily to decoys. Where ducks and geese will make several passes over a spot to make sure all is safe, the cranes descend directly.

Over the Pecos bluffs, as we stood there, the moon, almost full, lifted above the dark horizon line. At first its disk was soft-hued, orange-pink, banded with smoky trails of thin and slaty clouds. Then it soared into the clear sky. As the west darkened, its brilliance increased, spreading a misty, silvery light over the returning flocks and over all the scene around us.

More than once, as the twilight deepened, a long skein of returning cranes passed directly across the luminous disk of the moon, each bird in turn standing out in sharp-cut silhouette. Each performer in this silhouette parade flew easily, buoyantly, riding the air on wings whose spread exceeded the extreme length of the bird by as much as three feet. On a later day, at the Muleshoe Refuge in northern Texas, we watched more than 1,000 cranes, in ever-changing patterns, climb half a mile into the sky on a powerful updraft. Their forms grew small. Their calls faded away to a strumming sound. Gradually drifting toward the north, the birds seemed on an aerial outing, a pleasure sail in the blue expanse of the heavens. Then in long lines they spiraled downward to alight with gangling legs far outstretched. The flock had ascended half a mile vertically to move half a mile horizontally. Although it had taken longer, soaring on the upcurrents had consumed less energy. And what is time to a sandhill crane?

At Bitter Lake our elevation was about 3,500 feet. The chill increased quickly when the sun went down. We remembered the road runner and leaned back against the front of the car where hood and radiator still were warm. Waiting on in the dusk, while the stars came out, we watched the late arrivals returning home. Like waves on an ocean shore they swept toward us, skein after skein. We would think: "This is the last!" Then we would listen and catch the faint, far-off clamor of still another flock, unseen in the night.

In sunset and moonlight, how many cranes did we see? I do not know. We lost count. A careful tally, not long before, had recorded more than 20,000 at the refuge. So an estimate of 10,000, at least, seems reasonable. From night to night, the number of homecoming birds fluctuates. The following evening when we returned and took up this same station, after a morning of ice and snow and sleety rain, we saw but a few hundred cranes. The sudden changes of winter weather alter their plans. They simply move away temporarily. There is always a drop in numbers when snow falls and the skies are clouded at Bitter Lake. During one sudden cold spell, the count dropped from 30,000 to about 3,000. Cranes can cover long distances with ease. They leave local storms behind.

After the last flock came in, before we switched on our headlights and groped our way back to Roswell, we stood for a while longer in the moonlight and starlight. The events of that evening, the fading light, the chill, the rising moon, the calling of the cranes, the passing of their thousands of bodies across the sky carried our minds back to another evening when we were almost at the beginning of our travels with the seasons. Then we had watched all the glossy ibis of Florida come home to King's Bar, in Lake Okeechobee. The sunset was calm, the air warm, the evening filled with the smell of the great "Okeechobee Sea." And the dark birds came and came, flock after flock flying low across the water. That was Florida. This was New Mexico. That was the first season. This was the last. Skeins of homecoming birds bound the two together.

SAGUARO forms branches, top left, assumes grotesque
shapes, right; below, broken trunk and framework of rods.

ELEVEN

SNOW LINE OF THE GREAT PLAINS

I FIND in my journal that on January 21, one month to the day after winter began, Nellie and I were riding across the Texas line over the high western edge of the Great Plains. This semi-arid, almost treeless expanse, one of the famed prairie lands of the world, extends from Canada to Texas and from eastern Montana, Colorado and New Mexico to the central lowlands of the Mississippi Valley. Its average width is about 400 miles. At some points, the prairie begins less than 200 miles east of the Continental Divide. Tilting to the east, gradually descending, it drops from an elevation of between 5,000 and 6,000 feet at its western edge to a height of 1,500 to 2,000 feet at its eastern border.

The sun was bright, the temperature mild, as we rode onto the flat, high land of the Staked Plains. Coronado and his men had traversed it in the spring of 1541. The road we followed carried us through Lariat and Muleshoe and Needmore. Sundown lay off to the south, Circle Back to the east and Deaf Smith County to the north. No other state excels Texas in its picturesque place names. They descend the alphabet from Art and Ace through Bigfoot, Cross Cut, Dime Box, Gay Hill, Loco, Nimrod, Pep, North Pole, Pumpville, Quail, Seed Tick, Telephone and Wizard Wells to Zephyr.

Hardly had we turned north from the yellow rolling hills of the Muleshoe National Wildlife Refuge, that other wintering home of the sandhill cranes, when the changeable weather of the Texas Panhandle altered suddenly. The temperature dropped. The wind increased. Tumbleweeds bounded past us. Windmills spun, all facing the northeast. The mercury stood in the twenties by the time we came to Amarillo. It dropped to zero in the night.

Stabbing with cold, the winter wind was still sweeping over the plains when we started out next morning. Where tumbleweeds had lodged against a roadside fence in a porous wall a quarter of a mile long, a marsh hawk hung on the wind, supported by the updrafts of air vaulting over this insubstantial barrier. We watched it soaring down the line of the fence, its shadow passing over each post in turn.

This same wind that carried the hawk in effortless flight multiplied the cold for us. Scientists at the Army Medical Research Laboratory at Fort Knox, Kentucky, a few years ago worked out a scale comparing the thermometer reading with the equivalent temperature effect on exposed human skin, such as the hands and face, at different wind velocities. Even comparatively light winds, their researches showed, produce dramatic effects. When the thermometer stands at thirty-five degrees F. above zero, they found, a wind blowing only twenty miles an hour will produce a heat loss from bare skin equivalent to that of a temperature of thirty-eight degrees below zero in still air.

On this day, with the wind sweeping unhindered across the Great Plains and with the thermometer sticking at eighteen degrees, we left the car but infrequently. Then we hunched in the protection of its lee, continually wiping away tears that streamed from our eyes and made the use of binoculars almost impossible. It was under such conditions that we wandered over the flat land south of Amarillo looking for longspurs of the snow line.

When we think of a snow line, we think first of all of high mountain slopes clothed down to a certain point in permanent fields of white. But in winter the Great Plains have their snow line, too. Less stable, altering frequently, this southern limit of snow cover after storms extends across the same general area winter after winter. In Texas it usually crosses the region of the lower limits of the Panhandle.

A glance at the United States Weather Bureau's map of "Mean Annual Total Rainfall" reveals the swift drop in the amount of snow received by areas from north to south in Texas. West of Amarillo, in one area of the Panhandle, an average of twenty-four inches of snow falls every year. Around Lubbock, about 100 miles to the south, it is only half that— twelve inches. Go south another sixty miles and around Lamesa it is halved again—only six inches. Fifty miles more and at Midland it is but four inches. Before you reach San Antonio, the average yearly snowfall shrinks to only one inch. If you drive south from, say, Lubbock, in a winter storm, you almost always leave the falling snow behind within forty or fifty miles.

It is below this shifting boundary of the prairie snow line that longspurs tend to congregate in winter. For these birds of the open plains, where shelter is at a minimum, heavy snow is a special menace. In March 1904, several million Lapland longspurs met death in a single widespread storm of wet, heavy snow that fell in north-central states during migration. An estimated 750,000 were found dead on the ice of two small lakes. During the severest months of winter, the birds find below the prairie snow line increased chances of survival and of obtaining food. Some winters, we were told, the longspurs "swarm like ants" along the edges of one farm-to-market road that lies southwest of Amarillo.

It was this unnumbered country road, leading south across the wide, windswept plains, that we followed that January morning. Under the brilliant sun—in spite of the cold—the air pulsed and shimmered as with summer heat waves. Pools of mirage water appeared on the road ahead. To our right a natural trough, a shallow dip in the land, ran parallel to the road for a mile or more. There, slightly protected from the torrents of the wind, an immense flock of Brewer's blackbirds streamed northward below the level of the surrounding land. This dark current of moving birds, thousands upon thousands of them, flowed on without a pause, their forms wavering and vibrating in the shimmering air of the rangeland.

Not long afterwards, a small flock of sparrow-sized birds scudded across the road, turned and came swirling down in the heart of a gust. As soon as they landed, they ran about picking up seeds from the bare ground. Our glasses revealed a dark "t" marking on each white tail. The birds were Mc-Cown's longspurs. The hind toe of each foot of these prairie birds ends in an abnormally lengthy claw. Hence the family name of longspur.

From then on, we encountered flock after flock. In the fierceness of that winter wind, these small birds seemed frail, lost, helpless. Yet they were masters of their environment. They were no gust-blown leaves. They landed exactly where they desired. At times we watched them from a distance of no more than fifty feet. One large flock, a mixture of longspurs and horned larks, alighted close beside a cluster of Hereford cattle that stood stolidly on the range, backs to the January wind, their winter coats of longer hair giving them the appearance of ancient woolly mammoths.

Some miles beyond, when we were advancing slowly, a flock of 100 or more longspurs left the road ahead of us and landed just behind us. As we were emerging from the car into the wind, a jackrabbit bounded from a shallow roadside ditch no more than two yards away. It ran for twenty or thirty feet, stopped, ran for twenty or thirty feet in another direction, stopped again. It seemed more curious than alarmed. But then, just when we had focussed on the longspurs, some rabbity panic overtook it and it dashed directly through the flock, scattering the birds we wanted to see.

One of the largest flocks we met had descended at the edge

of a frozen pool near a windmill. There the birds crouched low, resting at midday. We mistook them, at first glance, for hundreds of small clods. It is often in the protection of real clods of frozen earth that these birds of the plains spend the bitter, windy nights of winter. On such nights, birds of many species seek shelter in widely differing places. Juncos and towhees have been found sleeping in the protection of English ivy, cardinals in masses of dead morning glory vines, bluebirds in deserted robin and flicker nests. Carolina wrens have sought out the pockets of old coats hanging in sheds. In big cities, starlings sometimes settle for the night on warm perches over the electric bulbs of theater signs. For the majority of small songbirds, the winter night passes while they are anchored in their sleep to some sheltered twig or branch. Along the lower side of the tendons that flex the toes and run below the toe bones of such birds a series of projections engage ridges on the inside of the tendon sheaths. As long as the bird's weight rests on the support, this arrangement locks the toes in a grasping position, holding the bird securely in place.

During this windy morning, all the longspur flocks we came upon were composed of one species, McCown's. But later, in the month of February, on our way through Oklahoma where the snow line swings to the north, we encountered Lapland, chestnut-collared and Smith's. Thus we observed in their winter home all four species of North American longspurs. Now, as we moved south through western Texas, we crossed the band or zone of their wintering area and left the birds behind.

But they were still with us when, before turning south, we descended into the Panhandle's spectacular Palo Duro Canyon, cut below the level of the plains by water that flows away down the twisting channel of the Prairie Dog Town Fork of the Red River. This stream is well named. The country through which it winds once held the largest of all prairie-dog towns, a rodent megalopolis that covered 25,000 square miles and contained an estimated 400,000,000 inhabitants. In early days a traveler on the Staked Plains could ride in a straight line for 250 miles and all the way be surrounded by the holes of these burrowing animals.

Toward the end of a day when, hour after hour, we had crossed the level land that once had been riddled by this immense city of tunnels, we came to Lubbock. There, on the east side of town, surrounded by a wall of concrete blocks, a hilltop in a public park forms the home of the last survivors of all those teeming millions of prairie dogs. We watched a hundred or more of the friendly, social animals enlarging their burrows, feeding in the sunset, carrying in bedding, giving territorial barks that ran in chain reactions across the colony. Living at peace, protected, following their ancient, instinctive patterns of behavior, they were hardly aware of our presence.

This unique sanctuary came into being in 1932 through the initiative and generosity of Mr. and Mrs. Kennedy N. Clapp of Lubbock. Mrs. Clapp, when I talked to her, recalled that in that year two prairie dog burrows were found on some new land added to the park. The question of how to get rid of them, what poison to use, came up at a meeting of the park board. Her husband, as president of the board, pointed out that in that region, where the historic dog town had formed the most dramatic feature of the plains, the animals had been killed by poison until they had become a rarity. A sanctuary was decided upon, and he and his wife contributed toward making the walled-in prairie dog preserve a reality. All the animals we saw, and many more that were underground at the time, have descended from the inhabitants of those two original burrows.

Today, the prairie dogs of Lubbock have made this western Texas community known even in far-off places of the world. A few years ago the private plane of the King of Saudi Arabia landed at the local airport. When it took off again it carried several pairs of the burrowing animals, destined to establish a new colony in that remote, oil-rich land of the Near East. Each recipient of prairie dogs from the Lubbock sanctuary signs an agreement never to keep the animals in a cage with a solid floor but always to house them in the open where they can exercise their natural instinct for digging.

The road that carried us south from Lubbock extends down the map almost exactly 100 miles west of the 100th meridian. This geographical line bisects the Dakotas and Nebraska, descends through western Kansas, forms the north-and-south boundary between the Texas Panhandle and Oklahoma, and leaves the United States below Eagle Pass on the Rio Grande. It has special significance in natural history, for it is widely accepted as the dividing line between eastern and western species.

For us the 100th meridian will always be remembered as the place of the crows. When we had come west for our rendezvous with the winter solstice on the Silver Strand, we had crossed this invisible line between Rule and Old Glory, south and east of Lubbock. Everywhere around us, in the morning light, the fields were black with crows. A continuous carpet of birds peeled from the highway before us. The air was filled with their flying forms. From the bottoms of the Salt Fork of the Brazos River where they had congregated for the night, the crows, in thousands beyond count, were spreading out for the day's feeding. Like the spokes of an immense wheel their flocks streamed away toward different points of the compass. One dense line of birds, extending as far as we could see, moved south almost exactly along the 100th meridian. How many miles would they fly in their feeding? Thirty or forty with ease. So the outspread wheel, of which the concentrated lines of moving birds formed the spokes, may well have had a diameter of sixty, eighty or even a hundred miles.

Near Lamesa, on the day we left the Lubbock prairie dogs behind, we came upon another concentration of dark birds, a flock of fifty or more ravens turning around and around in a tight circle about 200 feet above the plains. Almost in complete silence, this revolving aerial wheel passed over the road before us and moved away across the open land to the east. With increasing frequency now, other large birds, marsh hawks, passed by, drifting low in solitary hunting. For one long stretch, they averaged one a mile. In winter, they take the place of vultures along the highways of upper Texas. Often, early in the morning, we found them feeding on animals killed by cars at night.

At times as we worked south, we rode with the smell of raw petroleum strong in the air and nodding oil-field pumps all around us. At other times we were among vast cotton fields, already plowed and harrowed. Again, flat-topped mesas rose above overgrazed rangeland where mesquite was spreading. Across one field, a horse, with head held high and mane flowing, ran for the fun of running. So beautiful was it in action that we could understand how ninety per cent of the men in Britain who answered a survey question on what other animal they would prefer to be in case of obligatory metamorphosis chose the horse.

When we were nearing one small Texas town set in the immensity of the plains, we switched on the radio and heard a news announcer report that a jet pilot from this same community had been lost in the Pacific. We looked at the trees, the buildings, the dusty street corners. We were seeing them for the first time. We would probably never see them again. Yet, how familiar they had been to him!

Oftentimes, from some slight swell on the prairie, our road was visible so far ahead that it contracted almost to the width of a hairline. In such surroundings the far-away became the familiar. Distant features of the landscape accompanied us for long periods. I remember one cloud of smoke that lay before us for half an hour. When we reached the spot, we found men with flame-throwers burning tumbleweeds along a fence. We were surprised to note that these dry globes, which have the appearance of tinder ready for instantaneous igniting, burn rather slowly.

This is a roving chapter, a record of roving days. Somewhere near Midland we crossed the trail of the fabulous Cabeza de Vaca. More than four centuries before, this shipwrecked Spaniard had journeyed 10,000 miles on foot, had traveled from the Atlantic to the Pacific and survived years of hardship to reach the settlements on the west coast of Mexico. It was tales this wanderer had heard from the Indians that fired the imagination of Coronado and sent him in search of the Seven Cities of Cibola.

On our way west and across the Pecos River, we traversed the dusty expanses over which De Vaca had plodded. We were in a land where the infrequent motels featured "Big Boy Beds" for tall Texans. We were also, as we had been in parts of Arizona and New Mexico, in a land where fences served as public trophy rooms. We saw them draped with a depressing array of slaughtered birds and animals. More times than we like to remember, we passed coyotes, those wild dogs of the plains, hanging head-downward from fence posts. At one ranch, where sheep were busy skinning the land between creosote bushes, a gate was decorated with the decaying bodies of four wildcats. Another ranch gate supported the pronghorns of more than thirty antelope. Hawks dangled from barbed wires, and once we came to a place where, side by side, eight jackrabbits hung by their ears. All through the dry Southwest, the mighty hunters were exhibiting the results of their prowess.

At last our road lifted us off the plains. Near the western edge of the state, some 200 miles below El Paso, we climbed into the foothills of the Davis Mountains. Up the slopes and over the hilltops ran a sprinkling of ocotillo. When we stopped for the night at Alpine, we were 4,481 feet above sea level. Before us, away to the south, held within a great curve of the Rio Grande, lay our next day's destination—the highlands of the Big Bend.

TWELVE

BIG BEND

A HUNDRED miles to the next filling station! It was
that and more when we started south, next morning,
down the long and empty road from Alpine into the country
of the Big Bend. In all its length we met but a single car.

The modern naturalist, on such a trip as ours, is something
of a contradiction. He makes use of paved roads and improved
automobiles. He is aided by better tires. He depends upon
filling stations spaced along the way. He welcomes new and
faster films for his camera. In a word, he is assisted in innumerable ways by the products of modern technology. But
at the same time he wants wildness. He wants escape from a
too-civilized world.

To all who need a touch of wildness in their lives, to all
who seek contact, even fleeting contact, with nature untamed,
to all—now representing three out of four Americans—who
live in the man-made surroundings of the city and are able to
enter nature's environment only during short vacation periods; to all these the national parks of the country provide a
solution to an instinctive need. Nowhere else on earth is a
more magnificent system of wild parks available than in the
United States. Where else will you find the variety of a
Yellowstone, an Olympic Peninsula, a Yosemite, an Everglades, a Death Valley, a Grand Canyon? In later times,
America may be remembered for its great system of national
parks as older civilizations are remembered for their pyramids

and aqueducts. In these national preserves not only wildflowers and songbirds are protected, but hawks and weasels
also. Here we experience nature as nature is. We come in
contact with the wholeness of the out-of-doors.

One of the least tamed, most naturally wild and rugged of
all these public tracts lies below Alpine and Marathon, at the
western edge of Texas. There the Rio Grande abruptly alters
its course below the high cluster of the Chisos Mountains. It
cuts back to the north, tracing a ragged, openmouthed V on
the map before it resumes its southward flow to the Gulf.
Enclosed within this pocket of land lie the 700,000 acres of
the Big Bend National Park. Its few roads wind across a desert
floor where flash floods have unearthed the bones of dino-
saurs. They lead to river canyons where sheer rock walls shoot
up to a height of 1,500 feet. They climb among erosion-
sculptured peaks lifting 4,000 feet above the surrounding
country.

Near the end of our run southward from Alpine, we ex-
changed cholla for oak and juniper, desert landscape for
mountain scenery. Climbing up through Green Gulch with
towering masses of weathered rock pressing close on either
hand, we paused at Panther Pass, then dropped down a twisting road into the high basin that holds the park headquarters.
There we settled down in a stone cabin, 5,400 feet above sea
level. Towering above us, Casa Grande lifted its massive
monolith of rhyolite to an elevation of 7,300 feet. And all
around us rose the ancient Chisos, the Ghost Mountains of
the Apaches. Late in the afternoon, while I typed up my field
notes in the cabin, Nellie followed a mountain trail beside a
ravine. She returned with a new bird on her life list—the
black-chinned sparrow.

Centrally located, the cluster of the Chisos Mountains
forms the hub of the park. To natural scientists, the mountains also represent a biological island. Isolated from other
high mountains, the Chisos contain a surprising mixture of

species. On the upper slopes both the Douglas fir, associated with the Olympic Peninsula, and the drooping juniper, associated with Mexico, have a home. Here too grows the ponderosa pine. Nowhere in the United States except among the Chisos does the gray and yellow Colima warbler build its nest. More than 1,000 species of plants, some native only to the Big Bend, have been identified within the boundaries of the park.

On subsequent days, as we wandered along the trails on foot or followed the roads by car, we made the acquaintance of one of the most striking of these plants. Resembling dry and weathered tree trunks, the dead stalks of the century plant, *Agave scabra*, rose above the lower vegetation of the mountainsides. In the side of one we noted the round opening of a woodpecker hole. Several times we found our trail strewn with black and shiny seeds. They were the product of the one blooming of the agave's life. Slowly, over a period of a decade or twenty years—rather than the century of popular legend—the plant stores up food in its fleshy leaves. Then, all in a single season, the flowering stalk shoots upward to a height of as much as fifteen feet. In late spring and early summer, masses of golden blossoms appear at its tip. Then, life spent, the whole plant dies. At its base a smaller plant, or ring of plants, is ready to take its place.

One of our favorite trails led us up switchbacks past alligator junipers, with strikingly plated bark, and drooping junipers, with feathery, descending twigs, to an open slope where the huge rosettes of the agave were all around us. Each heavy, succulent spearhead of a leaf was tipped and edged with spines. Running the length of such leaves are the heavy fibers that the Apaches used for making sandals, rope and cloth. How much strength they impart we discovered when we stopped beside one rosette where a rock had lodged among the star points of the leaves. This stone was a foot or more square and almost as thick. Yet the leaves supported the burden without even bending. In former times Indians watched the century plants closely. As soon as the flowering stalks began to form, they pried out the plump buds and baked them over coals. Their flavor is described as resembling that of a roasted yam.

Near the end of our second day in the Big Bend, we came down the last twisting mile of the trail in falling rain. We could hear the drops drumming on the sounding board of the dead agave leaves. Like green troughs the living leaves channeled the water to the center of the plant. They carried it inward toward the roots.

Seventy-seven rainless days had preceded this downpour. Later the rain shifted to a flurry of snow, an event that occurs in the mild climate of the Big Bend but once or twice in a winter and then only in the mountains. By nightfall the air had cleared and above the rim of peaks we saw the familiar glitter of winter constellations that had become nightly companions of our wanderings. When these stars of the night had been replaced by the one great star of the day, we dropped down from the mountains and headed over the desert floor toward Santa Elena. So, on this last Friday in January, began a day of spectacular canyons.

The dirt road we followed led us through a region of arroyos, desert washes and tilted plains scarred by runoff. Clouds of fine dust trailed behind and billowed around us when we stopped. And we stopped often. Here we examined the purple-red of the Mexican rose prickly pear cactus, there the trails of wild burros crossing the road on their way to water. We solved the mystery of white curls lying beneath creosote bushes. They proved to be dead millipeds, coiled like spiral snail shells and whitened by sun and weather. We paused to watch red-tailed hawks hunting among the yuccas. Because of the variety of its elevations, the Big Bend Park is the home of six different species of yucca. In pioneer days, the long terminal needles on yucca leaves provided emergency aid that saved the lives of those bitten by rattlesnakes. Jabbed deeply into the fang-wounds, the spines caused bleeding and eliminated much of the venom.

Out in the open desert, we pulled up beside a large rock that lay shattered as though by a blast of dynamite. We examined it curiously. At Anza-Borrego, in Death Valley, among the Chuckwalla Mountains, we had seen similar disintegrated boulders. What reduced them to fragments? The primary ingredient, we learned later, is desert heat. The soaring temperature of the day is succeeded by the rapid plunge of the thermometer at night. In the Sahara, a temperature drop of 130 degrees has been recorded in less than twelve hours. Heat expands minerals in rocks; cold contracts them. Different minerals expand and contract at different speeds. This sets up internal stresses that even the strongest rocks may be unable to withstand. Again, a cold shower of rain striking a superheated rock may cause it to split. In still another way, water and heat produce the disintegration of desert rocks. During evaporation, water deposits salt crystals in crevices. Heated by the sun, these crystals expand with tremendous power. Sometimes, like driven wedges, they shatter a rock to fragments.

A century before, across this expanse of desert, a strange procession had wound toward the Rio Grande. Under Lieut. William H. Echols, a U.S. Army detachment from Fort Stockton, experimenting with camels as beasts of burden in the Southwest, had traveled as far as Santa Elena Canyon. Santa Elena is the first of three gorges through which the Rio Grande flows during the 107 miles of its course along the southern boundary of the Big Bend Park. It was not until thirty years after Major John Wesley Powell's exploration of the Grand Canyon that the first scientific expedition made a passage of this trio of gorges. In October 1899, Robert T. Hill of the U.S. Geological Survey started down the river with five companions in specially constructed boats. For a month they dropped out of sight. Then they reappeared, emerging safely from the third and last of the canyons.

Down a sandy path that coyotes, javelinas and armadillos had used before us, we came to the north bank of the Rio Grande. Standing at the edge of a sandbar, we looked across the stream, then up and up. On the opposite side of the water, a sheer wall of limestone soared above us, towering to a height of more than a quarter of a mile. Issuing from this wall, at the bottom of a titanic vertical slit hardly wider than the stream itself, flowed the Rio Grande. To the right of the river, the rock rose in the United States, to the left in Mexico.

For eighteen miles this Santa Elena Canyon extends up-stream. Most of the way it is so narrow and deep that the sun's rays never reach the bottom. Through geological ages the limestone had risen slowly against the cutting action of the debris-filled river. Downstream fifty miles or so, at the bottom of the triangle, the southernmost point of the Big Bend, the Rio Grande flows through a second gorge, the al-most inaccessible Mariscal Canyon, and still farther along its course, near the eastern boundary of the park, the river enters the longest of the three chasms, the twenty-five-mile-long Boquillas Canyon.

Here at Santa Elena, as we walked by the edge of the stream where clumps of willows grew, black phoebes and Say's phoebes and golden-crowned kinglets flitted among the branches. Pale gnats danced beside the river and, under the overhang of clods, the fine, dry dust was dimpled with the pits of ant lions. Winding down from the north, across land that once held one of the world's richest deposits of quicksilver, Terlingua Creek joins the Rio Grande at the mouth of Santa Elena. In its partially dry bed we came upon small plants already in bloom. As I bent close to examine one stalk of tiny pale blue flowers, a honeybee, its golden bands shining, alighted and hung for a moment, its tongue outthrust, probing the blooms, harvesting there the minutest droplets of winter nectar.

But always our eyes were drawn back to the door of the canyon and the sheer walls that pressed close against the stream on either hand. Here was another Split Mountain, a Split Mountain floored with water. Out across the desert, the morning heat was mounting. But beside the stream, under the towering rampart of the rock wall, the air remained cool and moist and delicious. It bore mysterious scents. Rich in the moister air of the canyon's mouth, one smell predominated. It was rank, medicinal, yet rather pleasant, reminding us of witch hazel. It was the scent of the creosote bush.

To anyone who has known the western desert after rain, this is the dominant smell that memory evokes. We encountered it first in New Mexico when we were going west. In the darkness after a shower, the damp air was filled with a heavy, wild, unknown perfume. We met it again when wet snow was falling in the Joshua Tree National Monument. And now we smelled it once more, beside the Rio Grande, in Texas.

Always it is increased humidity that brings forth the scent. In dry desert air the bush is odorless. Each leaf of its lacy evergreen foliage glistens with a waxy shine. Its upper surface is coated with resin. But on the underside of the leaf diminutive porelike stomata open and close in response to changes in humidity. When there is more moisture inside the leaf than outside, the stomata remain tightly shut. But as soon as it rains or the humidity rises to a point where the air contains more life-giving water than the leaf, like so many doors flung wide the openings admit the temporary supply of additional fluid. By means of this mechanism, the creosote bush, *Larrea divaricata*, conserves its water supply in times of drought and adds to it in brief periods of rainfall.

More than 2000 years ago Aristotle wrote: "If there is one

NELLIE walking in a valley amid the wind-formed gypsum dunes, top, and identifying a desert plant, below.

GYPSUM COLUMN in the White Sands dunes. The fine rootlets of a desert sumac hold the material together.

WHITE DUNES of gypsum extend for miles across the Tularosa Basin. Below, a yucca rises above wind-rippled sand.

SUNSET IN THE DESERT. Above, clumps of ocotillo wands; below, cholla cactus glowing in the backlighting.

way better than another it is the way of nature." He set down these words centuries before the discovery of the continent on which the creosote bush grows. Yet he might well have been referring to the ingenious mechanics of this desert plant. So effective as a water conserver is the bush that, near Bagdad on the Mojave Desert, it survived the historic drought that extended from 1909 to 1912, when thirty-two months passed without a drop of precipitation. Its roots plunging to depths of as much as thirty or forty feet, the creosote bush occupies sunbaked soil where no other bush can survive. It is the most widespread and conspicuous shrub of the Southwestern deserts.

As nesting birds have their feeding territories, the creosote bushes have their growing territories. Spreading out in a maze, their lateral roots monopolize the moisture around them. The rainfall supports only so many bushes, so far apart. These persistent, flourishing forms of desert life never appear in groups or clusters. They grow singly, held apart by their desperate need for moisture. Over hundreds of thousands of acres they dot the desert landscape, so evenly spaced that they suggest vast orchards set out by hand. At times they give the impression of a woven pattern holding the empty land together.

West of Death Valley, we had seen a dramatic instance of how the slightest change in available moisture is reflected in the height of the creosote bushes. Running ruler-straight up the floor of the Panamint Trough, a narrow line of hardtop parallels the mountains. Throughout its length, this desert road is bordered by twin lines of darker green. The creosote bushes nearest the road side are noticeably higher and more luxuriant than those farther away. Afterwards we encountered this same condition in many places. Rain, seeping under the hardtop, had evaporated less rapidly, had remained available slightly longer. There the roots had tapped a little additional moisture. The higher bushes, with their darker and richer foliage, had resulted from that small advantage.

Winter and summer, the evergreen creosote bush looks the same. Even in prolonged dry spells it retains its foliage by going into a kind of "drought dormancy." Probably because of the rank, resinous character of the leaves, livestock avoid the bushes. On rangeland, the creosote bush, indicating the driest soil, is considered a "poverty plant." Pioneers steeped the twigs and leaves in hot water to produce an antiseptic lotion effective in treating saddle sores on horses. They also used an acid extracted from the leaves to keep fatty foods from turning rancid. In the region of Death Valley, Indians employed the waxy resin that coats the upper surface of the leaves for waterproofing baskets.

Although books refer to the strong desert scent as "creosote-like," neither Nellie nor I could recognize the resemblance. I remember mentioning this to Dr. Jaeger as we sat by the campfire in the Chuckwallas. He was of the opinion that the plant had been named about the time creosote was being introduced widely and the fact that both had strong chemical smells had led to the choice of the name. How long the leaves retain their scent I do not know. But I have just dipped a few, shriveled and dry and several years old, in a saucer of water on my desk. As I lift them to my nose, I catch the same powerful, penetrating scent, evocative of deserts in the rain, reminiscent of the moister air we found that day at the mouth of Santa Elena Canyon.

Riding from this canyon, on the western edge of the park, to Boquillas Canyon, on the eastern edge, we traversed mile after mile of orchardlike tracts of creosote bush. Boquillas is the widest as well as the longest of the three chasms. The most vivid memories I have of the hours we spent there concern white-throated swifts in the sunset. Less than seven inches long, this western swift is credited with being the fastest winged creature in North America. One observer reports seeing a white-throated swift pull away from the stoop of a peregrine falcon. Its speed was estimated at nearly 200 miles an hour. In the top ranges of its flight its wings are said to give off a whirring sound.

Everything that we saw as we walked along the river's edge, climbed the high slides of sand, followed the windings of the canyon as far as we could go, is linked in memory with the shuttling forms of the swifts. Feeding on small flying insects, they plunged down the sheer faces of the rock walls in meteor descents, almost blurring in their speed. The air was calm. All was still. We were alone in the canyon. On one small bank of shining mud, we saw the imprint of the huge webbed hind foot of a Rio Grande beaver. And endlessly down from the canyon walls came the swifts. They ripped past us at the end of tremendous dives, twisted away over the water and sky-rocketed up again. High above us, in crevices in the rock, the birds had cemented together, with their adhesive saliva, plant material and feathers to form their nests. On the coldest days of winter these crevices are used for a different purpose. Then the swifts retreat into them and lie dormant.

By the time we had left this hunting ground of the white-throated swifts, the sunset had ebbed away and the brief January dusk had fallen. Our headlights, on the ride back to the basin, picked out pale desert jackrabbits, looking like al-binos in the glare. Beside our stone cabin in the darkness that night, we heard the long, fluttering trill of some unfamiliar cricket. More than a mile above sea level, it was continuing its serenade in January. The day ended with that sound. Frail and musical, it seemed huge in the intense stillness of the mountain night.

Hardly had the late dawn of the next day broken when we rode out along the war trail of the Comanches toward Mara-thon. Somewhere near the curious Scollop Mountains, which rise and fall in a fifteen-mile series of arcs, we saw a cluster of white dots expand into half a hundred beehives. In this region the insects are "herded" for long distances by truck. One bee-keeper of Marathon distributes his hives over an area of hundreds of square miles. Bees of the Big Bend are famous for mesquite and cat's-claw honey.

During an oil change at a Marathon filling station, I talked to a young attendant about the golden eagles. Once common in the Big Bend, these great birds are now a rarity. In a relentless war inspired by ranchers, light planes based at Marathon and Alpine carried hunters armed with shotguns close to the soaring birds. Such sky-hunting is now illegal, but the damage has been done.

"We don't see them much any more," the young man reported. "They seem about gone. Everybody's glad."

"Not *everybody* is glad," I told him.

That conversation reminded me of another I had had a few days before in New Mexico. I asked a man if anybody in his region was interested in natural history. He scratched his head, thought a long time, then said:

"No, I guess not. We run to hound-dog men around here."

With the purring of the motor, the whistling of the wind, the blur of pavement beneath our wheels, with mile after mile of flatland, cactus wastes, mesquite and rangeland streaming to our rear, we followed the Rio Grande south during the two succeeding days. The speeding car and the loaded gun both are heady wine. Step on an accelerator and annihilate distance; pull a trigger and annihilate life. Both provide a sense of overwhelming power at the expense of little effort. But both are filled with danger.

In all our travels with the seasons, we have had no accident on the road. Each trip has been begun with the primary object of returning home safely—to tell the story. A crash would have wrecked our plans as well as our car and maybe ourselves. Setting our own pace—usually well below the legal limit— being ready to stop at every crossroads, cutting our speed to let passing cars get by as quickly as possible, assuming that every other driver would do the wrong instead of the right thing, we traveled in safety. Even so, we no doubt had luck.

At times, as we ran on, our road was bordered by overgrazed ranches, their raw fields outspread in the sun like flayed carcasses. Disconsolate sheep wandered about in a final skinning of the land. The world is always ready to ask: "*Can* he do it? *Will* he do it?" But rarely does it ask: "*Should* he do it?" For a long time man has been "overcoming the wilderness" and "conquering nature." The conflict has held the spotlight. The results were around us in many places. This was the conquered earth.

As we went south down the long, dry roads to Del Rio and Eagle Pass, Laredo and Zapata, we followed the Rio Grande four degrees nearer the equator. Mockingbirds increased in number. Vultures replaced marsh hawks as highway scavengers. Meadow larks appeared in the more fertile fields. Once when we pulled to the side of the road to eat a lunch of sandwiches, a quart of milk and cat's-claw honey from Marathon, we noticed that a yucca, close by, was topped with a creamy mass of flowers.

Now we were leaving the desert behind. All the way from the Silver Strand to lower Texas we had been in and out of deserts. These dry lands occupy more than 150,000,000 acres within the boundaries of the United States. At first, as I have said, the desert formed for us a world aloof and forbidding. Like a man who needs his glasses to find his glasses, we seemed to need the end to achieve the end—we needed to understand the desert to appreciate the desert. Now, as it moved away behind us, we parted company with it with real regret.

The radio reported blizzards sweeping over the Rockies and roaming across the upper plains. Five hundred cars were stalled on snow-blocked highways. But our road followed the river into the warmer south. Ahead lay the delta of the Rio Grande. For the time being, the harsh winter of the north seemed far away.

THIRTEEN

SUMMER IN JANUARY

"NEVER put off until tomorrow what you should have done yesterday."

"Always put off today what you may not have to do tomorrow."

Nellie's rebuttal, being more in accord with our inclinations, prevailed. We postponed repacking the car and set off in the bright sunshine of our summer-in-winter surroundings. We had come to the southernmost point of our wanderings. In the vicinity of Mission and McAllen and Brownsville, we were almost as far south as Miami, Florida. The climate in this lower Rio Grande Valley is subtropical. Around us grew citrus groves, palms and banana trees.

Yet there is a basis for the paradoxical proposition that winter comes earlier to Brownsville than it does to Labrador. If we give the name winter to the coldest one-fourth of the year and fix its beginning at the average date on which the coldest thirteen-week period commences, George H. T. Kimble has pointed out in *Our American Weather*, we find that this date is November 25 for the lower Rio Grande region, mid-December for northern Michigan and nearly Christmas for Labrador.

A pebble, caught in the tread of a rear tire, proved a lucky stone that morning. As I got out to pry it loose, we heard a loud "weeeep!" or "weeeer!" and looking up saw a large-headed, bright-hued bird, almost the size of a belted kingfisher, perched on a dead limb overhead. Its face was strikingly patterned with black and white. Its wings and back were rufous. Its underparts, catching the morning sun, shone brilliant yellow. We were seeing, in the one small area in the United States where it nests, the kiskadee or Derby flycatcher. From the lower Rio Grande Valley of Texas its range extends southward to Argentina. With the exception of the scissortailed—which owes its superior size entirely to its abnormally long tail—it is the largest of our flycatchers.

The first hoarse "weeeep!" was followed by a loud, far-carrying "kiska-dee!" or "git-a-here!" Darting out, the bird snapped a flying insect from the air. When we drove away we left it riding buoyantly in the breeze on the tipmost twig of a mimosa tree. Like others of its kind, the kiskadee feeds mainly on aerial insects. But in surprising ways it often varies its diet. I heard of one that snatched up and swallowed a good-sized lizard. From time to time, a kiskadee will hover, kingfisherwise, over water, then plunge down, strike the surface with a splash, and fly away with a tadpole, a small fish or an aquatic insect. For long periods this fish-eating flycatcher will perch on some limb projecting out over a pond or stream, scrutinizing the water below. While a kingfisher can dive repeatedly, the flycatcher, after every two or three splashes, must perch in the sun and dry its water-soaked plumage.

One of the kiskadee's favorite habitats is among the dense vegetation along watercourses. In such a setting we saw the bird again, the next day, when Philip Myers and Edward Sutton, of McAllen, led us on winding trails through the Santa Ana Federal Wildlife Refuge. Enclosed within this sanctuary is the largest remaining tract of the original woodland that once bordered the lower reaches of the Rio Grande. With the luxuriance of a tropical jungle, it provides one of the country's richest bird habitats. Here nest species found nowhere else in the United States except in the lower Rio Grande tip of Texas. Hardly had we begun following the shaded trails that wind under overarching trees, when we came upon the largest of these rare birds.

Gray-brown, suggesting half-grown turkeys, with smooth, almost silky plumage, a flock of more than twenty chachalacas fed along the path. Most pecked at the ground like domestic hens. One dusted itself. Another lay on its side, with tail and wings spread, sunning itself where a shaft of light descended among the trees. But always these jungle fowl, primarily a Central American species, were alert and wary. In the wild they are secretive, difficult to see, inhabiting the densest thickets. Here at Santa Ana they had become less shy. But they were given to sudden alarms. All would disappear with a rush of wings. But soon we would see them coming back, hopping from limb to limb, returning to feed on the open trail. Not far from where we stood, Philip Myers had once seen two weasels dash from the undergrowth into the midst of a flock of feeding chachalacas. Every one of the alert birds escaped.

This flock was only the beginning of the succession of rare and beautiful birds we saw that day. Green jays, white-fronted doves, red-billed pigeons, golden-fronted woodpeckers—hour by hour Nellie and I added new species to our life lists. Down one side-path, where limbs were decorated with tufts of the air plant ball moss, we came upon the largest ebony tree in Texas. Unrelated to the ebony of tropical Asia and Africa—as is our persimmon tree—this species, *Pithecolobium flexicaule*, belongs to the *Leguminosae*. It is a relative of the mesquite and locust and acacia. Its range extends north from Mexico as far as Matagorda Bay on the Texas coast. Highly valued by cabinetmakers, its wood is hard, heavy and close-grained, with a rich red-brown color tinged with purple. In the Lower Rio Grande Valley it is considered the most valuable native tree.

Like the live oak, the ebony sheds its foliage a few leaves at a time. Ordinarily it is clothed in rich, dark green the year around. But this winter, abnormal cold and severe freezes had left its branches almost bare. Over the ground, scattered beneath it, were the beanlike pods that Mexican children collect to paint and use as decorations at Christmas. South of the border, the seeds within such pods are roasted and eaten like peanuts. At Santa Ana they form one of the main winter foods of a bird that has been called "the gem of the forest."

This is the green jay. Wherever we went along the Santa Ana trails, we saw or heard this ornate bird. Its strident squawking is known in the Rio Grande region as "green-jay static." As far south as Honduras and Venezuela and Bolivia, the flashing green of its plumage is familiar. In one opening in the woods we came upon half a dozen of these noisy, eye-catching birds feeding on the ground with three Sennett's or long-billed thrashers. The green jay is one of the tropical birds that have been observed "anting with fire," anointing their plumage with smoke from smoldering logs.

Not far from the bank of the Rio Grande, where the horses of the Border Patrol had left a well-worn path, we walked through a junglelike stretch sheeted in the gray of Spanish moss. Once more we were in a magical place, such a place as Marjorie Kinnan Rawlings had led us to in *The Yearling* country, in the Florida spring. In this gray and spectral habitat, barn owls make their home. Ten had been recorded in the area a few weeks before. In the crotch of one tree, curtained with hanging moss, the deserted nest of a kiskadee remained intact. Three of these flycatchers, that day, were sweeping back and forth across the Rio Grande. They called their names, now in Mexican trees, now in American.

It was amid the eerie beauty of this moss-hung forest that we encountered the bold black and white and orange pattern of our first alta mira. A rare nesting species in the Rio Grande Delta, this Lichtenstein's oriole ranges south to Nicaragua. It was not until 1939 that it took its place on the avifauna list of the United States. Whether we saw a male or a female we shall never know, for the sexes are indistinguishable in the field. The nest of this largest of our orioles is a skillfully woven bag of rootlets and vegetable fibers which at times has a length of more than two feet. Instead of hiding its nest, the alta mira hangs it in a conspicuous place. One nest, a year or two before, had been suspended from a television antenna.

Upstream along the Rio Grande, on another day, when Pauline James, a biologist friend from Pan American College, joined us in following the trails of the famous Bentsen–Rio Grande Valley State Park, we saw one of these elongated bags dangling from a live-oak limb above a dry stream bed. Like Santa Ana, the Bentsen sanctuary is the jungle home of the chachalaca, alta mira, kiskadee and green jay. The lushness of bird life in this region of Texas is matched by the variety of its trees. I was told of a priest, living at Mission, who had made a collection of 125 canes, each made of a different kind of wood that grows in the lower Rio Grande Valley. Several times we came upon a striking tree, almost like a canoe birch, standing out in contrast to its darker background. It was the native hackberry. Because of the whiteness of its trunk it is known locally as "palo blanco."

During the latter days of January, the grass is usually green in the valley and the huisache is in orange bloom, perfuming the air for miles around. But the plunge of the thermometer to a full twenty degrees below freezing, a few weeks before, had left only the yucca, the allthorn and the guyacan clothed in their normal green. At times we seemed to be walking in a summer drought. But the sounds around us were the sounds of spring—the bubbling "okaleee!" of redwings beside the Rio Grande, the pensive, woodwind calling of mourning doves in the heat of noon. We saw more orange-crowned warblers on this day than we had seen in our whole lives before. Many birds seemed poised for northward passage. In this exotic setting, with its gray sheets of Spanish moss, we encountered such old friends as the yellow-bellied sapsucker, associated with New England orchards in the spring.

Before we turned downstream toward Brownsville that afternoon, we swung past a ranch pond that teemed with waterfowl—pintail, gadwall, shoveler, blue-wing, green-wing and cinnamon teal, coot and gallinule. Here, for several years, Pauline James had been studying the amber-eyed, least or Mexican grebe, the smallest of its kind. We saw a score or more bobbing about on little waves amid the rafts of ducks. No larger than robins, they have a call surprisingly loud for so small a bird, a kind of "clang!" that has been compared to a trumpet note. In their odd habits, they are birds of considerable charm. Pauline has watched the male bringing tiny fish to feed the chicks as they rode about over the water on the female's back. Almost as soon as they are hatched, the young are taken for dives. Usually they ride under their mother's wings. Coming ashore after such an excursion, the parent shakes her plumage, opens her wings, and out tumble as many as half a dozen baby grebes.

Along the road to Brownsville, burrowing owls perched in the brilliant sunshine beside highway culverts. All over southern Texas, during the winter, such owls find shelter in these concrete-lined drains—ready-made burrows provided by the Texas Highway Department. Another thing we noticed was that shrikes and sparrow hawks seemed evenly spaced along the roadside. We had seen this previously but now we observed it with new appreciation. For, not long before, a student at Pan American College had placed a pet sparrow hawk out in his backyard without realizing it was part of the winter territory of a wild hawk. Before he could rescue the pet, the wild bird, considering its area invaded, had attacked and killed it. Among such predators winter territories apparently are as fiercely defended as summer ones.

In the region of Brownsville, at the mouth of the Rio Grande, the seasons intermingle as they do in lower Florida. Autumn and spring are part of winter. Each morning, we found the air bland and warm. Each midday, in summer heat, we welcomed a breeze from the Gulf. Small, noisy groups of boat-tailed grackles, locally known as jackdaws or Mexican blackbirds, alighted in the palm tops. White-necked ravens, which congregate in the area in winter and virtually disappear in summer, walked across lawns and alighted in refuse dumps. We drove to Boca Chica and Port Isabel, on the Gulf, and once, across the vast flatland of the Federal wildlife refuge at Laguna Atacosa, we skirted shallow bays with the sad, sweet whistle of hundreds of long-billed curlews around us.

Another day, a few miles west of Brownsville, we stopped at the edge of a wide field to watch a flock of two or three hundred lark buntings. They were feeding on plowed and harrowed ground. In the manner of a wheel slowly turning, the flock advanced across the open field into the wind. The buntings at the rear would take wing, flutter to the head of the procession and alight. This movement from rear to front continued without a pause until the whole flock reached the opposite side of the field. Then the birds moved over and repeated the process going in the other direction. In this way, with the flock literally rolling across the ground, the area was covered thoroughly and speedily. When the movement was into the wind, the progress was less rapid than when the flock rolled with the wind.

I timed one group that alighted at the front edge and found that they fed, with rapid, nervous movements, for only about half a minute before they took wing again. The path of their rotary movement formed a long oval, like the revolving tread of a Caterpillar tractor. By land and by air, in steady marches, the birds moved back and forth across the field. While we watched, they traveled in their feeding well over half a mile.

We were at Brownsville when we tore the first sheet from our new calendar. January was behind us. February had arrived. We had reached the midwinter month. But, wandering in the sunshine of the lower Gulf Coast on that first day of the second month of the year, we felt far removed in distance, in elevation, in temperature from the winter of the mountains and the winter of the north.

In the open range country, as we rode up the coast next day, ranch hands were using flame throwers to burn away the spines of the flat *opuntia* cactus. Behind them the cattle fed. Soon the cactus segments resembled lollipops nibbled at the edges, and we could hear the crunching sound of the chewing a hundred feet away. At one point a flock of wild turkeys crossed the highway. At another, six deer fed peacefully on a little rise. Without a curve for fifty miles, our road traversed the immense King Ranch. For us this stretch was a highway of hawks. Red-tails and Harris' hawks were all along the way. Here we saw, for the first time, Mexican black hawks at rest and in the air. And always, somewhere in the height of the sky, we caught sight of circling vultures.

According to an old Texas superstition, to see one vulture means bad luck; to see three, good luck. So frequently met are these scavengers that propitious omens must be the rule. On this February 2 another superstition was making headlines all across the northern states. This was Groundhog Day. The woodchuck, America's most revered wild weather prophet, is supposed to appear on this day, look for his shadow, and, if he sees it, retire into his burrow for six more weeks of winter.

In the folklore of the country, numerous superstitions relate to winter weather. Back-country farmers examine their corn husks—the thicker the husk, the colder the winter. They watch the acorn crop—the more acorns, the more severe the season. They observe where white-faced hornets place their paper nests—the higher they are, the deeper will be the snow. They examine the size and shape and color of the spleens of butchered hogs for clues to the severity of the season. They keep track of the blooming of dogwood in the spring—the more abundant the blooms, the more bitter the cold in January. When chipmunks carry their tails high and squirrels have heavier fur and mice come into country houses early in the fall, the superstitious gird themselves for a long, hard winter. Without any scientific basis, a wider-than-usual black band on a woolly-bear caterpillar is accepted as a sign that winter will arrive early and stay late. Even the way a cat sits beside the stove carries its message to the credulous. According to a belief once widely held in the Ozarks, a cat sitting with its tail to the fire indicates very cold weather is on the way.

Nellie and I recalled such odd beliefs as we followed the northward trend of the coast. The King Ranch and Corpus Christi had been left behind and we were 150 miles north of the Rio Grande Delta when we came to another area famed for its winter wildlife. Along the Aransas River, northeast of Sinton, 7,800 rolling acres—once a single pasture of the vast Rob and Bessie Welder ranch—now form a unique refuge and research center. Here, financed by oil wells and cattle herds, the ecological studies of the Welder Wildlife Foundation are under the direction of Dr. Clarence Cottam, research biologist and formerly assistant director of the U.S. Fish and Wildlife Service.

For a day we wandered with this admired friend across the twelve square miles of the scientific sanctuary. Four hundred species of birds, 1,300 species of herbaceous plants, 142 species of grasses, fifty-five species of mammals and fifty-four species of reptiles and amphibians have been recorded from the area. Our day was one of javelinas and wild turkeys, deer feeding on hills and hundreds of fulvous tree ducks, with squealing whistles and the flash of velvety black underwings, springing from the surface of ponds. In one stretch of open woodland, we surprised a flock of nearly fifty wild turkeys, their wings decorated with red, orange, white, chartreuse or blue markings. This color code enabled research workers to identify individual birds in studying the activities of the flock. Similarly, during other investigations, deer have been marked by dipping their tails in brilliant-hued dyes or by attaching small pieces of colored plastic to their ears. In this way, while living their natural lives at the Welder refuge, creatures as varied as quail, deer, jackrabbits, bobcats, wild turkeys and armadillos have contributed to scientific knowledge.

When we came back to the forty-acre compound that holds the administration buildings, the laboratories and the residences of the staff, we noticed the wire-mesh snakeproof fence that encircles it. This is diamondback country. Yet, where the road enters the area, a gap is left open in the fence. Two wings of the wire mesh extend out fifty feet or so, paralleling either side of the road. The snake that follows the fence and comes to one of these wings is shunted away from the opening. Experience has shown that, instead of doubling back when it comes to the end, it tends to keep going in a straight line. So far, although the gap remains open day and night, no rattler has entered the compound.

Somehow, before Nellie and I left for the coast, twenty miles away, late that afternoon, the conversation turned to the curious ways in which wildlife is stimulated by human sounds. There is the case of a flock of wild turkeys that gobbled each time a country blacksmith pounded on his anvil and another of frogs in a southern swamp that set up a chorus of calling whenever a carpenter used his hammer and saw. In the heart of New York City, I recalled, a woman who kept crickets as pets for her children noticed that, invariably, when the bells of a nearby cathedral rang, the crickets began to chirp. Dr. Cottam added another instance of the kind. At the Welder refuge, each time a jet plane passes over at evening, it sets the coyotes, all across the hills, to howling.

FOURTEEN

SEVENTY-NINE CATS

THE gray trunks of the live oaks flared inland around us. Like giant water weeds flowing with the current they stretched almost horizontally above the thick green undergrowth. The trees seemed bowing before some silent, unending gale. All along the edge of this part of Aransas Bay, thirty miles north of Corpus Christi, the oaks, like the cypresses of Monterey, have been sculptured by winds from the sea.

As we stood there a long, gray-green Cadillac turned onto the white shell road under the trees. It slowed to a stop and a woman slipped from behind the driver's wheel. She carried a paper plate heaped high with cottage cheese and hamburger. Setting it down, she called:

"Zeke! Zeeeeke! Come on, boy! Come, boy! Zeeeeke!"

Out of the undergrowth strolled a yellow cat.

We were seeing an event that occurred each day at about 4:20 P.M. It was part of what appeared to us a magnificent Texas gesture. In other states, people sometimes adopt a stray cat or maybe two. In Texas, where things are done on a bigger scale, Mrs. Sibyl Means has adopted more than 100 stray cats. Her home, about a mile from the point of land on which we stood, is surrounded by twenty-seven acres of landscaped lawn. It is also surrounded by cats.

In talking to her, while Zeke cleaned off the plate, we discovered that she had read my books. She felt she knew us both. Back at her home, as we followed a winding drive lead-

CASA GRANDE lifts its massive monolith of rhyolite
among the Chisos, or Ghost Mountains, of the Big Bend.

FOOTHILLS of the Chisos Mountains. Below, birds of the lower Rio Grande: green jays, left, chachalaca, right.

ing up a slope from the bay to a low, rambling house set among other leaning oaks, we saw white cats, black cats, gray cats, yellow cats, black-and-white cats, striped cats, tortoise-shell cats, long-hairs, short-hairs, well-fed and contented cats.

Until his death, caused by a heart attack in September 1961, the day after the hurricane Carla ended, Earl Means— who had made a fortune in Texas oil—had been as fond of cats as his wife. When he opened his bedroom window to give them a last snack at night, they used to pour in ten at a time. Before the Meanses moved to their home above the bay, where four yard men spend their time caring for the grounds, they traveled widely. They often fed strays they met along the way. Once they shipped a cat home from California by air express. As soon as they settled down in their new home, the cats began to accumulate. Their number varies from time to time. Homes are found for many. When we made this digression from wildlife to tame, they numbered seventy-nine— seventy-nine lucky cats.

It was time for the afternoon feeding when we drove up. The cats get a light meal in the morning and a main one in the afternoon. In the kitchen we found two Mexican girls opening cans and emptying their contents into an immense wooden bowl. Six cans of jack mackerel were followed by seven cans of dried dog meal, six cans of cat food, a pint of tomato juice, half a dozen eggs and seven pounds of lean hamburger. The Means cats are the local butcher's best cus-tomers. Every month of the year they get about 300 pounds of hamburger. The eggs, cracked and therefore unfit for selling in stores, are obtained at reduced prices from a poultry dealer. A veterinarian, who cares for serious illnesses, also alters the animals on a wholesale basis. Mrs. Means buys flea powder in bulk. She led us to her private hospital built under a spreading live-oak tree back of the house. Here she once saved the lives of five cats that had pneumonia at the same time.

We soon noticed a curious thing about this multitude of

felines. Although there was almost no fighting, each animal chose one side of the house or the other and stayed there. A cat that has chosen one side, Mrs. Means told us, almost never changes. If, by mistake, she puts one out of the house on the wrong side, it promptly returns to its home territory. Once when two sister cats arrived, one picked one side, the other the other. Apparently antipathy to some other cat plays no part in this decision. The animals just make their choice and stick to it. One gray angora shyly rubbed against my legs, purred, and followed me about, trying to make friends. It seemed to want individual attention. It left its dinner and attached itself to me and stayed close as long as we remained on its side of the house. But it made no attempt to follow me around to the other side.

Because Mrs. Means's father was a Baptist minister, many of the cats have Biblical names: Hannah, Peter, Timothy, Phoebe, David, Samuel, Jonathan, Hezekiah. Others get their names from their appearance, as Domino, a black-and-white male; or from their character, as General Eisenhower, a fighting cat; or from some event connected with their coming. In the latter group is a cinnamon-hued tortoise-shell that bears the name of Tree-sitter. Someone left it by the front gate, and it climbed a tree and stayed there for two days before it came down.

More cats keep arriving as time goes on. A few days before, a family in the region had moved away to a Houston apartment where they could not keep pets. On the morning of their departure they deposited fourteen cats and kittens at the entrance of the drive that winds up to the big house that is the happy home of so many varied felines. They all were made welcome. Three dogs, Bonnie, Gretchen and Dr. Schweitzer, live in the midst of this multitude of cats. They all get along amicably. In fact, one of the dogs, a large black collie, acts as a kind of shepherd for the feline flock. If a marauding tom appears and starts fighting with one of the

Means cats, the dog often rushes in to intervene.

Understandably, there are no mice at the Means place. One of the cats is a great mole and gopher hunter. It crouches by a mole tunnel, waits until it sees the ground move, then pounces. It also goes across the road to a small inlet where the incoming tide carries water through a narrow channel. Here it waits on the bank and scoops young mullet from the water with a sweep of its paw. This same hunting cat once was discovered walking around and around a coiled Texas diamondback with ten rattles on its tail. On one occasion, when it caught a squirrel, forty or fifty other cats sat around in a ring and watched it eat it.

Only occasionally do the well-fed cats catch birds. Aggression is on the other side when the pugnacious mockingbirds nest in low trees and shrubs on the grounds. They dive on any cat that comes near, pecking at the back of its head. For some unknown reason, one cat in particular attracted the attacks of the mockingbirds. It had scabs all over its head. Once, when Mrs. Means was carrying it across the yard, a mockingbird swooped down and whacked it on the head while it was in her arms.

We saw one small gray cat, bearing the name of Lucy, climb a tree, lean far out from a crotch and meow to attract attention. It does this each day at mealtime. Apparently unable to compete with the larger cats when the food is placed in dishes on the ground, it ascends the tree where it is fed by hand. Oldest of the seventy-nine cats is sixteen-year-old Kitty Girl. She had traveled with the Meanses all over the country, as far away as Nova Scotia. One large tom, as soon as it had finished its meal, climbed a tree trunk and jumped to the roof of the house. It spends most of its days sitting on the ridgepole.

At the time of Carla, the worst hurricane to strike the central Gulf Coast in many years, all the cats survived. They took shelter in the house. Even Zeke was brought home from the point. In a box of his own, he spent the period of the hurricane. But as soon as the storm was over and he was let out, he returned to his retreat among the live oaks of the point.

There he has spent the last half dozen years. He gets on well with the other animals at the house. But apparently there are just too many cats for him. He is overwhelmed by numbers. He likes to live alone and has chosen the thickets under the live oaks of the point for his solitary existence. A house cat living in the wild is an intelligent animal. Through the years, Zeke has escaped the dangers of wildcats and diamondbacks and great horned owls. When we returned with Mrs. Means for another feeding the next afternoon, we noticed how well and strong and self-reliant he looked. On several occasions, he has disappeared for two or three days, once for a week. Each time Mrs. Means thinks he is gone for good, that some accident has befallen him. But he has always reappeared, as well as ever.

During the hottest nights of summer he sleeps in the trees, stretched out full length on one of the gray, leaning trunks of the live oaks. The rest of the year he apparently sleeps on the ground—just where, nobody knows. Although he is solitary, a cat recluse, he is friendly and comes readily when called. One year, a mother cat with a litter of kittens ate with him in the afternoon. Another year, an opossum with five young used to feed with Zeke. Still another time, a family of raccoons shared his meals. Around the place where he is fed, Mrs. Means often finds the ground rooted up where armadillos have hunted for scraps of food.

Watching Zeke eating alone that afternoon, we observed how a pair of cardinals hopped among the bushes and drew closer and closer to the feeding cat. No sooner had he moved away than the redbirds darted down, alighted on the edge of the plate and began picking up bits of cottage cheese that had been left behind. The cardinals recognize Mrs. Means's voice. As soon as she begins calling for Zeke, they come flying. We noticed that even when the birds were only a foot or so above his head in the underbrush, the yellow cat paid no attention to them. More than once Mrs. Means has seen one of the birds dart down and snatch up food even while Zeke was feeding. But usually the cat eats first, then the redbirds. When he had finished his afternoon meal, Zeke waited for a time to be petted. But soon he strolled away and disappeared among the thickets, resuming his solitary ways, a cat individualist who did not want too many cats—or too many people—in his life.

FIFTEEN

STRANGE BIRDS CALLING

WE BLINK our eyes on an average of twenty-five times a minute. Each blink lasts about one-fifth of a second. Thus during every minute we are awake our eyes are shut one-twelfth of the time. They are shut for five seconds out of every minute, for five minutes out of every hour, for more than an hour and a quarter out of every sixteen-hour day. Nowhere in all the 20,000 miles of our winter travels did we regret more this loss of time through the necessity to blink than we did amid the wild birds of Rockport.

When we remember Rockport, we remember first of all a woman four feet, eleven and a half inches tall, weighing a hundred pounds or less, in her seventies as intense and alert as a hummingbird—Conger Neblitt Hagar. While Connie Hagar did not make the birds of the Texas coast, she has made them known. Singlehanded, she has added twenty new species to the avifaunal list of the state. Twice a day for a quarter of a century, storm or fair weather, she has patrolled the same four-by-seven-mile area beside Aransas Bay. The number of different birds she has seen in the vicinity of Rockport is now nearing the 500 mark. Her discoveries have attracted thousands of ornithologists and advanced bird watchers to her small section of the central Gulf Coast.

Connie Hagar was the first to find the snowy plover nesting in Texas. She was the first to report buff-breasted sandpipers and ash-throated flycatchers and mountain plover overwintering in the state. She was the first to see a cattle egret and the first to note a flamingo there. She discovered the state's first nesting pair of warbling vireos. She was the first to observe that blue-gray gnatcatchers migrate in waves down the central Gulf Coast. It was Connie Hagar who discovered that hummingbirds of nine different species—including some "not supposed to be in the state"—move southward through Rockport in the fall. Within a mile of her home, on three successive days in the spring of 1952, she observed what was unmistakably an Eskimo curlew, a bird generally considered extinct. Because, over the years, she has kept note of the numbers as well as the species, Connie Hagar's day-by-day observations provide an invaluable record in the study of the fluctuations in bird populations in the region.

At the end of our wanderings with *Autumn Across America*, on our way home from California, we had first met Connie and her husband, Jack. At the conclusion of our *Journey into Summer*, we had made the long swing south from Pikes Peak to spend another two weeks at Rockport. Now, in the midst of this last of our seasonal travels, we had come back again.

In the days that followed, on white shell roads, under live oaks bent by the sea wind, among oil wells, where bay-side houses were roofed with oyster shells, we drifted about in leisurely roaming, surrounded by birds from morning till night. No other state in the Union approaches Texas in the number of birds in its avifauna. Lying half way between the two oceans, it is a place where eastern and western species, northern and southern species, overlap. Here birds of mountains and plains and sea intermingle. A century ago, John James Audubon, after visiting only the eastern part of the state, estimated that two thirds of all the species of birds inhabiting the United States could be observed in Texas. That prediction proved remarkably accurate. Dr. Harry C. Oberholser, in his exhaustive study of the bird life of this commonwealth, has listed more than 800 species and subspecies.

Situated at the foot of the plains and at the edge of the Gulf, Rockport receives wandering birds from both land and sea. It also lies at the small end of a vast migration funnel. During a single day in the spring following our first visit, Connie Hagar and Clarence D. Brown, of Montclair, N.J., listed 204 species seen between dawn and dusk. In the history of American bird-watching, this stands as the all-time "big day" for two observers. Once, Connie told us, she counted 3,000 ruby-throated hummingbirds in her yard. Another year, upwards of 40,000 indigo buntings descended on Live Oak Peninsula, on which Rockport is situated. Each migration time, when birds pour south or birds pour north, Rockport provides a reviewing stand for one of the great avian parades of the world.

It was this fact that drew Connie Hagar to the spot. She was nearing fifty when she and Jack moved to Rockport in 1934. They came south from Corsicana, the northern Texas city christened by a man from Corsica whose wife was named Ana. It was there, in the high-pillared home of an eminent jurist, that Connie had been born on June 14, 1886. Early in her life her father interested her in nature. As a girl she set out to learn all the birds and all the wildflowers, butterflies and shrubs in her county, an area twenty-six square miles larger than Rhode Island.

Through the later events of her life—her musical education at the piano; the discovery of oil on her father's land, which opened up the first commercial petroleum field in Texas; her marriage to Jack Hagar, a New Englander who had come south selling automobiles and had stayed to invest in oil properties; her activity in numerous organizations; her prominence in Corsicana society—through all this Connie's interest in nature remained undiminished. She first saw Rockport in the early 1930's when a physician prescribed salt-water bathing for her sister. Brought up as she was on the dry, dusty prairie, the seashore and the lush bird life it supported were a revelation to her. The only water bird she was sure she recognized was the brown pelican. The next year she came back at migration time. And the following year, to the bewilderment of her friends, she left Corsicana for good and settled in Rockport. Twenty years later, one friend was still bewailing the fact that "with social eminence right in her lap, she threw it all away and went to live on the outskirts of a village *with birds!*"

To keep himself occupied, Jack bought the Rockport Cottages, a curving line of white cabins set amid palms and wind-tilted live oaks. Connie had stayed at these cabins on her first visit to the shore. At the time, the cottages were a mile and a half from Rockport, with only one house lying between. The community was so quiet, Connie recalls, that, except when it was mailtime at the post office, "you could shoot a cannon down the main street and not hit anybody." Since then, oil derricks have sprung up in the region and the town has doubled in population. Traveling salesmen and casual tourists were the earliest guests at the cottages. But as reports of Connie's ornithological discoveries spread, more and more bird people arrived. Each year at migration time, Rockport has not only an invasion of birds but an invasion of bird watchers. Visitors come from abroad, as well as from virtually every state in the Union. Many return year after year. The registery list of the cabins now is a veritable Who's Who of American ornithology.

Riding the roads of the Rockport region with Connie on successive mornings—to Redbug Corner to see a black-throated gray warbler, to Tule Lake to watch gull-billed terns pursuing dragonflies, to the fishing piers of the Fulton Road where snowy plover fed on a low-tide beach—riding thus we heard, little by little, the story of her gradual mastery of the teeming bird life of the Gulf Coast. At first there was no one to help her, no one to consult. She used to wade in ponds in hip boots and a bathing suit, using a dip net to scoop young grebes from under water for close study in her hand. The only reference books she had were a small Reed's pocket guide with colored illustrations "some good, some terrible," and Arthur Cleveland Bent's *Life Histories of North American Waterfowl*, published by the Smithsonian Institution in Washington.

"I tell you, it was rough," she commented. "When Roger Peterson's field guide appeared, I felt let out of the cage!"

Inheriting a phenomenal memory from her father, Connie Hagar has had to make few notes. Once a detail of plumage or song or the habitual action of a bird has been observed, it seems indelibly recorded in her mind. This, in a way, is a great misfortune. The copious notes that otherwise would have formed a whole advanced bird guide were never written. For, through the years, in addition to noting the more obvious field marks, she has concentrated on all the fine points, on all those innumerable little mannerisms and differences that set similar birds apart and enable the skilled observer to recognize them instantly as we recognize a friend coming down the street by the way he swings his arm or holds his head. Such things Connie has recorded, not on paper but on the tablets of her memory.

The winter dawns at Rockport come with soft, delicious, scented air, like June dawns in the north. This is the season of the three-month calm, the time when the trade winds, the benders of the live oaks, no longer blow in from the sea. Almost on the dot of seven each morning, Connie starts off on her six-mile circuit. She has learned that she can see more and alarm birds less if she stays in her car with the motor running. Many of her comments along the way come back in recollection. We passed a farmyard swarming with birds of common species. ("Isn't it comforting to be able to look out there and say to oneself: 'I know all those birds'?") We saw a small dead animal on the road ahead. ("Never run over a dead animal. It may be a skunk.") We passed a hall where a weekly bridge club met. ("They don't understand why I won't join them. When I was forty-five I quit being a child and I refuse to return to childish ways.") She hummed a snatch of a tune as we rode along. ("Every morning I wake up with a different tune running through my head. Sometimes it is a patriotic song, sometimes a hymn, sometimes an Irish jig. This morning it was 'Pretty Redwing.'") We stopped to study a bird that a friend of hers had long wanted to see. ("When I find a bird somebody else wants to see so badly, I feel as though I had gone to the circus and left the children at home.")

By eight Connie was back, crossing the cattle guard at the entrance of the long drive to the cottages. During the rest of the day, on roads now grown familiar, Nellie and I drifted this way and that, our hours filled with birds. This was the winter season. Yet here we were surrounded by concentrations and varieties of species hardly rivaled at home in the midst of the spring migration.

For nearly ten miles, beside shallows where herons and egrets feed, a shore road follows the winding edge of Aransas Bay. Along its length we sometimes came upon as many as 300 willets massed in a light-gray shoal where they rested on some barely submerged bar. Again we would see a hundred black skimmers in buoyant flight, their long bills cutting the surface of the water. Or we would stop to watch a marbled godwit, with food in its bill, twist and dodge and finally elude the running pursuit of ring-billed gulls.

Out in a dripping world, after a deluge of "Texas dew" one afternoon, we came to the edge of the bay just as the dark, swollen sky beyond was cut by the glowing arch of a rainbow. Beneath its curve, across the yellow-tinged water of the wind-roiled shallows, great blue herons stood hunched against the gusts, their forms extending away in long curves that, like a series of surveyor's stakes, marked the course of hidden sandbars.

Not infrequently as we followed this shore road in the sunshine, we stopped and walked about, examining the unfamiliar plants. I remember the beauty of the coral bean, its pods opened to reveal the brilliant red seeds that Indians once collected and used for making necklaces. Several times we stooped over a ground-hugging plant for a closer view of its leaves. They were round as coins and of several sizes. Children, playing store, use such leaves for money. The colloquial name for the plant is "nickels, dimes and quarters."

All across Texas, a host of other picturesque names have been bestowed on the wild plants of the state. They run from angel's trumpet, dry whiskey, dew flowers and careless weed to shame vine, barometer bush, love-in-a-puff, fluttermill, baby slippers, cloth-of-gold, lazy daisy and kiss-me-and-I'll-tell-you. On one published list that Connie let me read, I found frog fruit, good mother, tiny Tim, big-drunk bean, nimble Kate, Polly-prim, sunbonnet babies, poor man's patches, prairie lace and widow's tears. Such colorful local names represent a rich addition to our language.

Day after day, at one point along the shallows of this bird coast, we used to come to a halt to watch the antics of a reddish egret. It was the clown of our three-ringed circus. Like an awkward child burlesquing a ballet, it performed a ludicrous dance. It leaped into the air, seemed to clap its heels together, landed off balance, staggered drunkenly, minced backward a few steps, fell forward, stabbing wildly at the water. All the time it peered about with its head held at odd and comical angles, its crest feathers raised like a shock of unruly hair. Usually, during this dance, a ring-billed gull circled low or a willet edged nearer. For by playing the fool in the shallows, the egret in reality was stirring up food on the bay bottom. More than once, its wild stabbing brought it a prize.

Forty yards from shore, farther down the bay on an afternoon when the tide was out, we caught sight of a great blue heron hunched in an abnormal position. It appeared to be leaning against a line stretched between two low posts. Through our glasses, we saw that its wing was caught on a large fishhook, one of many strung along a trot or set line left for high water to cover. Leading across the mud of the ebb tide, a ridge of stones extended to the bar where the bird was trapped. I approached it warily, a thick sweater wrapped around my left forearm as a buffer against its javelin bill. Five minutes passed while I worked to release the muscles and tendons from one of man's most vicious primitive inventions, now refined by modern art. Then the wing was free of the barbed hook. When we left, the heron was standing beside an open channel. Its injured wing drooped slightly. But, unlike a hawk, it did not depend for its livelihood on flight. It could catch fish and feed itself while the tendons healed.

Later, on the Port Aransas breakwater, we saw a brown pelican released from a fishhook embedded in the skin of its pouch. It had scooped up a baited line. The hook was removed, the bird was liberated, and almost immediately it returned to the same spot where the accident had occurred.

Once, at the tip of Cape Cod, some twenty years ago, I encountered another instance of birds caught on trot lines. Near Provincetown, where the ribbed sand of the bay shallows extended out for a quarter of a mile or more, I noticed a swirling cloud of herring and ring-billed gulls. In their midst a boy of about twelve was racing back and forth, waving his arms and shouting. Gulls would rise from the water, flutter upward half a dozen feet, be snubbed, and drop back again. I waded out. All along a trot line, which the boy had baited with shining minnows, gulls were swooping down, snatching up the small fish and being caught on the hooks that pierced the fleshy skin behind their bills. I remember we hauled in and released bird after bird. But the job was not finished until all the minnows were gone, until not a single baited hook remained. For water birds, the barbed steel of the fishhook is a constant menace.

If you turn aside after crossing Copano Causeway from Live Oak Peninsula to Lamar Peninsula, you follow a road that leads you to one of America's notable trees, the largest live oak in Texas. Its immense trunk, suggesting four trees fused together, has a breast-high circumference of twenty-five and a half feet. We first saw this giant late one afternoon. Viewing it against the rays of the declining sun, we saw glinting bands of light flowing, like sunshine on ripples, among all its twigs and branches. Thousands of silken threads, gossamer that had carried wingless spiderlings on an airborne dispersal flight, streamed in the breeze with a shifting play of reflected light.

Beneath the tree, in a slow drift, leaves whirled down, part of the year-long shedding and renewal of the live-oak foliage. Everywhere under the wide expanse of the outstretched limbs the sand was densely strewn with the pits of ant lions. Never have I seen so many under the shelter of any other tree. We began counting the little craters. The total exceeded 1,000. On the very edge of this mine field of pits, each with a caliper-jawed predator hidden at the bottom, a colony of ants was thriving. We watched the insects hurrying about, threading their way among the excavations, many returning with bits of live oak leaves in their jaws. For we were seeing no ordinary ants. We were seeing agricultural insects, fungus growers. Leaf fragments form the soil of their subterranean gardens. On this decaying material, they plant and fertilize and care for the fungus that provides the only sustenance for themselves and their larvae.

To do justice to the Rockport region, to the fascination and variety of its wildlife, even a Texas-sized chapter will hardly suffice. Memories come crowding back, memories of tree snails strewn like white pussywillows along the branches of a bush, of a glittering metallic green scarab beetle plodding down a rangeland cattle path, and of a centipede, red of head and nearly half a foot long, flowing over the ruts of a dirt road. In that curious area of low mounds known as the Pimple Prairies, we watched sandhill cranes leaping high and parachuting down on partially opened wings, already beginning the strangely graceful, airy dance of their spring courtship. Not far from the spot where Connie had seen the Eskimo curlew, we looked out across the bay one morning and beheld nearly a thousand redhead ducks floating in long rafts on the water. Another time, without changing position, we had five species of plover within focus of our glasses.

Individual birds return in recollection. On one particular sandbar, a pugnacious little ringneck, a semipalmated plover that apparently considered the bar its private preserve, dashed endlessly this way and that, scattering smaller sandpipers and even launching an attack on an alighting willet, a bird twice its size. Each day, we saw the same vermilion flycatcher perched on a duck blind before a large live oak, standing out against its dark background like a glowing coal on a green hearth.

There were some mornings around Redbug Corner, on the way to Rattlesnake Point, when birds were so numerous and so active that branches all around us seemed jumping and vibrating with their alighting and taking off. Our eyes encountered species we had never beheld before. Connie pointed out black-crested titmice and gray-tailed cardinals. Farther afield, we saw such life-list species as white-rumped shrikes and white-tailed hawks and—out near the Tin Barn and the Lard Road, which a rain turns into gumbo— mountain plover, killdeer-sized birds with white foreheads and white showing under their wings as they flew. In the excitement of those hours I found myself referring to "Bedbug Corner," saying "cottontails" when I meant cattails, and even, as Connie and Nellie always afterwards agreed, talking about somebody's "bird guide to the mammals."

For nearly fifteen years, until his death in 1959, Patch, a black and white terrier, was Connie's companion on every trip she made. He was a bird watcher's bird-watching dog. More than once, he called Connie's attention to some hidden bird beside the road. And in the spring, when great flocks of willet suddenly reappeared and flew, a thousand at a time, over the Rockport Cottages, it was his habit to race and bark until she came out to see them.

Almost invariably when distinguished visiting ornithologists climbed into the car at the start of their first trip with Connie and Patch, they would glance in his direction. Their expression said:

"Is *he* going along?"

Then they looked resigned:

"*Well, here go the birds!*"

But at the end of the trip they viewed Patch with a new expression. Usually they commented:

"I never saw such a quiet dog."

Bumps in the road made him bark. Red automobiles and garbage trucks drove him into a frenzy. But in the presence of birds he remained still and quiet. He never gave chase unless Connie clapped her hands, a signal that she wanted the birds put up in order to study them in flight. At the time of his death, Patch, without doubt, had seen more species of birds —and more species of bird watchers—than any other dog in history.

Because his life was filled with a long succession of visitors who came, stayed a few days, then disappeared, he made friends slowly. Sometimes he took a dislike to a stranger and spent the whole ride sitting in the front seat growling. Fortunately, he seemed to take to Nellie and me. I say fortunately, because I long suspected that Jack Hagar gave visitors the dog test. He tended to like people, but the ones he liked best, I felt, were the ones his dog liked too.

Filled with good spirits, good sense and the ability to get along with visitors of many kinds, Jack enjoyed running the cottages as an avocation until he passed away in the summer of 1962 at the age of eighty-five. Although he continually kidded bird watchers, he was immensely proud of Connie's achievements.

"When I get to riding six horses at once," she told us, "Jack calms me down. I'm always riding two, but when it gets to be six that's too many."

During the October days we spent at Rockport, following our wandering course through summer, Connie was close to the sixth horse. Much was happening to get excited about. Passion flowers bloomed. Dragonflies migrated down the coast. Black-necked stilts flew past with trailing legs or slept, lined up like trains of cars, in the shelter of islets on windy days. Sanderling flocks—in fall so white that natives call them "ghost birds"—followed the wash of waves on the beaches. Once we saw half a dozen feeding roseate spoonbills, following a shower, shake themselves and send a sprinkle of water drops flying.

Across the bay from the outer islands, along the trail Cabeza de Vaca is supposed to have followed four centuries before, monarch butterflies were winging their way above a parade of shrimp boats coming in from the sea. We saw them rocking and tilting in the disturbed air amid a flock of milling ring-billed gulls. But always they advanced, as on a compass course, in a westerly direction. Why the migrating butterflies, year after year, turn inland at this point, instead of continuing south along the coast, is an absorbing mystery. One monarch that Connie Hagar banded in October 1955 at Rockport was recovered two days later 260 miles inland from the Gulf. It had advanced over the land, probably with the aid of favoring winds, at the rate of more than 100 miles a day.

It was other migrants, however—swift, pulsing, blazing with metallic colors—that formed the center of excitement those October days. We had arrived in the midst of the spectacular hummingbird parade. Until Connie Hagar reported it, this annual movement down the central coast of Texas, embracing nine species, was unknown to science. Its discovery probably represents her outstanding contribution to ornithology.

Day after day we had hummingbirds before breakfast. Along the white shell road that skirts the bay, Mexican mallows were clothed with the rich red of their blooms. These bushy plants, with their large and velvety leaves, are variously known as rose mallows, red mallows and Mexican apples. The latter name comes from the fact that Mexicans eat the small red, apple-shaped fruit. The five-petaled crimson flowers that attract the hummingbirds are rolled lengthwise into tubes. Even in the full sun, they do not open completely. The flowers bloom, a few each day, from spring until late in fall.

Around them we saw the hummingbirds, on blurring wings, swarm like larger, more colorful bees. Never before had we seen such numbers of hummingbirds or such varied kinds of hummingbirds. Broadtails, down from the high mountain meadows, were squeaking like so many mice. Ruby-throats, drained from across the eastern half of the continent, darted about—on occasion with heads yellow and mealy with pollen. Black-chinned nectar hunters hovered now before the crimson of a mallow, now before the blue of a morning-glory. One rufous hummingbird perched on the same twig during periods of rest for three days in a row. According to the angle of the light, its tail appeared rufous or cinnamon-hued. Turning in the sun, a female Anna's hummingbird, larger than a ruby-throat, flashed on and off like the beam of a lighthouse, a dazzling red spot that shone jewellike at its throat. Once Connie pointed out the slightly decurved bill and deeply forked tail of a lucifer hummingbird.

In all, during those memorable days along a hummingbird road, we saw six of the nine species Connie has recorded on migration. The males seem to come first. Then the females build up in numbers. The most numerous, and the last hummers to go through each fall, are the ruby-throats.

Some years ago, when Laurence J. Webster and his wife were pioneering in feeding ruby-throated hummingbirds at Holderness, N.H., they sent Connie eight of their specially designed feeding tubes. She attached them to a hedge outside her bedroom window. Day after day, ruby-throats streamed through the yard, paying no attention to the red-tinted feeders. Then early one morning—with a "swoosh" that awakened both Connie and Jack—a small group of new migrants arrived. They went directly to the feeders. Six at a time, they tried to get at the sugar-water. Obviously they recognized the tubes. Obviously they had fed at such feeders before. When she wrote the Websters, Connie learned that their ruby-throated hummingbirds had left New Hampshire and started south just five days before.

One of the first experts to observe her migration of hummingbirds was an ornithologist from the West Coast. After watching the birds for some time, he remarked that she definitely had a number of species and also a possible this and a possible that other species.

"Now, none of this possible business," Connie told him. "You know these hummingbirds. I have to go home. But you stay here and look at them until you are sure they are or they aren't what I say they are."

Later, he came in and said:

"Yes, Mrs. Hagar. The birds you said were there are all there."

In the early days when Connie, pioneering in this area of avifaunal riches, began sending lists of birds she had seen to the celebrated Dr. Harry C. Oberholser, of the U.S. Fish and Wildlife Service in Washington, D.C., that careful and exact scientist became worried. She was seeing birds out of their range, birds nesting where they were not supposed to nest. He made a special trip to Rockport. All day long, as he and Connie drove about the country, he would interrupt the conversation with "What bird is that?" or, shooting out a forefinger, demand: "Identification!" By evening, he was satisfied with Connie's care and competence and thereafter became her sponsor among professional ornithologists.

But to come back to the adventures of our winter visit. One morning, near the end of our stay, Nellie and I followed a cattle path beside Copano Bay, half a mile from Rattlesnake Point. We were looking for a new bird, the Sprague's pipit. Near this same spot, on another morning, we had watched five coyotes, probably a family, hunting jackrabbits in a pack, like a group of yellow dogs. After we had seen the pipit—small, striped and buffy—we were returning well content when a commotion at the edge of the bay attracted our attention.

A dozen white pelicans were thrashing the water with their wings. Hidden behind clumps of mesquite, we watched through our field glasses. In a ragged line, the huge birds advanced upon the shore. Their beating wings drove the fish before them. By the time the line of pelicans closed about the mouth of a small baylet, its water was swarming with prey. Then the feast began. Over and over, the birds dipped their heads and lifted them, their pouches bulging with water and fish. Other birds joined the banquet. Cormorants and egrets, both snowy and common, came flying. With the white pelicans wheeling like stately battleships and the white egrets darting about like small destroyers, they reaped an abundant harvest. For the first time in our lives, by that morning's good fortune, we were witnessing the famed cooperative hunting of the white pelicans. I remember we rode home, that day, puzzling over the mystery of how such closely related species as the white and brown pelicans could have evolved fishing techniques so different, one diving in individual hunting, the other obtaining food by cooperative endeavor.

Nearly 20,000 times, Connie Hagar has made her six-mile circuit of the roads of her four-by-seven-mile tract at Rockport. She has traveled within it in excess of 100,000 miles. This small foothold in the immensity of Texas has provided her with an interest that has never waned. When people invited her to make trips elsewhere, she always replies that she will as soon as she knows all there is to learn at Rockport.

How many hundred thousand persons do you suppose we talk to in the course of a lifetime? How many billion words do we hear spoken? Yet, how few are those we remember. One short sentence, only five words long, ending in a question mark, has returned to my mind innumerable times from our days at Rockport. For it condenses Connie Hagar's outlook. It explains the endurance of her enthusiasm.

I had commented on the fact that at Rockport you see rare species often enough and you see them in sufficient numbers to become really acquainted with them. You see them head-on and tail-to and from the side and top and bottom. You observe their characteristics. Elsewhere, after diligent search, you might find a single specimen of a rare species and see it only in a fleeting glimpse.

"The beauty of Rockport," I concluded, "is that here you have *enough* birds."

To which Connie replied:

"Are there *ever* enough birds?"

SIXTEEN

WHITE CRANES IN THE WIND

DURING one of our last days at Rockport, a blue norther struck. The sky became bright burnished blue. Robins, fleeing the cold, appeared in flocks. This particular blue of the sky and the arrival of robins from the interior are winter weather signs along the coast. Then the cold front hit. In five minutes the temperature dropped fifteen degrees. All night the wind blew. The next morning we saw herons hunched against the cold in the shallows and waves racing across Aransas Bay. At the top of its high pole, the Coast Guard's red warning flag for small boats—the "starvation rag" of the charter fishing captains—flapped wildly, continually collapsing and darting out again in the shifting gusts. It was under such conditions that we left the protection of the Rockport jetty in Willie Close's twenty-eight-foot, 250-horsepower *Missy III*. We were starting out in unusual weather to see unusual things.

Pounding through waves, we charged across the open water. Amid the spray that streamed away behind us, rainbows lengthened and contracted, disappeared and came to life. Thus, riding with rainbows, we crossed the bay and entered the Intracoastal Waterway. Once before, while traveling through the spring, I had come to this lowland canal along the edge of the Gulf. Then, also pounded by the wind, I had raced ahead of a storm across the Louisiana marshes to make my first and only ride in a mudboat.

The *Missy III* possesses "two of everything"—two rudders, two gasoline tanks, two 125-horsepower engines. It was built at Port Aransas especially for taking out sports fishermen. But the dramatized plight of America's almost-extinct whooping cranes had brought the owner a lucrative sideline. With him, we were riding on a fifty-mile trip down and back along the Intracoastal Waterway, through the Aransas National Wildlife Refuge on Blackjack Peninsula, the winter home of these rare birds.

Once ranging from Central Mexico to the arctic coast and from beyond the Rockies to the Atlantic, the shy cranes had steadily retreated before the advance of the homesteaders. Their numbers decreased with the plowing of the prairies and under the pressure of pioneer hunting. This decline accelerated as gun clubs increased and firearms became more deadly. Although Close is only a little past middle age, he can recall a time when a local gun club erected numerous duck blinds in the area. There, when ducks were scarce, hunters blasted away at every passing crane, letting it lie where it fell.

Man's inclination toward—and enjoyment of—destruction almost, if not completely, counterbalances man's inclination toward—and enjoyment of—creation. Natural predators never kill *all* the prey. Natural parasites never destroy *all* the hosts. But man possesses the power and the inclination to kill all wildlife as he has killed the heath hen and the passenger pigeon. Man represents a new kind of predator and parasite in nature's world. The hawk, the weasel, the mountain lion weed out the diseased and unfit. They play their part in evolution. The hunter seeks the finest victims. He represents evolution in reverse.

When, in some better day, man—The Great Predator—recognizes a Bill of Rights for Wildlife, two propositions will head the list:

1. Wildlife was not put on earth for man's use and accommodation merely.

2. Getting pleasure from causing pain is morally indefensible.

The belief the Lord created all living creatures with no other purpose than to aid man is man's own idea. The wish is father to the thought. Moreover, no idea has been more comforting to the plunderers of the forests and the slaughterers of wildlife than this sophistry that the mink was given life merely to provide mink coats for women and the honeybee to produce sweets for man.

In time, the attitude of the hunter—"What a beautiful day. Let's go out and kill something!"—may stand no higher in the scale of moral values than the acceptance of human slavery. Seeking pleasure by bringing suffering and death to fellow creatures, which also enjoy the beautiful day and desire only to escape and continue to enjoy it, will appear, in time, part of our own Dark Ages." I believe I have found the missing link between animals and civilized man," Konrad Lorenz wrote. "It is us." Why concern yourself, the hunter asks, with cruelty to wild creatures when wars destroy so many human beings? Always you can point to a greater wrong to justify a lesser wrong. But does that make the lesser wrong less wrong?

Fundamentally, it is those who have compassion for all life who will best safeguard the life of man. Those who become aroused only when *man* is endangered become aroused too late. We cannot make the world uninhabitable for other forms of life and have it inhabitable for ourselves. It is the conservationist who is concerned with the welfare of all the land and life of the country who, in the end, will do most to maintain the world as a fit place for human existence as well.

The hungry man hunting to feed his hungry family has some moral grounds for his act. The well-fed sportsman, going afield to find his pleasure in destroying the pleasure that some other creature knows, has none. Yet, too often, it was only to bring such pleasure, merely to gratify the whim of some bored gunner, that the great white cranes were brought lifeless to the ground.

Slow in reaching maturity, low in rate of reproduction, demanding expanses of wild and open land, easily disturbed on their nesting ground, retreating always before advancing civilization, the cranes grew fewer year by year. Even before the beginning of the present century, alarmed conservationists were writing the species off as doomed. By 1923 a national magazine was reporting that the whooping crane might already be extinct. It was primarily to save the remnants of the species that, in 1937, the Federal government set aside 47,000 acres of the Blackjack Peninsula as the Aransas refuge.

Along the edge of its vast expanse of tan and russet-colored tidal flats and salt marshes, the *Missy III* advanced steadily. Before us stretched the wide brown path of the Intracoastal canal, the quieter water tinged with green at its shallower edges. And over all boomed the great wind. Cormorants passed us, fighting their way into the gale with laboring wings. Once, sixteen long-billed curlews took off from a sheltered spot, turned with a gust and went hurtling by over our heads. Another time, at our approach a whole raft of white pelicans lifted out of a little bay and dissolved into strings of buoyant birds soaring away across the outspread land. But in spite of several false alarms—for, in the far distance, the white signs of the U.S. Fish and Wildlife Service suggested feeding cranes—nowhere did we catch sight of the rare birds we had come to see.

The first annual census of the Aransas cranes took place in the winter of 1938–1939, the year after the refuge was established. It showed that the great flocks of a century before had dwindled to a total of only eighteen individuals. Three winters later, the count had dropped to fifteen. Slowly it crept upward to thirty-four in 1949. In 1952 it had dropped back to twenty-one. Again the figure crept ahead, to thirty-three in 1959, to thirty-eight in 1961. Then came a year of disaster.

Ten of the rare cranes were lost. The total dropped to twenty-eight. Once more, the painfully slow build-up commenced. At this writing, in the winter of 1964–1965, the number of wild whooping cranes in the world has risen to a new high—a total of forty-two. Ten of the birds are juveniles.

These ups and downs in the bird's fight for survival made front-page headlines. So did the discovery, in 1955, of the long-sought northern nesting ground of the Aransas cranes. In the remote interior of Wood Buffalo National Park, near Great Slave Lake, in the Northwest Territories of Canada, more than 2,000 miles north of the Gulf, the birds rear their young. A round-trip migration of nearly 5,000 miles carries them north and south each year.

Millions of North Americans who have never seen a whooping crane have become engrossed in its desperate fight against extinction. So great is the interest in its welfare in Canada that, in 1961, the first railroad to enter the wilds of the Northwest Territories was rerouted and nineteen miles were added to its right-of-way to carry it farther from the nesting grounds of these shy birds. For the whooping crane is one of the most easily disturbed of all wild species. It takes alarm, on the open land of the Aransas refuge, if a man on foot approaches within half a mile. However, to some degree it has become accustomed to the boats that use the waterway. Close has learned that by idling along with the engines running, he can draw nearer to the cranes than can a man on foot or on horseback. But if the sound of the engine stops, the birds take flight at once.

When we did sight our first whooping crane, our good fortune was tripled. The stately birds stood grouped together only a couple of hundred yards inland from the canal. Two were white adults. The third, standing between them, was a young bird, its neck rusty with immature plumage. These cranes are among the few birds that continue to live together as family groups after the breeding season has passed.

The three had flown south together. Only five or six weeks after it first had used its wings, the fledgling had begun this long aerial journey. All winter the trio would form a unit, the parents guarding their young, the mother at times catching and breaking up food, the father defending the territory the pair had chosen. Even pairs that come south with no young remain together during the winter months and fly together to their northern breeding ground in the spring.

The three birds stopped their feeding. They lifted their heads and watched our approach intently. Their piercing yellow eyes were raised almost five feet above the ground. For the whooping crane is North America's tallest bird. Through our glasses we could see the bare, carmine patches on the heads of the adults. As we drew nearer, the birds moved away, retreating inland with measured, stately tread. But always their eyes were on us. Although their movements were unhurried, their long strides carried them over the ground with surprising speed. Even before we drew abreast, they had lengthened the distance between us to 300 yards or more. Brilliant of hue in contrast to the immaculate white of the adult cranes, a roseate spoonbill, closer at hand, sprang into flight and was swept away by the wind. Thus most birds take to the air when alarmed. But the cranes, unless closely pressed or suddenly startled, tend to move away by land rather than by air, trusting to the ground-covering ability of their long legs.

Less than five minutes went by before we sighted our fourth crane. It stood watching us near a fence that ran across the open land. Half a dozen common egrets stretched up their slender necks around it, dwarfed by the stature of their solitary companion. In this treeless land the cranes were exposed to the full force of the gale. Yet none of the big birds we saw that day seemed bothered by the wind. Mainly they fed facing into it. At the Aransas refuge each pair of cranes stakes out and defends its own feeding territory. These areas may cover as much as 500 acres.

When Robert Porter Allen was making his intensive studies of the whooping crane at Aransas, he found its food included such varied things as snails, frogs' eggs, water beetles, snakes and acorns. The total list included seventeen vegetable and twenty-eight animal items. One basic food is the marine worms that live in astronomical numbers in the coastal mud. It has been calculated that one acre of such Texas tidal land will hold at least 8,000,000 worms. Once, Close told me, when he was skirting the edge of the refuge, he came upon a young crane swallowing a small rattlesnake. He judged the reptile to be about two and a half feet long. The rear of the body hung from the bird's bill, and he could see the tail tip twitching and the rattles vibrating as long as they were visible.

On that windy day, traffic was light along the canal. We had just passed a tugboat pushing before it a string of oil barges when we surprised two cranes feeding at the water's edge. Both leaped into startled flight. They flapped into the air, loomed up for a moment gigantic, then were borne away on black-tipped wings with a spread of more than seven feet. On several occasions, far out across the flatland, we saw other cranes in flight. Sometimes they beat against the wind, sometimes they cut across it, sometimes they rode with the gusts. But always, in the air as on the land, their advance was stately. Characteristic of cranes, the powerful down-drive of their wings ended in the flip of a faster upbeat. More than once, where low ridges of excavated earth ran beside the canal, we saw cranes, taking flight, sweep up and over the embankment to fly parallel to the waterway, hidden from sight.

At first, whenever we lifted our heads above the protection of the cabin to scan the level expanse spreading away from our water lane, the wind from the north battered our faces and brought tears streaming from our eyes. But, as the morning advanced, the strength of the gusts diminished. To see wild things, go forth in wild weather. That was Thoreau's counsel.

And it may have been that this time of violent wind aided us in seeing more cranes closer at hand. At any rate, whereas on some trips Close sees only six or seven cranes, our tally reached and passed the twenty mark by the time we came to the end of the refuge and swung about for our return.

Going back, we started a new tally, for we had no way of knowing how many of the cranes we saw now were ones we had seen before. Our new list rose to ten, then to a dozen. We had traversed about half the passage back along the waterway when we reached a small cove edged with an open beach of sand and mud. There the greatest adventure of the day awaited us. Almost in a straight line, their long necks stretched down, eight whooping cranes fed near the water's edge. Some rich source of food held their attention. Close, a veteran of the waterway, had never seen so many in one spot before. With the engine almost idling, we crept slowly nearer.

Just then, another crane, previously unnoticed on the opposite bank of the canal, sprang into the air and mounted up and up with powerful downward drives of its great wings. Instead of turning away from us, it came in our direction, growing more immense moment by moment. Its long white neck was outstretched. Its long black legs trailed behind. For a time we thought it would pass directly overhead. Instead, almost above us, its snow-white plumage luminous in the sunshine, it veered in a high wing-over, slanted off downwind and went scudding away just above the winter browns and yellows of the tidal flats.

We turned back to the feeding birds. They had taken alarm. All eight were in the air. We watched them making off in two straggling flocks of four birds each. Their forms receded into the distance. But while they were still in flight, while the bird that had almost passed overhead was still airborne, two other cranes appeared on the wing far out over the level land. We looked back and forth from flying crane to flying crane, trying to arrest this superlative moment in memory. Eleven whooping cranes, all at the same time, were in the air around us!

Still another indelible memory, almost as stirring as the sight of those eleven huge birds in flight, came a little later. A lone whooping crane lifted into the air from the windswept expanse. As it rose, the far-carrying trumpet or bugle note of its call came back to us even against the wind. This famous call, a prolonged "ker-looo!" that, on calm days, carries as much as two miles across the coastal flats, is the product of a remarkable windpipe which is longer than the bird itself. More than two feet of this tube is coiled like a French horn behind the breastbone of the crane. Because early frontiersmen thought the call suggested the war whoop of an Indian, the bird received its common name. Another, less frequently used name—sky bugler—is also derived from the call. The sound, powerful, prolonged, musical, rang in our ears long after it had ceased, as it has rung in our memories since. It is a sound wild and untamed. And it is a sound that still may be forever lost to the world.

With the wind behind us we came home across the bay, tallying up the harvest of what we had seen and heard. On the outgoing trip we had listed twenty-three cranes; on the return trip, twenty-four. Taking the larger figure, we had seen, on this day of wind and flying spray, far more than a majority of all the wild whooping cranes on earth. We had watched family groups. We had followed with our eyes cranes striding across the tidal flats. We had observed eight feeding together. We had seen one immense and luminous bird tilt away almost above us. We had beheld eleven whooping cranes in the air at once. And we had heard the prolonged trumpet note of the call, the voice of the retreating wilderness, rolling over the open land.

That afternoon the norther blew itself out. Warm, almost tropical air flowed inland from the Gulf. We breathed it in deeply as we walked beside the salt water at the end of our last evening on this wonderful bird coast of Texas. Over now were our days west of winter; over now, our days south of winter. In the morning, we would follow the wind inland. Wanderers once more, we would head straight up the map toward the winter of the north, the white winter, the season of ice and snow.

SEVENTEEN

CATFISH MURPHREE

MIDWINTER, the halfway point between the beginning and the end of the season, had come and gone while we were on the Texas coast. A drifting, Indian summer quality had characterized the warm days of Rockport. Now, turning northward, we braced ourselves for a sudden leap into the deep freeze of ice and snow and winter wind. But, as we learned long ago, on such a trip as this events rarely occur exactly as we anticipate them. Instead of cold, we met warmth; instead of a deep freeze, we encountered a heat wave. Across the Gulf Coastal Plain, onto the Edwards Plateau, over the high prairies beyond, we rode with a soaring thermometer. We shed our coats. We opened all the car windows. We saw the mercury climb close to the ninety-degree mark. Almost as far as the Oklahoma line we were surrounded by a February thaw, Texas-sized.

About ten o'clock on the second morning, we crossed the Red River into the red land of Oklahoma. Almost suddenly, the far west seemed left behind. On every hand, as we advanced, we were reminded of the Midwestern country we knew in childhood. Blue jays screamed in the hardwoods. Sycamores appeared in the creek bottoms. Once more we heard the nostalgic sound of Midwestern spring and summer days, the clear, whistled song of the eastern meadow lark. The fascination of the strange—desert and mesa, canyon and Gulf Coast, creosote bush and saguaro—had been succeeded by the

WHITE PELICAN of Aransas Bay. With others of its
kind it cooperates in driving fish into shallow water.

CONNIE HAGAR on a field trip with Patch, the bird-watching dog, and Sibyl Means feeding Zeke, the recluse cat.

attraction of the familiar. During the next few days, as we made a loop up and over and down in Oklahoma, the impression strengthened that we were coming home, that we had returned to a land we knew.

Awaiting us at Norman was a pleasant evening with George Miksch Sutton. Thirty years before, on the edge of the arctic tundra near Hudson Bay, this artist-naturalist had been the first to discover the eggs of the Harris' sparrow. South of Norman we saw this same beautiful sparrow feeding among cottonwoods on its wintering ground. And along the edge of the local airport, amid dry winter grasses, Marvin Davis showed us the rest of the North American longspurs—the Lapland, the Smith's and the chestnut-collared. Again and again, we heard the "rattle-chew" of the Lapland's call. Each time it ended in a definite, emphatic "chew!"

Atoka, Konawa, Tishomingo, Muskogee—the country we wandered over in succeeding days was strewn with such aboriginal names. They reflected the historical fact that, only a few decades before, all this land bore the name not of Oklahoma but of Indian Territory. Somewhere south of Eufaula, a bridge carried us across the wide red bed of the almost-dry South Canadian River. Along the banks of this Oklahoma stream, willow thickets form the home of cottontails of unusual size. When a scientist of the University of Oklahoma, R. E. Bird, studied their life cycles, he discovered that in winter these animals are in the habit of tearing open the cocoons of Cecropia moths and feeding on the pupae within.

Not many miles upstream from the bridge we used, workmen, on a winter day, were using a drag line and a clamshell bucket to haul sand from the dry bed of the river. Several times, as the bucket dumped its load, out poured not only sand but huge channel catfish. As streams dry up toward winter, these fish follow the water underground. They wriggle and push their way downward, usually choosing areas of gravelly sand that will not pack too tightly around them.

Then, safe from drying out, they lie dormant until the rivers rise once more. Along the South Canadian River, these whiskered fish have been reported working their way underground to depths of as much as fifteen feet.

In the strange world of the fish—where most species cannot turn their heads and never see their own bodies, where certain minnows have a sense of taste more than 500 times as keen in detecting sugar as that possessed by humans, where the blinded pike is able to find its food by vibrations in the water, where individuals can remain frozen in solid ice for months and revive as soon as they are thawed out—in this world, the primitive catfish have some of the most remarkable habits, adaptations and abilities of all.

Infinitely older than all the American lakes and rivers in which our species live, their lineage is almost as ancient as that of the armored sturgeon. They form one of the most widespread, hardy and prolific groups of fishes. Including those that live in the sea, the catfish of the world number well over 1,000 species. They range in size from midgets so small that they live in the gills of other fish to giants ten feet long and weighing up to 600 pounds. Some feed on algae which they scrape from submerged stones. Others gnaw holes in the sides of larger fish and drain away their blood. By chemical means in the tissues under its skin, one African catfish generates electricity. With discharges as powerful as 400 volts, more than three times the average house current, it wards off enemies and stuns its prey.

There are blind catfish that spend their whole lives in the darkness of caves. There are species confined to the vicinity of waterfalls. There are others that produce a braying sound. The familiar bullhead of ponds and ditches possesses taste organs on many parts of the exterior of its body. In times of drought, when ponds dry up, these fish sometimes survive for weeks buried in a kind of cocoon of hardened mud. Other species are able in emergencies to leave the water and travel overland. Not only can catfish obtain oxygen through their smooth, scaleless skins in the manner of frogs, but they can gulp down air in bulk and employ stomach respiration. Numerous species build nests and stand guard over the eggs and the teeming fry. In at least one case, the male even carries the eggs about in its mouth until they hatch.

Wherever we went in the Oklahoma country—near Platter Flats, along the Clear Boggy River, beside the Blue River whose water is green—we saw evidence of the importance of catfish. "Worms for sale" signs bore pictures of whiskered fish. Wayside restaurants featured catfish dinners. And north of the Verdigris River, above Muskogee, we came upon another of those outdoor trophy rooms such as we had seen in the Southwest. The immense heads of nearly fifty channel catfish hung in a row from the topmost wire of a roadside fence.

In Oklahoma channel cats have reached a weight of sixty pounds and a length of three and a half feet. Mud cats sometimes tip the scales at eighty pounds. Silver cats may even go as high as a hundred and, in the Mississippi, that fan-tailed giant, the blue catfish, has attained a length of six feet and a weight of 150 pounds. It was no doubt such monsters that startled Marquette and Joliet when they first explored the Father of Waters. "We met from time to time," Marquette notes in his journal, "monstrous fish, which struck so violently against our canoes that we took them to be large trees, which threatened to upset us."

At the western end of the long Roosevelt Bridge at Lake Texoma, we came to a well-known feature of the region—a huge white fishing barge riding on more than 2,000 empty metal drums and anchored in a sheltered cove. Under its roof, protected from rain and wind and snow, warmed by heaters, with bait and tackle, with rest rooms and a lunch counter close at hand, a score or more of silent anglers were enjoying a de luxe version of their sport. At this time, bundled-up fishermen in the north were dropping their lines through holes in the ice. Here anglers were dropping their baited hooks through holes in the floor.

For a dollar for twelve hours, or a dollar and a half for twenty-four, men in overalls and women in party dresses were intent on their all-weather sport. Many anglers stay through the night. One woman drives down from Oklahoma City several times a year and fishes eighteen hours a day for as long as a week at a time. Even the man who washes dishes in the kitchen and the woman who waits on the lunch counter have trap doors they can open in the floor to let down a hook when work is slack. Many a fine catfish has been pulled up through the railed-in, rectangular openings in the floor of this angling barge.

In recent years, the commercial raising of catfish has assumed new importance in the South. I talked with one scientist at the University of Oklahoma, Howard P. Clemens, who had received a grant of $125,000 to study methods of speeding up their propagation. By injecting hormones, he had found, he could cause channel catfish to deposit their eggs in an aquarium approximately when he wished. On the average, spawning occurred thirty-three hours after the hormones were injected. Added impetus to the commercial growing of these fish has come from government restrictions on the raising of rice, limiting crops to one year in three. By stocking their flooded ricefields with year-old, quick-growing catfish, owners in the South have discovered they can produce a valuable meat crop during the two years their land lies idle. Demand for young fish now far exceeds the supply.

Largely responsible for this expanding industry is the work of John Murphree, of Durant, Oklahoma. Known throughout the region as Catfish Murphree, he is the pioneer who first raised channel catfish under hatchery conditions. When I pulled into his yard, on the eastern edge of town, I found him to be a tall, spare man, square-jawed, gray-eyed. He had just retired as head of the nearby state fish hatchery. Speaking in a soft, musical southern drawl, accented now and then with bursts of animation inherited from his French ancestors, he proved a superb storyteller. He began recalling dogs he had known. He remembered a "fishing dog" that used to sit at the water's edge and bark when the float on a line bobbed under. That reminded him of an "alarm-clock dog" he once had trained to watch the clock in the morning and to set up a barking as soon as the hands pointed to seven. When we had run out of dogs, we got down to the great interest of his life—catfish.

About 1900, when he was a child, he had been taken on "a traveling trip" to Missouri. One of the places visited was a state fish hatchery. From then on, the work he wanted most to do was raising fish. His first job was as an assistant at the Durant hatchery. Later he transferred to Pratt, on the southern Kansas plains not far from the spot where Nellie and I had experienced the dramatic night of the falling stars. It was here he began experimenting with catfish. When the ponds were drained and restocked in 1919, he discovered that sixty-four channel catfish had been accidentally included. The head of the hatchery asked him what he was going to do with the catfish. He said he guessed he would try to raise some. He was reminded that that had been tried innumerable times without success.

But Murphree had a new idea. These fish often spawn in hollow logs and in holes in stream banks. So he obtained thirty-two nail kegs, knocked out the tops and bottoms, and laid them in a horizontal position in the water. Uncertain how deep to place them, he arranged them like descending steps in one of the ponds. The bottom of the topmost keg was only an inch or so below the surface. The bottom one was sunk in four and a half feet of water. Which keg would the catfish choose? To his surprise, they picked the one that had the shallowest water in it, the topmost of the thirty-two kegs.

Their next choice was the second from the top.

Each day Murphree carefully removed the eggs. He placed them in a fine wire-mesh basket, with spaces too small for any to slip through and be lost. This he lowered into a gentle current. A slight motion of the water over the eggs is important. Under normal conditions, when the fish guard their eggs they keep the water around them agitated by a deliberate fanning motion of their lower fins. If the water remains completely stagnant, silt is more likely to settle around the eggs or fungus form on them. On several occasions, while studying catfish in aquariums, Murphree has seen a guardian male discover an egg on which fungus has developed. Each time, it has backed away, come down on a slant, sucked up the contaminated egg and got rid of it by swallowing it.

By the end of the first year of his experiment, Murphree had 3,275 baby catfish. They were about four and a half inches long, ready for stocking. As time went on, he discovered that it always requires just about the same total number of degrees of temperature to hatch the eggs of the catfish. In the case of the channel cats, the total comes to almost exactly 800 degrees F. It seems to make little difference how many days go by while the degrees are accumulating. When the total arrives at approximately 800, Murphree told me, the eggs hatch. Egg laying usually begins when the water temperature rises to sixty-eight degrees F.

In his later experiments Murphree employed as many as 200 kegs at a time. Practice has shown that the fish accept these open-ended barrels to a depth of eighteen inches. After he had been working with channel cats for twenty years, at Pratt and later at the Durant hatchery to which he returned as head, he correlated his records of spawning. The great blasts of spawn, the largest deposits of the transparent, amber-colored eggs, had come almost invariably in the dark of the moon. Nearly seventy per cent of all the eggs were laid at times when there was no moonlight. However, during laboratory tests he found he could produce spawn regardless of the moon by controlling temperature.

Under natural conditions, Murphree calculates, not one new-born channel catfish in 10,000 survives to become an adult. The enemies of the small fry are legion. Bass and bluegills feed voraciously on them. Only by burrowing into the sand and mud when not feeding do the young fish escape their attention. Giant water bugs also prey upon them, clutching them with powerful forelegs, thrusting home their dagger beaks and draining away the life juices from their bodies. But of all the enemies that pursue them or lie in wait, Murphree found, the most destructive are the nymphs of the dragonflies. Moving sluggishly along the muddy bottom or clinging to water weeds, they wait until one of the minute catfish comes within reach. Then out shoots an extensible underlip that is carried folded beneath the nymph's body. Two incurving claws at its tip anchor themselves in the body of the victim and drag it back to the waiting mouth. In two weeks' time, dragonfly nymphs in a hatchery pond will consume virtually all the fry unless the little fish receive special protection.

Such protection was provided during the early days of Murphree's experiment by adding a riprap of flat rocks at one side of the pond. Here the small fish found a safe retreat in the deep horizontal crevices. Because the grasping underlip of the nymphs can be thrust only straight ahead, not to either side, it is when the fish swim directly in front of or above the predators that they fall victim. By making the space between the horizontal layers of rocks so narrow the fish could not pass above the nymphs but had to turn to one side or the other, Murphree eliminated much of the loss. Even more effective was keeping the hatchery pools dry until just before the young catfish were put in them. This prevented the dragonfly nymphs from becoming established in advance of their arrival. One of the chief elements of his ultimate success, Murphree believes, lay in studying the enemies of the young fish and taking precautions against them. His constant goal was: never let the enemies get a head start.

In the hatchery pools he fed the growing catfish twice a week. Before the summer was over, he found that by "shortening and sharpening" his voice he could call the fish like calling hogs. As many as 300 at a time would come swimming in his direction as he stood on the bank at feeding time. The growth of the catfish is usually rapid. Among the rice paddies of Louisiana it probably reaches its maximum rate. Here the water is shallow, sunshine is ample, insect food abundant and the feeding season long. By stocking four- or five-inch-long, one-year-old fish at a cost of about $100 a thousand, the planter turned fish-rancher is able to harvest a crop of large three-year-olds at the end of two years. Both as predators and scavengers, catfish consume a wide variety of foods. In one instance, a moderate-sized bullhead devoured eighteen leeches. Audubon, in his *Ornithological Biography*, tells of a large catfish taken from the Ohio River near Louisville, Kentucky, which had swallowed a suckling pig.

In searching for food in the murky light of muddy ponds and rivers, and in the blackness of moonless nights, catfish employ their barbels, the whiskerlike appendages that give them their name. These are equipped with delicate organs of touch and taste. The most widespread of the American catfish, the bullhead or horned pout, will sometimes move along the bottom of a pond, pause suddenly, tilt downward and bury its head in the muddy ooze to obtain some unseen food its sensitive whiskers have detected. Similarly, the barbels of the channel catfish enable it to follow scent trails left in the water of Oklahoma lakes by that favorite of all its foods, the little gizzard shad.

This soft fish, usually no more than six inches long, collects in vast schools and swims close to the surface. Sometimes, Murphree told me, as the afternoon drew to a close, their massed bodies cover half an acre. Bass follow such concentrations, driving up through the multitudes and feeding until satiated. Common mergansers eat enormous numbers. The hard little "gizzards" of the shad collect in the stomachs of these birds and remain undigested for some time. Scientists studying the habits of the mergansers can determine the number of these fish a collected bird has eaten simply by counting the number of undigested gizzards in its stomach. As they swim along, the shad leave a distinctive trail of scent in the water. A channel catfish, coming upon such a trail, rushes headlong in pursuit. In fact, the most prized of all baits for attracting the biggest of the channel cats are gizzards of these shad. Although they sell for two dollars a pint, the supply continually falls behind the demand.

All the rivers we crossed, next day, when Nellie and I rode east in southern Oklahoma—past Slim and Apple, Gay and Bluff, Swink and Frogville—held catfish bedded down in muddy beds. In depressions they had rooted out, they were spending their winter of inactivity. Beyond Broken Bow, we crossed the line into Arkansas. Then our attention shifted. It shifted from the world of water to the world of land. It made a giant jump from catfish to diamonds.

EIGHTEEN

THE DIAMOND FARM

BROAD, blue-black furrows, flattened by the winter rains, extended across the eighteen-acre field. Scattered over this ribbed ground, a score of persons wandered in different directions. They stopped, stooped, walked on slowly. Their heads were bent. Their eyes were downcast. They all were hunting diamonds.

This was the winter scene that confronted us when we came to a halt beside the high fence of heavy woven wire that encircled the field. One hundred and fifteen miles southwest of Little Rock, near Murfreesboro, in Pike County, we were in the diamond country of Arkansas. Sixty years before, the enclosed tract had been merely part of a conventional corn-and-cotton farm. It was plowed each year to produce agricultural crops. Now it is plowed, at more frequent intervals, to produce crops of precious stones.

This dramatic turn of events had its beginning on August 8, 1906. John Wesley Huddleston, the owner of the farm, on that summer day, decided to pan some of his soil in the vague hope of discovering gold. He found no gold. But what he did see on the bottom of his pan when the dirt had washed away were two shining pebbles. He had stumbled on a diamond field. In other parts of the United States, from time to time, isolated, widely scattered diamonds have been picked up. One was found by a laborer digging in a street excavation in Virginia, another by a schoolboy getting a pail of water from a

spring in West Virginia. But such stones are believed to have
been transported far from the spot where they were formed,
either by glacier ice or by running water. The Arkansas diamonds, on the other hand, are in their original location. They
lie in their matrix, in the volcanic material in which they
came into being millions of years ago.

Huddleston sold his farm for $36,000 and retired to
Murfreesboro. Subsequently, various attempts were made to
mine the diamonds commercially. At one period, Henry Ford
was interested in the project and, about the time of the Second World War, Glen L. Martin, the aircraft manufacturer,
purchased the tract. The present owners, Howard A. Millar
and his wife, have found it more profitable to maintain the
diamond farm as a tourist attraction. For a dollar and a half
admission, visitors can spend a whole day hunting for precious
stones. Any diamonds they find, they may keep. However, if
the stone exceeds five carats, uncut, the management shares
to the extent of one-fourth of its value. The field is open to
visitors every day the year around. Diamond hunting here is a
winter sport and a summer sport, a daytime sport and—with
the aid of floodlights—a nighttime sport, as well.

We paid our entrance fee and joined the searchers fanned
out across the furrowed field. Well over a quarter of a million
persons have walked back and forth across this ground. They
have arrived from every state in the Union and from such far-
away lands as Africa and Ceylon. Given special rates, school-
children arrive by the busload. Every week in summer, and as
often as the ground dries out in winter, the area is plowed with
a bulldozer and smoothed with a road grader to bring new
soil, and whatever it contains, to the surface. Just after such a
plowing, and after a heavy rain, conditions are best for seeing
the shining crystals.

These crystals were born amid volcanic action millions of
years before John Wesley Huddleston looked for gold. Lava
had poured from the crater of a volcano at the site of the

farm. Cooling rapidly in the waters of a prehistoric sea, it had plugged the opening from which it had come. Gases and hydrocarbons were trapped under tremendous pressure that transformed the hydrocarbons into diamonds. The rock that underlies the soil is Kimberlite, identical with that found at the famed Kimberley diamond mine in South Africa. Over vast stretches of time, erosion disintegrated this volcanic rock and released the diamonds. The dark-blue soil over which we wandered extends downward for from twenty-five to fifty feet before it reaches the solid Kimberlite rock. This soil is particularly rich in magnesium, lithium and iron. When peanut vines were planted here, they attained such luxurious growth that they were harvested for hay. Three times in early days, cotton raised on the diamond farm and transported seventy-five miles by wagon won first prize at the Texarkana fair. The enclosed field would be swiftly overrun by vegetation except for the almost continual plowing and grading of the soil.

The breeze blew out of the south that February morning. The day was bright and mild. Thermometers rose into the low seventies. Cardinals called from sweet gum and black oak, and eastern meadow larks sang of the "spring-o'-the-year." With the sun warm on our backs, we progressed slowly over the ground. Our expectations of treasure were slight; our enjoyment of the peaceful scene was great. This was a quiet interlude in our winter travels. Like fishing, diamond hunting offers a time of tranquil relaxation and, at the same time, the possibility of a nibble or a strike.

Only the week before, one visitor had gone away with a three-carat stone. All told, more than 2,000 precious crystals have been picked up by visitors to this field at the Crater of Diamonds. Millar, himself, has found a couple of hundred. Once he picked up a diamond from mud where some visitor had scraped his shoes as he was leaving. Most of the Arkansas stones are small, probably averaging about a quarter of a carat.

But on a number of occasions there have been large ones, too.

The great prize, so far, is The Star of Arkansas. On March 4, 1956, Mrs. Arthur L. Parker, a housewife from Dallas, Texas, caught sight of a glinting object in the dirt about fifteen feet away. When she picked it up, she held in her hand, that winter day, the finest diamond ever found in North America. A blue-white stone without a flaw, it was as big as a peanut shell. It measured one and five eighths inches in length and five eighths of an inch in width. It weighed 15.38 carats. This history-making stone, now cut, is valued at $85,000.

Diamond hunting, apparently, is a sport that grows on visitors. They often come back again and again. When we talked to Millar, a soft-voiced former mining engineer, he recalled that one year he kept track and found that almost one out of five visitors had been to the Crater of Diamonds before. One woman, Mrs. Marge Christman, of Dallas, a descendant of the pioneer scout Davy Crockett, has come back at least fifty times. On one occasion she saw something glitter under a grader that was going back and forth across the field, stirring the surface soil. Holding up her hand like a traffic cop, she shouted: "Stop!" The startled operator brought the machine to a sudden halt. Mrs. Christman crawled under the grader and came out with a diamond that weighed nearly six carats.

For more than a decade, a St. Louis, Missouri, man, Ken Gibbons, has been driving down several times a year to spend a week-end hunting diamonds. He leaves home Friday evening after work, hunts all day Saturday and most of Sunday and then drives home in time for work on Monday. He has found almost forty diamonds, the record for one individual. Among women, the champion is Mrs. Helen Wills. Her total now exceeds thirty. Some years ago, when she and her husband were moving from Pennsylvania to California, they stopped off for a day at the Crater of Diamonds. She picked up a two-carat beauty. After they reached California, she and her husband turned around, returned to Murfreesboro, bought a house and settled down in order to be close to the diamond farm. Mrs. Wills receives an annual pass from Millar. Several times a week, and always after a heavy rain, she searches for diamonds.

Like all experienced hunters, she walks, whenever possible, toward the sun. This increases her chances of catching the glint of one of the crystals. Recognition, no doubt, is a large part of luck in finding diamonds. Nellie and I, as we walked toward the sun, discovered what a surprising variety of things, such as seed scales lying on the ground, catch and reflect the light. The only aid that Mrs. Wills employs is a pair of tweezers. But other visitors arrive with picks, shovels, garden weeders, sifting screens, rakes, post-hole diggers. We saw one woman in a red sweater wielding a grub hoe. The rule is that you can bring anything with you that you can carry in your hands.

Of all those who have entered the enclosure, the visitor who arrived with the most elaborate equipment was a man who drove up, one day, in a Cadillac with a California license. He wore elegant clothes. And he came prepared for diamond hunting de luxe. First he brought in a large umbrella, then a folding table, then a metal drum, then a blowtorch, then a tin pail, and, finally, a sifting screen. While he sat in the shade of the umbrella beside the folding table, a Negro boy brought him pailfuls of the dirt. This he dried on the top of the metal drum with the blowtorch. Then he sifted it onto the tabletop. There he stirred it with a stick, being careful never to touch the dirt with his fingers. When he tired of this activity after a few hours and drove away, he was accompanied by no diamonds.

Another wealthy visitor has come up several times from Florida in a chauffeur-driven Cadillac. Each time, he unloads a mine detector. So far, it has provided no assistance. Not infrequently, among the visitors to the diamond farm are dowsers who wander over the field holding out forked sticks of willow in the implicit faith that they will lead them to the precious stones. Judging by the results, their faith is not justified. Nor has any greater success been chalked up by an infinite variety of doodlebugs, homemade divining instruments —each reported by its maker to be infallible—that have been carried back and forth over the furrowed ground.

A few years ago, a man arrived with a long pole from the end of which a leather pouch holding an iron ball hung on a three-foot thong. When he held out the pole and set the iron ball swinging, he explained, the weight would come to rest in a vertical position if there were no diamonds to either side. But if a diamond was hidden in the ground to left or right, the ball would stop on that side of perpendicular. All day he walked about, swinging the pendulum first in one place and then in another, without finding a diamond.

That evening, at the motel where he was staying in Murfreesboro, there were a number of other diamond seekers. In the driveway after supper, he demonstrated his doodlebug. A small crowd gathered. One woman suggested a test to prove whether the device really could detect the presence of a diamond.

"I have a diamond ring. I paid $1,000 for it in St. Louis. You go behind the motel where you can't see what I am doing and I will bury the ring somewhere in the dust of the driveway. Then you come out with your doodlebug and see if it can show you where the ring is hidden.

The test was made. The iron ball came to rest in a dead center position.

"See," the woman said, "that proves your doodlebug doesn't work!"

"Oh, no," was his reply. "It doesn't prove that at all. It simply proves that the stone you think is a diamond is not a real diamond. Somebody has sold you a fake."

In a spectacular display of human credulity, the woman—who had watched the doodlebug fail all day long at the diamond field—was convinced. Without waiting for morning, she jumped in her car and started on the long drive back to St. Louis to confront the jeweler who had sold her the ring.

During June, July and August, the floodlights strung across the field on high poles illuminate the area as though for a night baseball game. To a naturalist they vastly increase the interest of the field. Great moths flutter about them, and the ground directly beneath is often covered with fallen beetles and giant water bugs. In the cool of summer evenings, Millar's cream-colored Cocker spaniel engages in a peculiar search of his own under the floodlights. Ever since he was a puppy, he has been enchanted by land turtles. When he finds one, he picks it up and carries it around in his mouth all evening. His sire had the same odd habit. Some evenings he will go around for hours transporting a turtle so heavy that he has to put it down and rest at frequent intervals. He never harms the animals. Just carrying them around seems, in some strange way, to give him pleasure.

By the time we left the diamond field that afternoon, we had a considerable collection of small stones—some chalcedony, some agates, some quartz, none diamonds. Precious stones had been found previously and precious stones would be found again, but fortune favored none of the visitors on this day. The Law of the White Queen prevailed.

"The rule is," the White Queen told Alice," "jam tomorrow and jam yesterday—but never jam *today*."

Working northward toward the Missouri line on subsequent days, we first turned west and followed the windings of the Arkansas Valley. Country stands featured jars and jugs of sorghum molasses. Many-pointed starlike seed balls covered the sweet gums like ornaments on a Christmas tree. Hound dogs, worried of expression, stoically padded along the roadsides casting sidelong glances as we went by. At Fort Smith we turned north. The road we followed rose and fell along the western edge of the Ozarks, then climbed among these ancient and picturesque mountains, older than the Rockies. At times, we rode on lofty ridges with mountain vistas, blue-tinted, spreading away on either hand. We were in a land of "yarb doctors" and "ridge runners" where local superstitions abounded. Among the curious ideas about winter that have been handed down from generation to generation in the Ozarks is the belief that there will be as many frosts in May as there are thunderclaps in February.

As we wandered up the map, over the state line and toward the Missouri River, we became aware that we were leaving birds behind. For a time, turkey vultures circled overhead. Bluebirds flashed among the tans and yellows of the oak leaves. But they grew fewer as we advanced.

Toward the end of an overcast day, we came to Jefferson City, on the banks of the Missouri River. Here we encountered a local contraction of a place name like many we had met from coast to coast. When a name is long, the local pronunciation or contraction often takes the path of least resistance. San Bernardino, California, becomes "San Berdoo" and Elizabethtown, Kentucky, "E-town." And so Jefferson City, the capital of Missouri, is known locally as "Jeff City." When we were inquiring the way to the diamond farm, I discovered that when I was talking about Murfreesboro and a filling station man was telling me about "Murfboro," we were talking about the same place. I asked a waitress in the town if people always called it Murfboro. She said:

"They do when they're tar'd."

In a wide brown flood the Missouri River rolled past us at Jefferson City. Up this stream Lewis and Clark had ascended on their venture into the unknown. This was the water highway followed by the canoes of French trappers and the barges of fur companies in a day when the wealth of the west was measured in beaver pelts. Even today, a century and a half later and amid modern conditions—as I soon was to learn—beavers still make their homes along the banks of this historic river.

NINETEEN

GIANT BEAVERS

IN THE summer of 1843, when John James Audubon ascended the Missouri River in a fur-company boat loaded with 10,000 pounds of gunpowder, a trader at Fort Union told him that the largest beaver he had ever encountered weighed sixty-one pounds. Nearly 120 years later, on December 2, 1960, a farmer named Henry Mullins trapped a beaver weighing virtually half as much again on a tributary of this same river near Otterville in central Missouri. Its length was almost five feet, and it weighed ninety pounds.

A few years earlier, on December 12, 1956, a beaver weighing seventy-two and a half pounds was taken on the Roche Perce River, less than fifty miles from the capital of Missouri. On March 19, 1953, Clyde Ramsey, of Hazelgreen, trapping along the Gasconade, caught a female beaver that tipped the scales at eighty-eight pounds. It held the record until Mullins' catch seven years later. The average beaver weighs about thirty pounds. I handled the skull of Ramsey's animal and examined the huge cutting teeth, orange in front and yellow behind, when I called at the Missouri Conservation Commission to inquire about the giant beavers taken in recent years.

At one time, the beaver was almost extinct along the lower reaches of the Missouri River. Today it is common. It is found in all the tributaries as well as in the main stream. It lives in the Moreau River within the city limits of the capital. A beaver weighing sixty pounds was caught, a few fears ago, less than five miles from Jefferson City. Mike Milonski, of the State Conservation Department, showed me one den in the north bank of the Missouri within sight of the dome of the state capitol.

For nearly 100 miles, Milonski and I rode up the river and along its tributaries to view the work of these animals. In this region almost all are bank beavers. Instead of building dams and lodges, they burrow into steep banks produced by the undercutting of the river currents. The largest beavers are always found in areas of ample food, in cottonwood bottoms and where corn land runs down to the river. However, plentiful food is only a contributing factor, not the entire explanation for the larger animals. For other beavers, with exactly the same foraging opportunities, may stop growing at a weight of less than thirty pounds. No matter how ample the food supply, the animal never exceeds its individual potential for growth. Nor do the larger beavers belong to a special race. Individual beavers, like some human beings, are just larger than others. A strain of giantism appears to have cropped up among these aquatic animals of the lower Missouri.

Underneath a limestone bluff crowned by ancient Indian burial mounds, Milonski and I pulled on boots and started across a wide black floodplain that extended to the river's edge. This alluvial soil represents some of the richest ground on earth. At this time of year, in a February thaw, it stuck like tar. It balled up under our boots. By the end of fifty yards my feet seemed to be dragging a ball and chain. I recalled Charles Darwin's experiment with the dried mud he found adhering to the foot of a partridge. From that tiny ball of soil had germinated eighty-two plants of five species. What potential gardens, I wondered, were being dragged across that floodplain in the huge masses of mud adhering to my boots?

Along the river bank we came upon little coves edged with barkless sticks. We halted beside stumps of felled cottonwoods. We watched peeled sections of branches go drifting by on the brown flood of the muddy Missouri. Everywhere around us there were evidences of the feeding of beavers. And at a sharp turn on one of the tributaries, where spring freshets had strewn a jumble of debris up the bank, we peered into the mouth of a beaver den. This opening was only a foot above the water line, well hidden from view by the tangle of branches and logs.

Toward the end of that afternoon, as we were traversing an area dense with giant horsetails, the scouring rushes of the pioneers, Milonski recalled an eerily beautiful sight he had glimpsed on a winter day. In the midst of a swirling snowstorm a bewildered flock of snow geese had flown low toward him and turned almost overhead. The white birds were virtually invisible in the white storm. All he could see was a multitude of black wing tips moving in seemingly bodiless flight. I envied my companion that dramatic moment of beauty, just as earlier I had envied another companion who told of seeing migrating yellow-headed blackbirds alight on a field near the Salton Sea in such numbers that for acres the level ground seemed carpeted with gold.

The next day was February 15. Dawn came slowly. The sky, overcast and dark, pressed low. Cold rain began falling as I left Nellie snug in a motel room on the outskirts of Jefferson City and started for Otterville. On a farm somewhere in that region lived Henry Mullins, the man who had seen and handled the ninety-pound beaver.

For fifty miles I rode west, up the Missouri. The gray falling rain added to the gray of the winter hills, the sodden cornfields, the streamside sycamores. When I came splashing into Otterville, all of its 400 or so inhabitants were indoors. The streets were deserted. Outside a furniture store I spotted the one telephone booth in town. But when I looked under "M" in the directory, I found no one named Mullins. For a time I circled about on puddle-studded streets seeking the post office. When I discovered it, it was closed and empty, in the process of being repainted and renovated. Eventually I traced the temporary post office to the rear of a grocery store. Henry Mullins, I learned, no longer received his mail from Otterville. He was on another route, out of Smithton, five miles farther on. There, at the local feed store, where a dozen farmers in overalls and muddy rubber boots were swapping news on this rainy day, I received conflicting directions until the proprietor appeared.

"He can tell you," the farmers chorused.

He did. Go back to an orchard. Turn left on a county-line road. Go to a crossroads. Keep going to the second mailbox. That was it. It seemed easy and simple. But when I swung off on the county-line road, I stopped. It was unpaved, a road of soaked dark-brown earth. And I had already had experience with Missouri mud. However, the surface of the road seemed fairly solid, and there were fresh tire tracks coming out. So I started gingerly ahead.

The road rose and fell. In each hollow I came to, the mud seemed a little deeper. But my cleated snow tires, the tires that had caused so much comment in Death Valley, carried me through. As I neared the crossroads, a bluebird and a cardinal, flying almost side by side, appeared and disappeared. That fleeting glimpse of gay plumage gave a momentary brightening to the gray and misty landscape. The country grew wilder. It seemed more lonely and remote. I met no one, saw no one. Some distance beyond the crossroads I came to the first mailbox. On it red letters spelled: JOE MULLINS. A hundred yards beyond, a second mailbox bore in black letters the name; H. W. MULLINS. Opposite it wheel tracks led through a gateway. They dipped down a wide stretch of meadow, forded a stream, then lifted steeply up the slope beyond until they reached a weathered farmhouse set far back among the fields.

I looked for a long time before I started down. If I got across the stream, I would be all right. With sheets of water fanning away on either side and tires biting into mud and gravel, I shot across and reached the solid ground. All was well. At the top of the rise, I entered a narrow lane, made a right-angle turn around the house and came to the barnyard. Now there was no turning back. One low, wet spot lay ahead. All the rest was higher ground. My luck had held so far. I rushed the spot, hit it with spraying muddy water, and then, with wheels spinning, sank to the floorboards in the soft glue of the Missouri mud.

I climbed out. Nobody was in sight. Nobody came to the door. The rain fell with a soft, steady patter on the roof of the car. For a long time after I knocked at the farmhouse door, nothing happened. Then a woman in her seventies appeared. I asked for Henry Mullins.

"He can't come to the door," she told me. "He isn't well. He's in bed."

"I was interested in the big beaver he caught."

"Oh, that wasn't this Henry Mullins. That was our grandson. He doesn't live here. He's in the woods today cutting posts."

I looked at my white car splattered with mud and anchored fast in the barnyard.

"I'm afraid we can't help you any," the woman volunteered. "We are old and my husband is sick. There isn't anybody else here. I guess you'll have to just work your way out as best you can."

A few minutes later, as I stood in the rain looking at the car hopelessly mired, her husband, an elderly man with an immense white handlebar mustache, appeared from the farmhouse. He leaned on a post and surveyed the scene.

"There's only one thing to do," he told me. "Go to the next place." He waved toward the distant roof of Joe Mullins' house peeking above a hilltop. "They have a tractor. Maybe they can pull you out."

I started off with my raincoat collar turned up and my hat

pulled down. The winter air was chill but not piercingly cold. The winter rain fell steadily but not in a deluge. Ascending the slope, I found it dense with dripping weeds. Before I was half-way up, I was soaked above my knees. Water sloshed in my shoes. For this higher ground, instead of being comparatively dry, was a running sheet of water. From top to bottom, a network of intertwining rivulets covered the hillside. Once, almost at my feet, a woodcock flew up from among the weeds of the sodden ground.

I was a long time making the climb. The house seemed to recede before me. It was nearly noon when I came out into a muddy barnyard where rusting machinery stood about in the rain. There was another long delay before anyone answered my knock on the farmhouse door. Then a girl of about ten explained that there was nobody there to help me. Her parents had gone to town. When would they be home? About two o'clock she thought. That frail—and, as it proved, ill-founded—hope buoyed me for a long time that day. Did any other farm around have a tractor? She didn't know. However, she thought the place back down the road might have one. How far was it? Oh, not so far. To keep warm, I decided to continue to be active, to find another tractor if I could, but at least to keep walking until her parents returned. I headed down the rutted and muddy lane toward the road. It was a long, long lane.

On the road, the mud under my feet had a particular greaselike quality. It did not ball up beneath my feet as had the mud of the black river bottom. But it let my feet slip at every step. Ascending the rises, I slid back almost half a step at the end of each forward stride. Stopping at the crest of each successive elevation, I scanned the fields around. No house was anywhere in sight. I was alone, the only human being in all that wide, deserted, dripping landscape. The sole sign of life I saw for a long time was a sow and a litter of small pigs lying in the mud of a fence corner. I paused to look at them, then plodded on. The rain increased as I advanced.

Slipping at every step, my progress was slow. It was almost one o'clock when I came to the crossroads. Now there was no bluebird, there was no cardinal. But down the side road to the right I glimpsed a house. As I drew nearer, plodding through the mud, I saw behind it well-kept farm buildings. But most important of all, under the protection of an open shed there stood, on huge mud tires, a bright-red tractor. My troubles were over! With high hopes I knocked at the door. I knocked again. I knocked and knocked and knocked, unable to believe my bad luck. Nobody was home. On this rainy winter day, every farmer in the region seemed to have gone to town.

For a long time I stood on the farmhouse porch, leaning against a post, staring at the rain, listening to it drumming on the roof, regaining some of my energy. Then I started back toward the intersection. Just visible over a hill down the side road to the left, I saw the ridgepole of another house. I plodded toward it. Water raced beside me down the ditches on every descent. When the house came into full view, I saw that it was well-painted. The farm buildings were substantial. Wires led in from poles along the road. I was thinking in terms of telephones, of the possibility of calling a garage in Otterville, seven miles away, for a tow car—of at least letting Nellie know where I was. Then I neared the house. A large, recently installed picture window stared from the front. But behind the glass I could see no furniture. The room was empty. I circled to the back. Each window revealed an empty room. The whole house was empty. At the rear I found piles of pipes and lumber. I had come to an uninhabited house, a house in the process of renovation.

Now I was completely discouraged. Slowly I retraced my steps to the crossroads. Nobody seemed to dwell in all this drenched and deserted land. I turned left along the county-line road in the direction of the far-off hard-topped highway. I could see a higher rise down this road and decided to climb to the top on the chance of sighting a house somewhere beyond. For what seemed an interminable time I struggled in the rain, slipping and sliding in the mud. From the top of the hill I swept my gaze in a great circle over the landscape. The expanse that met my eye contained nowhere a single sign of human life except wheel tracks leading away down the muddy road and the fences that bounded the immense and desolate fields. I turned away. I seemed bewitched, isolated, in a nightmare, inhabiting a land as barren of life as a moonscape.

It was now long after two o'clock. Only the thought that the Mullinses might be back from town lightened the great burden of discouragement I carried as I struggled on the slippery footing of the mud back along the county-line road, back to the crossroads, up and down over the interminable rises and descents.

My hope, my sole hope, now was pinned on their return, on the tractor I had seen dripping with rain in the barnyard. I remembered the Old Country saying: "Every mile is two in winter." In my mind I added: "And every mile is ten in winter mud." I walked slowly, moved mechanically. My feet now dragged as well as slipped. I counted my steps as I walked: "One, two, three, four, five," and then began again, distracting my mind from my predicament. I imagined myself coming back down this muddy road in a liberated car. I imagined how good it would feel to be back on the hard-topped highway again. I imagined what it would be like to be taking a hot shower and eating a hot supper. How far away they seemed!

I was about halfway to my destination when I heard the sound of an automobile. Where, I could not tell. It is curious how, in our day, the noise of a machine is the familiar indication of human life. When hunters are lost in the Maine woods, chain saws are now set going to guide them out of the forest. The sound of the car grew louder. A green Plymouth station wagon lifted into view over the crest of the rise ahead.

A young farmer in a heavy jacket, rubber boots and a leather hunting cap sat at the wheel. At my uplifted hand, he slowed to a stop.

"I'm mired down in a farmer's yard," I told him. "Do you know anybody with a tractor to pull me out? I was looking for Henry Mullins, the man who caught the big beaver."

"I'm Henry Mullins," was his reply. "I caught the beaver."

It developed that he lived with his father, Joe Mullins, next door to his grandfather. He had come home early from cutting posts, intending to go to town by a back road. If he had done so, he would have missed me entirely. At home, his young sister had told him a man had called and was stuck somewhere in a car. Thinking it was a customer interested in buying his posts and that the car probably had skidded into a ditch, he had started off down the road.

So luck was with me after all. I climbed into the green car. We turned around at the crossroads and headed back.

"That tractor," he volunteered, "is tricky. Sometimes it starts. Sometimes it doesn't. I don't know what it will do in this rain."

Then came the most encouraging words I had heard all day.

"If it doesn't start, we can always hitch up the horses."

Rocking and splashing up the muddy lane, we came to a stop beside the weathered International Harvester "Farmall" tractor. As soon as we climbed out, we were surrounded by more than a dozen hunting dogs. They had been in the woods with Mullins. Mainly they were coon dogs and fox hounds.

Starting the balky tractor proved to be much like cranking a giant old-fashioned outboard motor. Mullins wound a hay rope around the belt wheel used in sawing wood. Then, with the end of the rope in our hands, he, his eleven-year-old brother and I pulled, as though in a tug-o'-war, running through the mud, spinning the wheel, turning over the big engine.

Once we ran. Twice we ran. Three times we ran. Over and over, panting, we splashed through the rain and mud without eliciting a cough from the engine. I began to look to see if I could catch sight of the horses. Then we tried once more. With the first sound it made, the engine took hold, thundered, never halted, never sputtered, never ceased its clattering uproar. I have rarely heard a more welcome sound than its ragged thunder. Mullins flattened out a cardboard carton and put it as a dry cushion on the metal bucket seat where a pool of water had collected. His brother climbed on the framework beside him and I climbed up on the other side. So we started off down the field of dripping weeds which I had climbed hours before.

One small front tire was almost flat. But the great mud tires on the rear wheels drove us, bucking and slewing, amid the hummocks and ruts and mudholes along the way. Behind us trailed the hounds. I looked back. Strung out in a long pack, they padded along, lifting their heads to the sky. Their mouths were open. They were baying on our trail. So, with the tractor lurching and the mournful voices of the hounds rising and falling behind us, I interviewed Mullins on his capture of the giant beaver.

He was twenty-eight, rather gaunt and Lincolnesque, friendly, deliberate of movement and speech. It was on the second day of his second trapping season that he caught the ninety-pound furbearer on the Maine River, about four miles from his home. Corn land bordered the stream. For several years the beaver had been growing fat, feeding in the fields at night, clipping off the cornstalks and carrying them back to the water like succulent saplings. In one cornfield it had cut away an extensive open area like a clearing in a forest. A beaver in a cornfield, Mullins declared, will do more damage than a dozen raccoons. On the morning he caught the giant animal, he had two other beavers in his traps. They weighed about thirty pounds apiece. The largest other beaver he ever caught weighed forty-nine pounds.

The pelt of the big beaver was rather coarse. It brought only about twelve dollars. What happened to its skull is still a mystery. One of the Conservation Department men called a week or so after the capture to see if he could get the skull for the collection at the capital. For hours he and Mullins hunted everywhere without turning it up. After he had skinned the beaver, Mullins had thrown the carcass to the dogs. They had gnawed on it, worried it, dragged it "every which way," crunched up or buried the bones. All remains of the skeleton had disappeared.

While we had shouted back and forth, question and answer, lifting our voices above the clatter of the tractor and the long-drawn baying of the hounds, Mullins had steered a winding course down the slope, avoiding the worst stretches. Now, in the barnyard, he wheeled into position, hooked on a chain and slowly dragged my car to higher ground. Eventually I was turned around, headed out, hauled to the entrance of the lane and pointed down the hard slope toward the road. When, in saying good-bye, I paid him for dragging me from the mud, Mullins mildly remonstrated:

"I never took anything for helping people out!"

Going back down the muddy road where I had walked with so much labor, back to the highway, free at last, I switched on the heater in a white car now plastered and mottled with dark Missouri mud. The rain slackened in the late afternoon as I drove east in my wet clothes through fifty miles of hills mantled in mist. I realized how lucky I was. I might still be mired down, still seeking help, with night falling on my moonscape of mud. I felt like a small boy determined never to run away again. But, even then, I remembered the fairyland beauty of feathery grasses spangled with droplets of water, which I had stopped in the rain to enjoy. For still another time, as I rode home from my adventure, my mind flashed back to Alice. Hers had been a kindred emotion when, in the midst of the complications of Wonderland life, she had declared:

"I almost wish I hadn't gone down the rabbit hole—and yet—and yet—"

TWENTY

EAGLES OF THE ICE JAM

D OWN the final twisting miles of the Missouri's course, next morning, we descended with the river. A hot shower, a good supper, a long night's sleep, had left me none the worse for my adventure in the mud.

Like the course of the river, our trail through winter had led us down from the mountains, across the plains, into the central trough of the Mississippi Valley. Less than ten miles from the Missouri's mouth, more than 2,400 miles from its source in the highlands of Montana, we crossed for a final time this longest river in North America. Beyond, we made our way past flooded woods and over wide alluvial bottomland, then soared up and up on concrete that spanned the width of the swollen Mississippi. We descended on the east bank just below the Alton Dam.

During our stay on the Gulf Coast, the Alton Dam had been in the headlines. The worst ice jam in forty years had piled up against it that winter. Twelve hundred acres of floes extended for miles upstream. In places the jagged cakes were massed to a thickness of twenty-five feet. Lowland woods along the banks were left in splintered wreckage. Nearly a score of barges were swept away. Mississippi River traffic was paralyzed. Only a few days before, in the warmer weather of a February thaw, the break-up of the jam had commenced. With a grating rumble, the cakes began to slide apart and float away downstream. During this spectacular ice jam, both fish and ducks had been injured or killed by the grinding of the cakes. Attracted by this feast, bald eagles had concentrated in the area.

From Alton we followed the Mississippi upstream to Grafton, to the mouth of the Illinois River and beyond to the Pere Marquette State Park. But we saw no eagles. It was late in the day when we found ourselves installed in the only lodgings we could discover in the vicinity. Saying this, however, brings echoes of Edmund Burke's classic story of the defense of the pickpocket who explained that in the excitement of a panic he had reached out and held onto the first thing his hand encountered—which happened to be a man's watch. For "the only lodgings we could discover" proved to be a de luxe room in one of the limestone guest cottages at the Pere Marquette Park, provided by the State of Illinois apparently for the comfort of visiting millionaires. In the space of twenty-four hours, I thus made the leap from rain and mud and a Missouri farmyard to hanging drapes, shaded lights and wall-to-wall carpeting. In these surroundings we were delighted to encounter an old friend, one we had known far up the Missouri in North Dakota during our autumn journey. This was a black-and-red box-elder bug hibernating in luxury.

After sunset Nellie stepped out with her bird glasses. The bird she saw lifted our spirits. An immature bald eagle was passing directly overhead. Its flight was carrying it in a north-easterly direction. This fact, as we later discovered, was a point of special interest. That evening I called up John Wanamaker, a biologist friend at Principia College, in nearby Elsah. He was free next morning. We would start early on an eagle day.

The bald eagle, ever since a late June day in Philadelphia in the year 1782, has been America's most celebrated bird. On that day, June 20, the Continental Congress selected it as the emblem of the nation. Since then its image has appeared on United States currency, has formed the central figure of the

CIRCLING STARS in the northern sky on a winter night trace concentric circles during an hour's exposure.

ICE STORM encases teasel heads in transparent shells.
Below, ice freezes in curving lines on a winter brook.

Great Seal, has been part of every treaty and important document of state. Yet, during more than a century and three-quarters, the bird itself has been harried and warred upon and pushed toward extirpation. In all the United States outside Alaska, it is calculated, there are now only about 3,500 bald eagles. Interest in our national bird has been accentuated in recent years by its alarming decrease in numbers. Revered in image and persecuted in life—that has been the paradoxical story of the American eagle.

Old-time bird books commenced with an eagle. It was the King of Birds. In mythology the eagle was Jupiter's favorite, the carrier of his thunderbolts. North America's bald eagle, in repose or in the air, is a natural symbol of dignity and power and freedom. Clinging to some lofty perch, it habitually sits erect, its white head of impressive size held high, its yellow eyes surveying with that piercing, concentrated gaze peculiar to its kind the scene spread out below. In every line it imparts a feeling of majesty, of unflinching independence. And this is the eagle quiescent.

It is the eagle active, soaring in a vast, windy sky on a day of brilliant sunshine, that becomes transcendently the symbol of all freedom from restraint. With its size and weight, the soaring eagle, above all other birds, gives an abiding impression of power and purpose in the air. It advances solidly like a ship cleaving the swells and thrusting aside the smaller waves.

Many years have passed since that day, but I remember well seeing one such bird as it mounted above my canoe floating on a forest lake in the Adirondacks. With wings outspread, riding the updrafts in effortless ascent, white head and tail gleaming in the sun, it left the earth, the lake, the forest, the mountains behind. My paddle forgotten, I watched it recede into the shining sky of that August day. It shrank to sparrow size, this bird with a wing span of nearly seven feet. As long as I could see it, it turned endlessly in spirals and graceful curves, writing its poetry of motion on a blue page of the sky.

And so the bald eagle has moved through the history of this land. It no doubt circled over Ponce de Leon when he roamed Florida searching for the Fountain of Youth. It met Henry Hudson when he sailed into the river that bears his name. It looked down on the Jamestown colonists and knew the Plymouth shore where the *Mayflower* came to anchor. It flew at Kitty Hawk long before the Wright brothers. It watched the pioneers roll west. Ages before Washington became the nation's capital, it patrolled the Potomac. And here along the Mississippi it soared above the river steamers of Mark Twain's day just as it had sailed above the birch-bark canoes of Father Marquette. This was the national bird, the American eagle, we hoped to see in numbers next day.

Eating a cold sandwich in lieu of a hot breakfast, Nellie and I were ready to start when Wanamaker and his laboratory assistant, Homer Hoffman, knocked at the door in an overcast and misty dawn. The Illinois River slid by, gray and chill on its way to join the larger stream. Two hundred and twenty-seven miles to the north and east we had seen the birth of this river when, on our summer trip, we reached the junction of the Des Plaines and the Kankakee. One hundred and thirty-five miles upstream, we had watched it flowing beneath Starved Rock while on our autumn travels. And now, in winter, we had reached the end of its descent. During the driest time of late summer, the water of the Illinois covers its 227-mile course in twenty-three days; during the flood time of late winter, it makes the same journey in as few as five days.

Hoffman was the first to sight an eagle. He had set up a twenty-power telescope on a little point of land a few hundred yards from the twin springs where, nearly 300 years before, Marquette and Joliet had camped at the beginning of their homeward journey. Sweeping the opposite bank of the river, Hoffman brought his telescope to rest on a large bird perched in a dead tree half a mile away. We peered through the eyepiece. With its white head impressive even in the gray light of the winter dawn, the eagle turned without haste as it surveyed the river scene around it.

I could imagine the intensity of that gaze. For once, years before, at the Bronx Zoo in New York City, I had rashly tried to outstare a bald eagle. Its yellow eyes, with their untamable depths, never wavered. In the end, that gaze, so fiercely concentrated, produced a curious illusion, the feeling that there was weight and substance and penetration in its glance. A bald eagle, soaring in the sky, has been observed to detect, and head directly for, a fish floating on the surface of a lake three miles away.

As we walked about, alert for other eagles, small birds became active around us. A sparrow darted to a limb nearby. In our glasses we noted the black ear spots on the gray cheeks. We heard its *chip*, higher pitched than that of the house sparrow. In a first meeting we were seeing that little immigrant from abroad, the European tree sparrow. In 1870, this bird was introduced at St. Louis. After almost a century, it is found nowhere in the United States except in this city and in the surrounding countryside. Here, near the Pere Marquette Park, we were at the northern limit of its restricted range.

Twice as we walked along the river's edge, we came upon large dead fish with flesh torn away by feeding eagles. Over our heads flew skeins of geese, and from the river flocks of golden-eye ducks took off with a high whistling of their wings. The sound reminded Wanamaker that he had seen these ducks, as well as scaup, swimming close beside ice cakes on which eagles rode. Neither bird paid any attention to the other. Once he saw an eagle eating a duck on a floe while other ducks swam nearby without showing the least concern. As a rule, it is the sick or wounded bird that is preyed upon. During the great jam, eagles sometimes fed on waterfowl that had become frozen in the ice.

Before we left the point of land that morning, we had seen four eagles. The last and best of the four was spotted by

Nellie as it came up the river. A majestic adult, flying straight, cleaving the air with powerful wing strokes, it passed almost above us at a height of no more than a hundred feet. Sometimes bald eagles are found perching on posts or even on the metal frame of a Shell gasoline sign on the point. But not this day. In fact, that passing bird was the last of the eagles we saw that morning. Although we rode for miles upstream and down, we sighted no more. However, all those miles were filled with interest.

They carried us through the spectacularly beautiful Principia College campus, perched like an eagle's eyrie high above the Mississippi. They brought us to an uncultivated bluff top, where we found that giant plant of the virgin prairie, the tall bluestem grass, *Andropogon furcatus*. Here the dry, rustling clumps rose higher than our heads. We measured one stem. It was eight feet tall. We could imagine how easy it must have been to become lost on a treeless plain dense with a sea of this grass. And we could visualize the speed—at times faster than a horse could run—with which prairie fires raced across miles of such grass in times of drought.

At one point we walked out on a line of palisades where sheer limestone cliffs were fluted and broken along their tops and where, far below, the wide, smooth sheen of America's mightiest river spread away upstream and down. Less than a dozen miles to the south, the Mississippi is joined by the flow of the Missouri. About seventy-five miles farther downstream, John James Audubon, near Ste. Genevieve, Missouri, on a late winter day in 1811, collected the large eagle he named the "Bird of Washington." As long as he lived, he believed it represented a new species. Now it is generally accepted that it was an unusually large immature bald eagle. For these birds are frequently larger than the adults when they leave the nest. The contraction of bones and the more strenuous exercise account for the later reduction in size and weight. But during their early months of flight, they may exceed their parents by as much as a pound in weight and a foot in wingspread.

During the summer of 1831, on another high bluff near Dubuque, Iowa, some 200 miles upstream from where we stood, an Indian's bullet had brought down a bald eagle. When the hunter picked up his prize, he found a silver bracelet encircling one leg. It had been placed there the week before by a silversmith at Cortland, N.Y. An ardent admirer of Henry Clay, he had engraved on the metal clasp, a greeting to his hero. On the Fourth of July, the bird had been released and, with shouts and musket fire, started in the general direction of Clay's Kentucky. In the seven days that followed, this banded bird had traveled at least 725 miles and had reached the banks of the Mississippi. Its week's wandering supplied science with its first precise information about the wide-ranging character of an eagle's flight.

It is curious how slow in accumulating has been our knowledge of the life and ways of our national bird. Ninety years passed after the flight of the Cortland eagle, 140 years went by after the action of the Continental Congress, before any serious scrutiny was made of the day-to-day home life of the bald eagle. In the 1920's, Francis Hobart Herrick, biology professor at Western Reserve University, began recording in notes and photographs the activity at nests near Vermilion, Ohio, on the shore of Lake Erie. He carried on this work in blinds at the top of steel towers erected close to the nests. One of these structures, anchored in concrete and containing four tons of metal, rose to a height of ninety-six feet.

During more recent years, Charles L. Broley, the retired Winnipeg banker whom we had accompanied on a banding expedition on the Kissimmee Prairie of Florida when we came north with the spring, has further widened our knowledge of these birds. Ascending trees to lofty nests until he was nearly eighty, the famed "Eagle Man" placed numbered metal bands on the legs of more than 1,200 fledglings. As the life of a bald eagle is normally long—some estimates have placed it at as much as 100 years—the fruits of Broley's work may well continue to be harvested for decades to come.

Cradled at the foot of the bluffs beside the river, the old and picturesque village of Elsah (population 165) appeared remote and peaceful when we reached it by a winding road. It seemed living in a Mark Twain past, its quiet likely to be broken only by some such sound as the whistle of a paddle-wheel steamer coming in for a landing. Yet day by day that quiet was more closely threatened. The concrete of a four-lane superhighway was drawing nearer along the river's edge. Its completion would bring the world to the village door in a way the river had never done. Already this activity was producing changes for eagles as well as for men.

As we walked along a stretch of the new roadbed, Wana-maker pointed out a small ravine eroded into the bluffs at the edge of the Principia campus. It ended in the circular amphi-theater of a hanging valley where red oaks grew. For years these trees had formed the nighttime roost of overwintering eagles. As many as thirty-five came winging home at sunset. Beneath the trees Wanamaker sometimes picked up handfuls of feathers shaken loose by the perching birds.

Once they have begun nesting, bald eagles—in common with many other birds—keep on in spite of severe distrac-tions. There is an instance of a robin that built its nest on the arm of an inactive oil-well pump and then, after the pump had gone into action, brooded its eggs and fed its young in a nest that continually rose and fell a yard or more through the air. Bald eagles have refused to leave a nest even when bull-dozers worked beneath their tree and blasting occurred nearby. However, the overwintering birds, in the hanging valley among the bluffs, had no such powerful link to their surroundings. Soon after the highway construction began, they deserted the roost. Where they had moved to, where they were spending their nights at the time of our visit, were still a mystery.

Toward sunset, at the end of that short February day, Nellie and I thought we had found a clue. We had returned alone to the twin springs and the little point of land near the mouth of the Illinois River. Standing at the tip, with a cold wind blowing out of the southeast, we had hardly lifted our glasses to our eyes when a white head shone out above the dark trees of the opposite bank. An adult eagle crossed the width of the river, swept overhead, and continued inland toward the northeast. Another appeared downstream, flying in the same direction. It disappeared above the wooded end of a long ridge in the Pere Marquette Park. Less than five minutes afterwards, two eagles, one immature, one adult, one from down the river, one from up, turned inland and followed the same aerial path across the ridge end.

We seemed transported back into a time of eagle abundance. On that long-ago June day when, unknown to itself, it became the country's emblem, this bird had inhabited all but the most arid interior portions of the land. The decades since had marked a long retreat. Throughout the country, it had been shot for fun or to produce a stuffed trophy, or, more recently, in a self-righteous war on "vermin." Collectors robbed the birds of their eggs. Farmers and real-estate developers felled their nesting trees. Everywhere the decrease of the bald eagle has been the handiwork of man. Today, in numerous regions, those landmarks of a former time, the eagle trees with their immense nests of sticks, are but fading memories in the minds of the older inhabitants.

It was not until 1940, more than a century and a half after it had been honored by the Continental Congress, that the eagle received protection in the then forty-eight states. Twelve more years passed before that protection was extended, on July 1, 1952, to Alaska. From 1917 to 1952, a period of thirty-five years, every bald eagle in Alaska lived with a price on its head. Its destruction was rewarded with a bounty. For each pair of talons the territorial government offered first fifty cents, then a dollar, then a dollar and a half, finally two dollars. During these years, more than $100,000 was paid out to encourage the killing of eagles. Before the slaughter ended, about 115,000 were destroyed. Yet recent careful observations indicate that, contrary to charges made in the long and bitter attack of commercial fishing interests, most of the salmon taken by eagles in Alaska are dead or exhausted after spawning, fish that already have come to the natural end of their lives. No doubt, some live salmon are taken by the birds at a time when millions of fish are swimming upstream to spawn. But such has been the case for thousands of years while the numbers of salmon remained undiminished. Uncontrolled fishing, multiplying canneries, illegal seining by man—not the infinitesimal fraction subtracted by the eagles —have been the obvious cause of the decrease in northern salmon.

At last the long persecution of our national bird is over— officially. Nowhere now is a price set on its head. Everywhere under the stars and stripes the bird is protected by law. But other factors, more difficult to control than bounties and firearms, still work against the eagles. The spread of mechanized civilization, the growth of population, changing environment, the widespread use of DDT and other toxic sprays, the destruction of nesting sites, these continue to produce profound and adverse effects upon the birds. No longer is it possible to say, as the famed Illinois ornithologist, Robert Ridgway, did in 1913: "Along all the larger watercourses in our state the bald eagle is a more or less common bird, and may be met with at all times of the year." Today two widely separated places, Florida and Alaska, hold the bulk of the bald-eagle population. The former is a reservoir of the southern subspecies, the latter of the northern subspecies.

Our fifth eagle, that afternoon, came directly out of the reddened clouds that marked the winter sunset. One minute the sky appeared empty; the next, when I looked back, it held the great bird flapping toward us with deep and powerful wing strokes. It passed by low and a little to one side, giving us a magnificent view. In that moment, it was easy to understand why Thoreau, after a visit to Fair Haven Bay with his new spyglass in 1854, noted in his journal: "I think I have got the worth of my glass now that it has revealed to me the white-headed eagle."

We continued to sweep the river, up and down, with our binoculars. The cold wind seemed less cold as eagle after eagle went by. Our glasses showed us one immature bird passing over the Stump Lake above our point of land, an adult farther upstream and a second adult swinging in circles over the opposite bank, its white head and tail catching the glow of the sunset. Three times it turned before it straightened out and crossed the river. As we looked away from its retreating form, a ninth eagle appeared coming up our side of the river. Almost simultaneously a tenth came in over the water. Only a few minutes passed before we discovered an eleventh, flying higher, almost directly overhead—journeying, as all the others had been, toward the northeast, toward the end of the ridge and the wild interior of the Pere Marquette Park. It was there, we surmised, that the new roost would be found. A year or so later, its exact location in that area was discovered. The birds had moved nine or ten miles from the site of their former roost beside the river to congregate, as evening fell, in tall trees at the head of a narrow valley.

Each in turn, the eagles we watched arrived with disconcerting suddenness. They seemed to appear from nowhere. Almost all were flying low, just above the treetops, flying fast, flapping steadily, bent on covering ground, intent on reaching the same unknown destination. They flew, in the main, without digressions, without flourishes. It is at the time of the courtship flights that the eagle's mastery of the air is most dramatically demonstrated. Then the earthbound man fortunate enough to witness the spectacle sees twisting climbs, inverted flight, thunderbolt dives with half-closed wings. At its climax he may see the paired birds grasp talons and plunge for hundreds of feet through space, turning over and over as they fall like a wheel in the sky.

It was after sunset and we were climbing into our car when we hastily climbed out again. Three bald eagles, almost together, were crossing the river a little to the north. Two were adults, one was immature. Five minutes passed and a second immature eagle cut diagonally across the Stump Lake heading for the end of the darkening ridge. Another ten minutes went by. Looming up suddenly, our sixteenth eagle passed low above us, its great pinions driving it forward in swift and powerful flight. When one ornithologist counted and weighed all the vaned feathers on a bald eagle, he found that their number was 7,182 and that they comprised fourteen per cent of the total weight of the bird. They weighed more than twice as much as its skeleton.

Again we were getting into our car, chilled by the cold wind, thinking the eagle show was surely over, when a seventeenth bird, an immature, dark against the darkening clouds, passed close to our point of land. Crows had been streaming by, flock after flock, bound for their river-bottom roosts. Now, over the tail of their procession, still another eagle, the eighteenth, crossed the river from the west and, following the aerial path of its predecessors, disappeared over the fringed black line of the ridge end.

We were filled with eagle fever now and stayed on and on after the last tinge of red had left the western horizon, enduring the cold wind, scanning the river up and down and across, getting in the car to warm up, then getting out again. And we were rewarded. A nineteenth eagle, huge and dark, crossed our sky in unmistakable silhouette. With the bird Nellie had seen the night before, the four sighted at dawn, the nineteen going to roost, our total was twenty-four.

We drove away content. But even then our eagle day was

not entirely over. In the deepening twilight a little later, with
Wanamaker and Hoffman we crossed to the land that extends
in a long point down between the Illinois and the Mississippi
rivers, to an area with communities named Deer Plain and
Golden Eagle, there, at a famous back-country restaurant at
Brussels, to have a dinner of celebration. Going, as we crossed
the ferry I looked up and saw another silhouette. It was the
swiftly-moving form of a twenty-fifth eagle. It, too, was cleaving the air, hurrying into the northeast, homeward bound for
the roost where its companions were already settled for the
night.

TWENTY-ONE

THE WHITE SQUIRRELS

FOLLOW the sun. Follow the moon.

This we had done when we rode west across the continent to meet the fourth season at the Silver Strand, beside the Pacific.

Follow the roll of the earth.

This we were doing as we zigzagged east with the winter. Almost a hundred times, during our journey, the globe would revolve in this direction, each time carrying us toward an earlier sunrise. A minute a day, the hours of light were lengthening.

But, during the days we traced a wandering path across lower Illinois, down to the tip of its arrowhead shape and up again, closed-in skies hid the sun, delayed the dawn and hastened the dusk. We rode in gray light across a drenched, muddy, misty world, across the flat black land of the winter cornfields. Where lowland meadows were cut by little streams, cattle stood knee-deep in ground mist. In this time of February thaws, ditches brimmed and puddles everywhere mirrored in a dull sheen the somber light of the clouded sky.

It was in this section of the trip that Nellie began concentrating on the "fieldmarks" of automobiles. It was a mystery to me, I had pointed out, how anyone able to note slight plumage differences in sparrows and warblers and shore birds had difficulty telling a Ford from a Rambler or a Chrysler from a Buick. Her explanation, not without logic, had been:

"The trouble is, automobiles keep changing their plumages."

Other random memories of those days of open winter come back: Miles of roads bordered with the red hips of multiflora roses. Communities named Horseshoe and Red Bud, Equality and Muddy, Wisetown and Stubblefield. A country restaurant which we entered in the midst of a debate over whether an old farmer had, or had not, started the blaze in his woodbox in order to see the new fire engine. And the filling station man who looked at our Eastern license and remarked:

"You're going to have to drive pretty fast to get home for supper."

We came to Cairo, where the Ohio and the Mississippi meet. I had seen it last more than thirty years before. Then I had arrived by water, floating on the current, guiding to shore the fourteen-foot rowboat that had carried me 400 miles down this tributary stream from Louisville, Kentucky, to the river's mouth, an adventurous trip described in my book, *The Lost Woods*. Now all the landmarks had changed. I hunted for some time below the concrete flood wall before I found the place where I had tied up in the dusk at that journey's end.

Angling to the north and east, next day, over floodland and rolling hills, we came to Norris City. The name stirred a special recollection of something I had read. Near here, in the spring of 1815, two boys, returning from a log-rolling contest, had wagered on who could vault farthest, using their cottonwood handspikes as vaulting poles. When the sport was ended, they left the poles sticking upright in the soft earth. There they took root and grew into immense trees. One became a famous landmark of pioneer times. It was known as The Vaulting Pole Cottonwood.

As we neared Mt. Carmel on the Wabash River, later that day, the sun appeared briefly. A flurry of fine snow swept across the empty cornfields. Like the ditches, the Wabash was brimming. It flowed past Mt. Carmel, wide and muddy, its waters flooding the lowlands to the east. A century before, all this stretch of river and swamp had been part of the life of a remarkable boy whose name later became famous in American ornithology.

The son of a pioneer druggist, the first of ten children, Robert Ridgway was born at Mt. Carmel two days before the Fourth of July in 1850. When he was only four years old he made his first drawing of a bird. By the time he was ten, he had assembled a private museum of nests and eggs and was producing accurately colored paintings of the native birds. In his effort to record the exact hues of the feathers, he ground pigments and combined them with gum water of his own manufacture in a back room of his father's drug store. Many years later, this early interest in colors was to reach its culmination in his famous *Color Standards and Color Nomenclature*, which contained examples of 1,115 named hues, each produced by hand-mixed pigments. The process of creating them consumed a full three years. This work is recognized as one of the great milestones in the standardization of colors and their names.

One summer, when the water of the Wabash was abnormally low, the cargo of a sunken river steamer, the *Kate Sarchet*, was salvaged near Mt. Carmel. It included a rusty rifle. To provide the young ornithologist with a collecting gun of his own, Ridgway's father had the barrel bored out and the weapon transformed into a percussion-cap, muzzle-loading shotgun. By following a formula found in an old book, Ridgway mixed together chlorate of potash, yellow prussiate of potash and white sugar to manufacture his own gunpowder.

Knowing nothing of taxidermy or of preparing bird skins, he had no way of preserving the specimens he collected except by painting pictures of them. When he was fourteen, bright-colored songbirds, such as he had never seen before, appeared in numbers one winter around Mt. Camel. He named them the "roseate grosbeaks." Their identity remained a mystery for months. A neighbor suggested he send his painting to the Commissioner of Patents in Washington. The Commissioner, who knew nothing about birds, turned the drawing over to Spencer Fullerton Baird, then beginning his brilliant career at the Smithsonian Institution. Baird identified the bird as a purple finch. He suggested that young Ridgway send him drawings of any other birds that puzzled him. Thus began the most important correspondence of Ridgway's life.

Less than three years later, when he was still not quite seventeen, he returned home one March day, after climbing to the nest of a red-tailed hawk, and found a letter from Washington awaiting him. Baird offered him the position of zoologist on a U.S. expedition being sent to explore the fortieth parallel from the eastern slope of the Sierra Nevada, in California, to the eastern slope of the Rockies, in Colorado. Thus, about the middle of April 1867, Ridgway broke home ties. Driving with his parents to Olney, some fifty miles to the north, he boarded the first train he had ever ridden on, his destination the nation's capital.

Later he remembered that, at frequent intervals, in stretches of still primitive forest, the wood-burning engine stopped to load on fuel stacked beside the rails. The Fortieth Parallel Expedition, led by the noted government geologist Clarence King, embarked from New York in a side-wheel steamer bound for Panama. A similar craft carried the party up the Pacific Coast to San Francisco. There the group headed inland for two years of scientific exploration.

When this adventure ended, Ridgway returned to Washington to illustrate and prepare scientific descriptions for the monumental five-volume treatise on North American birds being written by Baird and Dr. Thomas M. Brewer of Boston. At the age of twenty-four, he was appointed Curator of Birds at the Smithsonian Institution. Only two other museums in America at that time had salaried officials in charge of a department of birds. For several years young Ridgway lived in one of the red-brick towers of the Smithsonian building and during more than half a century, until his death in 1929, he remained a member of the scientific staff of this world-famous institution.

Quiet and unassuming, he turned out a vast body of valuable work. He published more than 13,000 pages of material on birds. Two genera, twenty-three species and ten subspecies of birds were named for him. He was one of the founders of the American Ornithologists' Union. Between 1901 and 1919, eight volumes of his *Birds of North and Middle America* appeared under the imprint of the Smithsonian Institution. This was his magnum opus. It was hailed as one of the greatest works on systematic ornithology ever written. For it Ridgway received the Brewster Medal of the A.O.U. and the Daniel Giroud Elliott Medal of the National Academy of Sciences.

When, as a boy beside the Wabash, Ridgway began studying birds, he imagined that he was the only person in America, perhaps in the whole world, engaged in such pursuits. In a history of the United States he had come across references to Wilson, Audubon, Bonaparte and Nuttall. But they all were no longer living. He concluded that all ornithologists belonged to a past period, that they all were dead, that none was alive in his time. The only natural history books he possessed were Oliver Goldsmith's *Animated Nature* and Samuel G. Goodrich's *The Animal Kingdom Illustrated*. In contrast, I found when I visited the local library, the young naturalist in Mt. Carmel today has more than a score of excellent bird books at his disposal.

Nellie and I were talking to Ruth Lengelsen, the librarian, late that afternoon, when a young man on his way home from work stopped to return a borrowed book. The dust jacket caught our eyes. The book was *Journey Into Summer*. When we were introduced, the reader's astonishment was understandable. Here in his own library, in his own Wabash River town, suddenly appearing from nowhere were the very people he had just been traveling with for 19,000 miles through all the pages of a book. It seemed to me that our conversation had gone on for some time before the faint light of suspicion left his eyes and acceptance of the coincidence of this unexpected encounter took its place.

During all the years that Robert Ridgway worked in Washington, far from the Illinois country of his boyhood, he said he felt he was in prison. The sensitive, living man inside the shell of his reputation was, he once confessed, "homesick for forty-five years." In 1913, he could stand it no longer. He returned to Olney, where he had boarded the train that originally carried him away. There, with his wife, he settled down at Larchmound, a pleasant, elm-shaded home on the south side of town. Arrangements had been made for him to continue his Smithsonian work in these congenial surroundings.

The road—U.S. 50—that carried us into Olney next morning follows the line of an ancient buffalo trace, a natural highway across the open land left by the hoofs of centuries of traveling bison. Olney, thirty miles west of the Wabash, has a unique distinction. It is The City of the White Squirrels. No other community in the world contains so many albino gray squirrels. Hundreds climb among the trees or race across the yards. The insignia of a white squirrel adorns the shoulder patches of Olney policemen. It appears on the sides of Olney fire engines. It is part of the highway signs that welcome visitors to the city.

In Olney we found Lee and Ida Cantwell, two friends my books had brought me. Laden with facts about the white squirrels and Ridgway's Larchmound, they had driven down from their home in Mattoon, Illinois, to spend the day with us in the midst of our final journey with a season. We joined forces on a white-squirrel safari.

How did the Olney albino colony originate? Various answers to that question have been advanced. The volume on *Illinois* in the American Guide Series even suggests that the white squirrels may have been introduced by Robert Ridgway. However, the correct story seems to be the one published in the *Olney Daily Mail* and inserted in *The Congressional Record* for Tuesday, July 14, 1959, by Congressman George E. Shipley. It gives credit to Thomas Tippit, of Olney.

When we all called on Tippit, later that afternoon, I found him to be a small, erect, spry man in his seventies. He had recently retired after spending most of his life as a piano tuner. He recalled the arrival of the first white squirrels, about 1902, when he was fifteen. A farmer brought a pair of albinos to town and, for nearly a year, they occupied a cage in a window of Jap Banks' saloon on Main Street. When they were no longer wanted as an attraction, Tippit's father—a newspaper editor and one-time mayor of Olney—told him and his brother, Bert, to hitch up the cart, get the animals, and turn them loose in the wooded stretch beside their house.

After nailing the cage to the trunk of a big tree, the boys opened the door. First to come out was the male. Hardly had it begun to ascend the trunk, when a large fox squirrel raced down the tree and ripped it to pieces. Only the day before, Tippit's father had given him permission to fire his shotgun. He killed the fox squirrel, and the white female established herself in a hole in the tree. Some weeks later, baby squirrels, all albinos, appeared on the trunk. If, Tippit observed, he had not been given permission to shoot the gun, enabling him to protect the second squirrel, or if it had been the female instead of the male that had emerged first, Olney's famous colony might never have come into existence.

In Tippit's woods, the white squirrels multiplied. They spread out into the parks and backyards of the city and into the surrounding country. An informal census has placed their present number at between 600 and 700. Although they may interbreed with ordinary gray squirrels, for some unexplained reason the strain of albinism is dominant. Since 1925 a city ordinance has prohibited trapping, killing or shipping away any of the white squirrels. In 1943 the Illinois state legislature passed a law protecting the famed Olney squirrels. In this community, as *The Congressional Record* summarizes it: "The children love them, the people feed them, the Chamber of Commerce advertises them, and the law protects them."

For a time, we wandered through the remaining remnants of Tippit's Woods. This tract has been in the same family for three generations, since Matthew L. Tippit obtained it from the Federal Government in 1821. High on the mottled trunk of a sycamore we saw the opening of a hole where one family of white squirrels lived. After more than half a century of multiplying, the animals appear to be leveling off or slightly declining in numbers. One factor in this change has been the felling, in recent years, of numerous dead trees in Olney. Previously, they provided nesting places for the squirrels. In many yards, people are putting up kegs or boxes as a substitute for the hollow trees. At one of Tippit's neighbors—whose house number was embellished with a metal cutout of a white squirrel—we found three nesting boxes in the backyard. They all were occupied.

An even more important factor in reducing the number of squirrels is the mounting hazard of automobile traffic. Recently, Tippit has noticed the animals using electric cables to cross above the passing cars on busy streets. In this process, they sometimes rub off some of the insulating material and soil their white fur. At other times, the white squirrels appear from under parked cars blotched with black stains of oil or grease. As we were driving down a side street later that day, we came upon a sorry-looking squirrel. This albino had been scampering over a mound of soft coal piled in a yard outside a cellar door. Its white fur was thick with coal dust. An Olney saying is:

"The squirrels are prettiest after a rain."

Before the 1925 city ordinance was enacted, white squirrels were shipped to a number of other communities. Yet, in no other place did they obtain a foothold. Only in the region of Olney have they been able to thrive. Why so high a percentage of the offspring here should be white is still a riddle. But all over town, as we drove about, we encountered the albino squirrels. Even in the dull light of the overcast day, they were strikingly beautiful as they raced up the trunks or leaped among the branches of the bare winter trees.

The tree in which we saw the greatest number of squirrels was a lofty elm that overhangs the eastern side of the house at Larchmound. Five of the white animals climbed among its branches. As many as a dozen have been observed at the same time in this one tree. Ridgway used to sit at the bay window that overlooks the base of the elm and watch the squirrels and the birds that came to feeders he had fastened to the trunk. We looked out through that same window on a similar scene. And later, when the Cantwells guided us to Bird Haven, the wooded tract a few miles north of Olney which Ridgway maintained as a sanctuary, we followed the same winding trails he had followed among the trees. The eighteen acres of Bird Haven held a central place in the affections of the ornithologist. On its rolling land grow more than seventy species and varieties of trees. As a boy, Ridgway had seen hundreds of swallow-tailed kites performing their incomparably graceful evolutions over the open prairie. In the summer of 1910, he observed the last of this species he ever saw in Illinois, a single pair passing over Bird Haven.

In the fading light of that winter afternoon, Nellie and I walked alone along a trail through the woods, across a rustic bridge and up a hill. At its top, in the land that was dearest to him, Ridgway is buried. His grave is marked by a granite boulder bearing a bronze tablet inscribed: "Robert Ridgway. 1850–1929." Behind it, ranged in a semicircle, rose a thick stand of junipers. Dangling from the evergreen boughs, like tan-colored cones, hung a score or more of bagworm cases. They brought to mind all the insect life that, through innumerable stratagems, was surviving through the months of cold.

In one of the finest paragraphs in one of his finest books, *Nature in Downland*, W. H. Hudson reflects on the swift disappearance of the multitudinous insect life of summer days. "I moved and had my being amid that life as in a golden mist spread over the earth," he writes. "My ears were full of the noise of innumerable fine small voices blending into one voice; wheresoever I looked their minute swift-moving bodies appeared as thin lines on the air and over the green surface. Forms so infinitely varied yet so wonderfully fashioned, each aglow with its complete separate life, and all in harmony with all life and all nature, responsive in a million secret springs to each and every external influence, so well balanced in their numerous parts and perfect in their equipment, so intense in their lives as to seem fitted to endure forever. And now in so short a time, in a single day and night as it seems, it is all over, the feast and fairy-dance of life; the myriads of shining gem-like bodies turned to dead dust, the countless multitude of brilliant little individual souls dissipated into thin air and blown whithersoever the wind blows!" But, as Hudson recalls, even the winter earth is filled with seeds of life which another spring will awaken. Then "we shall know it all again, and in seeing renew the old familiar pleasure."

Everywhere we went these winter months, that new install-ment of minute lives lay dormant, ready to emerge. The chain of insect life, seemingly broken, remained intact. Under the fallen leaves, slowly decaying on the woodland floor, a host of tiny creatures had found a hibernaculum. Beneath the ice, in mud, in debris, beneath sunken stones, the inert bodies of aquatic insects lay hidden. Rocks and logs and tunnels in trees sheltered colonies of dormant ants. And from the pointed, silken bags that dangled from the junipers would come the bagworms of another season.

Within each hive of honeybees, dancing insects, enclosed in an insulating shell of other workers, were generating warmth and keeping the colony alive. The pale green luna moth and the eyed Polyphemus rested in pupal form within their tough cocoons, like seeds enclosed in husks. Below the frost line beetle grubs and cicada nymphs lay safe in their burrows. The same warmth that would stir them to activity would also bring the young of the digger wasps burrowing upward to the surface and awaken the fertilized queens of bumblebees and paper-making wasps that now were anchored in crannies or hidden under debris, hibernating with the flame of life turned low.

As we walked back along the dusky trail, we were vividly aware of all this life only temporarily imprisoned within a winter world, life hidden, life partly formed, but life ready to respond to the rise of the spring thermometer, ready to resume the endless relay race that is its species' existence. As we drove north and east, across the Wabash and into Indiana, leaving behind the white squirrels and all the scenes associated with Ridgway, this awareness of dormant, unseen life in the winter fields formed the final thread woven into the fabric of our memories of the day.

TWENTY-TWO

RETURN TO THE STARS

SLUSH streamed from beneath our wheels. Snow, wet and clinging, had begun falling soon after we left Terre Haute. Angling for almost 200 miles to the north and east, across Indiana and toward the Ohio line, we followed the Wabash upstream. All the way a soggy blanket of white extended across the black bottomlands. We stopped, when day was giving way to evening, not far from the Limberlost Swamp, celebrated in the writings of Gene Stratton Porter. The dusk deepened; the thermometer plunged; the slush froze. Night, starless and black, settled down.

When we had crossed the continent through autumn, one of our chief disappointments had been the closed-in sky that blotted out the stars the night we visited Leslie C. Peltier's backyard observatory in Delphos, Ohio. Although we gained two valued friends in Leslie and his wife, Dorotha, the telescope, that night, had been blinded by clouds. Now, in another season, crossing the continent in another direction, we were swinging far to the north to visit Delphos again. Day after day and night after night, ever since we had crossed the Mississippi, clouds had obscured the sky. We were gambling, in this return to the stars, on a single night of clearing weather.

But when we awoke the next morning, in the dawn of Washington's Birthday, clouds stretched solidly from horizon to horizon. It was early afternoon when we drove into Delphos. Two small spots of blue had appeared in the overcast.

By sunset, in great elation, we saw the whole sky swept clear of clouds. A night of crystalline brilliance followed—a single star-filled night in two weeks or more of cloudy weather.

When we turned into the drive leading to Peltier's home, we found a dramatic change. His fifteen-dollar observatory—the small rotating box in which he had discovered more new comets than any other amateur astronomer in America—was now overshadowed by the immense mushroom of a white dome rising almost as high as the treetops. Complete with a twelve-inch Clark refracting telescope, the big observatory—worth, literally, a thousand times the homemade comet-hunting box nearby—had been presented to Peltier as a gift in recognition of his accomplishments. Thus, in this one back yard in northwestern Ohio, America's largest and smallest private observatories stand side by side.

In the cold stillness of the night, bundled up in heavy clothing, we all walked out to the twin observatories. The white dome of the larger building loomed up in the starlight. Behind it, a pale cone of illumination lifted high in the western sky. Peltier pointed it out and my mind went back to the Green Flash Nellie and I had seen at the Silver Strand. For this nebulous glow was another celestial phenomenon we had never observed before. It was the zodiacal light that is noticed on infrequent occasions in the eastern sky before dawn and in the western sky after twilight. Sunshine reflected from swarms of tiny meteoroids in outer space is believed to be the source of the long-mysterious illumination. This faint, wedged-shaped glow in the sky is most often seen in the east in September, and in the west in winter, during the months of February and March.

Within the dark, cavernous interior of the big observatory, where our footsteps echoed hollowly, Peltier switched on the dull-red glow of a night light over a table littered with star charts and notebooks. Gradually our eyes became accustomed to the gloom. We could make out the heavy mass of the central pier of concrete on which the telescope is mounted. In the stillness we heard the steady ticking of a clock. It was part of the synchronized mechanism that automatically swings the telescope in time with the apparent movement of the stars.

Near the door, Peltier pulled down on a heavy rope. High above us, with a creaking rumble of rollers, the cover slid back from a long rectangular opening in the rounded roof of the observatory. Starlight flooded in. Against this narrow rectangle of glittering, burning stars, the black tube of the telescope stood out in silhouette.

Now nearly a century old, this tube and the lenses it contains were the product of the famous Cambridgeport, Massachusetts, firm of Alvan Clark and Sons. In American astronomy, a Clark telescope has the standing of a Rolls-Royce among motor-cars. This particular instrument was made in 1868 for the Van Vleck Observatory at Wesleyan University, in Middletown, Connecticut. In 1923, when it was replaced by a twenty-inch refractor, it was sold to Miami University, in Oxford, Ohio. There it was used for nearly forty years. When astronomy courses were abandoned, the university presented the telescope, the building and several smaller instruments to Peltier in an outright gift. From end to end, the tube of the big telescope measures sixteen feet. The concrete pier on which it is mounted weighs a ton, and the revolving dome above it weighs two and a half tons. Depending on the eyepiece employed, the instrument magnifies celestial images from 150 to 600 times.

"What would you like to see first?" Peltier asked us.

Our choice was the same:

"The stars of Orion."

In how many far-separated places—beside the sea, in the desert, among the mountains, on the shores of forest lakes—had we gazed upward at this favorite constellation of ours. It was the nighttime companion of our winter travels. Dominating the evening heavens from December to April, it is the most brilliant constellation in the sky. No other grouping of the stars can be confused with it. Like the giraffe among animals, the praying mantis among insects, the jack-in-the-pulpit among wildflowers, it is distinctive. Orion is familiar even to those who have never heard its name.

Now, one after another, we examined the component parts of the sword and belt. We saw the individual images of the stars magnified hundreds of times. Here was the blue-white brilliance of Rigel, thought to be a star in its prime. Here was the red of Betelgeuse, believed to be nearing the end of its immeasurable span of life. Here, at the center of the sword, was the Great Nebula of Orion, a mass of glowing gas sixteen light-years in diameter.

From Orion we swung to the brightest star in the sky, Sirius, in nearby Canis Major. If Sirius occupied the position of the sun in our solar system, its brilliance would appear to us to be thirty times as great. It has three times the sun's weight and twenty-seven times its volume. The beams that reached us from this first-magnitude star had traveled eight and eight-tenths years. This is a comparatively short time as celestial journeys go. Yet during that period man had entered the adventurous uncertainties of the Space Age. We wondered—as all who sweep their telescopes back and forth across the night sky must—what profound changes would occur before the rays that were beginning their journey even while we watched would reach other telescopes nearly a decade hence.

About the time the instrument through which we looked was being made at Cambridgeport, the largest refracting telescope attempted up to that time was completed by the Clarks. To test the quality of the image produced by its eighteen-and-a-half-inch lens, Alvan Graham Clark, the elder of the two sons, trained the new telescope on the brightest star in the heavens. As a result, his were the first human eyes to see the form of a faint companion star that revolves about Sirius approximately once in fifty years. This discovery solved the mystery of certain irregularities in the path of our brightest

star. Called "one of the strangest objects in the entire universe," this dwarf companion is only 1/10,000 as bright as
Sirius. So heavy is the material of which it is composed that a
cubic inch would weigh a ton.

If Christopher Columbus returned to the New World or
Henry Hudson sailed the *Half Moon* up New York Bay once
more, amid all the changes they would meet, the stars would
appear the same. The classical age of Greece and the Atomic
Age and whatever ages lie ahead are bound together by the long
endurance of the stars. This continuity of the heavens was part
of the fascination of our experience as the tube of Peltier's
telescope carried us this way and that across far outer space.
At the touch of an electric switch, flipped either to right or to
left, the ponderous dome above us rotated in the desired
direction. As the hours passed, with Peltier shifting the telescope and adjusting the eyepieces, we visited different portions
of the heavens. We saw the misty cluster of the Pleiades separate into individual stars burning bright. We looked long at
that island universe in the sky, the Great Nebula of Androm-
eda. This galaxy is the farthest object the naked eye can see.
Without the aid of the telescope, it appeared a mere dot or
wisp of light, as though a star were shining wanly through
mist. But as we peered into the eyepiece, the hazy dot expanded into a swirl of light seen through a stratum of hundreds of nearer stars which seemed to form a white mesh or
shining net in the depths of the sky. So vast is the distance to
this great galaxy that its rays were reaching our eyes at the
end of a journey that had begun a million and a half years
before.

Roaming thus among the stars and planets and constellations of the winter sky, Peltier stopped from time to time to
examine some variable star and make brief notes under the red
glow of the shaded lamp. For more than 500 consecutive
months he has sent to the Harvard Observatory his records
of these mysterious "flare stars" that wax and wane in brilliance. Nearly forty-five years before, on the first day of March,

in 1918, he had seen his first variable star. It was R. Leonis in the constellation Leo. He swung his telescope to this constellation now and showed us this small celestial body that, during a period of 313 days, changes from a star visible to the naked eye to one of only the ninth magnitude. Stars of the sixth magnitude are the faintest our eyes can detect. Each year, on March 1, Peltier makes a sentimental journey across millions of miles of space, revisiting this fluctuating star that had first appeared to him as a boy with a spyglass telescope on an Ohio farm. And now, we, ourselves, each year when March comes in, look toward the constellation Leo, remembering Peltier.

When the moon comes up, the stars are dimmed and serious observing is at an end for the astronomer. The east had grown lighter as we moved from one heavenly body to another. Now the late-rising moon lifted above the trees. I climbed to the top step of the astronomer's ladder—a structure mounted on casters and resembling a narrow section of the bleachers at a baseball park—and turned the telescope toward the east. Everything in the lunar landscape shone brilliantly clear in the reflected light of the sun. Objects on the moon the size of the Pentagon Building were visible through the high-magnification eyepiece. I seemed flying in a satellite just above the dead, yawning craters of the moon's face.

For a long time, while the clock mechanism ticked away in the darkness, we roamed across other parts of the sky. Then Peltier lowered the telescope, closed the slit in the roof and we stepped outside. We were greeted by a large collie named Canis Major. Around us the trees were dark, the ground silvered by moonlight. Above us lifted the dome, snow-white and shining in the frosty air.

On the way across the yard, I eased myself into the cramped quarters of the old observatory and looked through the six-inch glass. It was with this telescope and in this month—February—that Peltier had discovered the greatest number of the eleven comets he was the first to see. Although it is only one-fourth as powerful as the big refractor, the six-inch glass has a wider field. It magnifies a larger portion of the sky and this is a definite advantage to the comet-hunter. Through it I looked at Orion, at Sirius, at the mottled face of the moon, seeing what we had only imagined behind the clouds when we had first come to Delphos in our autumn journey.

Late in the night, after cups of hot chocolate at the house, we bade the Peltiers good-bye and started for our motel on the outskirts of town. Already, in the light of the moon, we could see clouds creeping back, rising all along the horizon. The curtain that had parted for our Delphos night was closing again.

We rode in silence, in a reflective mood. My mind had gone back to a lonely campfire on a lonely beach among the Indiana dunes. There, years before, Nellie and I had encountered Maurice Maeterlinck's words: "Can we, without putting constraint upon ourselves, confine our thoughts to everyday things at times when we are face to face with the night?" It all came back: the deserted shore, the darkening water, the first stars of evening, our little driftwood fire that glowed and fluttered beside a log half buried in the sand. The light faded, the sky filled with stars, and, under the stars, the waves broke and swept over the sand in a long succession.

I remember we talked of how every wave was formed of a new combination of water drops. Never would the identical composition be repeated. Each breaking wave was unique just as each human being is unique. No two other people would ever appear on earth alike in all respects to the two who then sat under the stars listening to the rush of water on the shore. The infinite originality of nature, originality in snow-flakes and sand grains, in waves and human beings—and stars —runs through all the universe.

TWENTY-THREE

ICE STORM IN INDIANA

DAWN came late the next morning. We watched the gray of its leaden light slowly increase beyond the window-panes. Gone were the undimmed heavens of the night before. All across the sky, as we started out, sullen clouds pressed low. We were once more in a time of winter rains. It was days before we saw the sun again.

Under the low ceiling of the clouds, we turned south down the eastern edge of Indiana. We traveled, that day, almost the length of the state, from just below Fort Wayne to Madison, on the Ohio River. And all the way we rode through a half twilight. Somewhere below Winchester, near Lynn, I remember we looked down a wet side road that led east a few miles to Greenfork Top. There, 1,240 feet above sea level, the crest of a little knoll in a cornfield represents Indiana's highest point of land.

Rain was falling when, a little before noon, we slowed down at the edge of Richmond. For Nellie and me, this was a nostalgic return to familiar surroundings. We drove about for some time, winding through the Earlham College campus, following Clear Creek, visiting a long-remembered clump of blue spruces on a hillside. Beyond the ceaselessly swinging arms of the windshield wipers, we saw scenes associated with the past. Every turn brought recollections. For it was at Earlham College that we first met. There our adventures together began.

First in rain, then in soft, wet snow, then in sleet that bounded in streaming white pellets from the windshield and hood of the car, we zigzagged southward through Liberty and Connersville and Rushville and Versailles. The sky grew darker. Rain had changed to snow when we came to Liberty. Snow had changed to sleet by Connersville. And sleet had become fine rain again when we reached Rushville. The roads were almost deserted. No one was in the fields. Both man and beast were under cover. I switched on the radio. Broadcasts were filled with warnings against freezing rain. An ice storm was imminent.

Winter blizzards and winter ice storms usually are born of opposite conditions. A cold front, sweeping down from the north, brings the blizzard. A warm front, moving up from the south, commonly produces the ice storm. Under the latter conditions, the temperature of the air is above freezing while that of the ground is below freezing. Moisture, descending through the air as fine rain, congeals on contact with the colder earth, thus forming and building up a transparent shell of ice around every object it encounters. Sleet, on the other hand, freezes before it reaches the ground. Its pellets are formed of raindrops that have turned to ice as they fell. As a general rule, ice or glaze storms are most widespread in the eastern half of the United States. In some instances, meteorologists have found, a difference of only one degree F. will determine whether moisture descends from the winter sky as rain or as snow.

We advanced with reduced speed. And as we advanced, we watched a transparent tube of glaze, a shell steadily growing thicker, form around the radio aerial that rose upright beyond our windshield. Telephone wires, dipping between their poles, glinted and shone. The plating of ice, all along their length, glittered even in the murky light below the darkened sky. Each leaf and spray among the roadside weeds and grasses appeared encased in glass. Mail boxes and fence posts and highway signs rose bearded with icicles, enclosed in a shining sheath that, minute by minute, increased in thickness.

At times, such shells of ice have become three inches thick. In one instance, in the Panhandle of western Texas, the hard glaze built up on telephone wires to the record depth of five inches. It has been calculated that in the historic ice storm of 1940, in England, individual wires became weighted down with as much as 1,000 pounds and that some telegraph poles were supporting eleven tons before they snapped off. Each severe ice storm leaves in its wake a widespread trail of wreckage. In 1951, one such storm swept in a 100-mile-wide path all the way from Louisiana to West Virginia. When power and telephone lines were repaired and the debris from broken trees was cleared away, the U.S. Weather Bureau calculated that the destruction wrought by the ice of this single storm amounted to more than $78,000,000.

If you look to the west as you reach the top of a rise some miles south of Versailles, your eye ascends a long slope to the summit of a higher hill. Scattered trees and patches of woodland vary with open stretches up the length of this incline. On this day, all the trunks of all the trees were gleaming; all the branches were crystalline. Even under the lowering sky, grass and bush and tree seemed bathed in a silver glow, the cold radiance of light reflected from the ice.

Not far beyond we crossed a small stream. The twisted limbs and bare twigs and blotched trunk of an immense sycamore, all sheathed in a transparent coating, momentarily towered above us. Nearby we saw the silvery-gray of a smooth-barked beech as through shining, purest glass. All the twigs and smaller branches drooped, weighted down with a growing burden of ice. For many a tree, in many an ice storm, the burden becomes too great to bear. I remember traveling through New England one spring after a particularly destructive ice storm in March. Friends told me of lying awake far into the night, listening to the sound of the laboring trees,

LONG-TAILED salamander at Mill Grove, John James
Audubon's first American home in eastern Pennsylvania.

CATARACT OF ICE flows down an Adirondacks cliff.
Above, spot where grouse hid in snowbank during storm.

their fibers pulled as though on a rack, until—strained beyond their strength—they snapped and, with a sudden splintering crash, some great limb gave way. Everywhere I went, I saw beloved elms of the village streets maimed or split apart by the weight of the ice.

Trees with deep V-shaped forks, like the elms, are most likely to be damaged severely by the ice. Among the other species particularly hard hit by ice storms are the poplars, the box elder, the willows, the black locust, the linden, and the silver maple. All other maples are fairly resistant to ice damage. So are the sweet gum, the honey locust, the tulip and the black ash. Among those at the top of the list of species best able to endure the ordeal of ice are the beech, the shagbark hickory, the hornbeam and the horse-chestnut. All the oaks, except the pin oak, are highly resistant to glaze damage. Birches are also likely to come through intact, with the yellow birch having the best chances of all. The brittleness or suppleness, the weakness or strength of the wood chiefly determines the fate of the tree in an ice storm.

Ever since Nellie and I had found ourselves back in the Middle West, we had been enjoying a traveling game—identifying distant winter trees by their shapes. As we rode south through the increasing glaze, we saw these different, distinctive forms each enclosed in a sheeting of frozen rain. One of the easiest trees to recognize and, for me, one of the most beautiful of all, is the sycamore, often with white, satiny branches twisting away from a trunk massive and mottled. As we advanced through the ice storm that day, we observed, encased within glaze, the spreading fans of the elms, the twiggy tops of the tupelos, the crooked branches of the persimmons, the scraggly vertical lines of the black locusts, the twisted clumps of the black willows, the feathery branch-ends of the beeches and the white oaks, round-headed, seemingly evenly sheared all over their tops. Thus we made our way through a world of glittering trees.

This hard, crystalline landscape that was taking shape around us brought with it a desperate time for all the wild creatures that inhabited it. Birds, most of all, suffer from an ice storm. Their wings may become coated so they cannot fly. In some instances, the feet of perching birds have been cemented to limbs by the glaze. Held prisoner in this way, they have even starved to death, unable to free themselves. Seeds and buds are locked away beneath the ice. Grouse, buried in snowdrifts, may find themselves unable to escape, imprisoned under a hard surface layer through which they cannot break. I remember reading, some years ago, of a flock of red-winged blackbirds forced down by a glaze storm onto snow on a small lake near Oklahoma City. They became so solidly encased that shells of ice had to be chipped away to free them. Usually, as soon as rain commences to freeze, the birds seek out some sheltered spot. On this day, from the time the ice storm began, we saw no birds in the air.

Fortunately for us, the dark hardtop of our highway was just enough warmer than the surrounding earth to keep the falling moisture from freezing. Our road was wet. Sometimes it became slushy. But it was never slippery with ice. On the hood and front of our car, the glaze built up, melted free, suddenly came sliding back to shoot up the windshield and go sailing away behind us. As I watched this same sequence of events—the ice building up and disappearing and building up again—an event I had not thought of for many years, a kind of universal allegory linked with the formation of ice, returned in memory.

I had heard the details of the event from an official of a Federal aviation agency who had investigated a crash in the southern Appalachians. In the early days of commercial aviation, on the dangerous north-and-south Appalachian Mountains run, one of the pilots determined that if he ever got into trouble in the air and saw he was going to crash, he would report over his radio everything he could observe. Something said might save the lives of other pilots. One winter night over the mountains, ice built up along his wings and—in a time before de-icers were invented—he plunged to his death. But he carried out his promise. All the way down, up to the moment of impact, he poured words into the radio reporting everything that might be of importance. He died thinking he had not died in vain, that he had done something to help. Yet the story ends on a note of pure tragedy, tragedy in the Greek sense in which disaster overtakes the hero through some flaw within himself. For, although his words were recorded, he talked so fast, his sentences tumbled over each other in such desperate haste, that even to this day nobody has been able to make out more than a few words of what he said.

As the afternoon wore on, we seemed more and more transported into a kind of Crystal Age. Everything around us had become smooth and unmarred, clean and shining, hard and transparent. We moved through a realm of cold and lifeless beauty. A breeze sprang up, but the dry music of the winter grasses was stilled. We heard when we paused—and then only rarely—the small tinkling sounds of ice striking ice. The beauty of a glaze storm is almost exclusively visual beauty.

But that beauty has endless variety. Like specimens preserved in colorless amber, each weed head was displayed within its envelope of ice. A teasel became a crystalline work of art, and all the woven fences bordering pasture fields were converted into gleaming meshes of ice and wire. Under a line of locust trees, every branch shining with its glinting burden, an embankment fell away in a steep descent. From top to bottom, it was clothed with wild honeysuckle vines. All the intertwining stems and tendrils were enveloped in ice. The picture presented suggested some tumbling waterfall, its airy grace stilled by cold in the midst of its descent. A little later, we passed a cornfield where all the stalks lay prostrate, each yellow line visible through its coating of ice.

We were nearing the Ohio when we came upon one of the

few large vehicles we saw abroad, a trailer truck loaded with automobiles. Each new machine was fringed with icicles. So was a roadside sign: "Caution. Deer Crossing." And, where a clump of evergreens grew beside the road, icicles lengthened among their drooping branches. Such northern trees, particularly the spire-shaped firs and spruces, are especially suited to survive under the harsh conditions of winter. Their branches are able to droop without breaking, then return to their former position when the burden of ice is gone. It has been noticed that, under certain conditions, icicles actually help support such trees. Descending from branch to branch and to the ground, they end by forming a kind of framework or skeleton of ice that reduces the strain on the individual limbs.

About an hour before dusk, on roads becoming slippery, we crept cautiously down the steep, winding descent into the town of Madison, beside the Ohio River. The freezing rain continued into the night. In the morning, our car was sheathed in ice.

When we had crossed the ridges of the southern Appalachians in early spring, we had noticed how, as our elevation changed, we went in and out of the season. We moved backward into late winter and cooler surroundings when we climbed, and forward into valleys gay with spring flowers when we descended. Similarly, the traveler in hilly terrain after an ice storm often goes in and out of the glaze-encrusted landscape. It is the higher ground that is most heavily sheeted in ice. The difference in temperature represented by an elevation of only 100 feet frequently is sufficient to determine whether trees are wet with rain or coated with ice. Oftentimes the glaze ceases in an almost abrupt boundary—a natural contour line depicted in ice.

Later that morning, when we had crossed the wide, brown, flooded Ohio—where floating islands of debris drifted downstream far below our bridge—we looked back from the Kentucky side and saw just such a contour line drawn along the

wooded hills of the Indiana bank. Above the line, the hilltops
rose in glinting crystalline masses; below, the woods were drab
and wet. For half an hour or more we followed the river upstream, and all the way we saw the ice-crowned hills in double
image. We saw them lifting above their darker bases like shining cumulus clouds. And we saw them again, below, inverted,
reflected in the brown mirror of the stream.

TWENTY-FOUR

BIG BONE LICK

BETWEEN Beaverlick and Rabbit Hash, during a lull in the subsequent days of rain, we dipped on a muddy road into a small valley among the Kentucky hills. We were less than two miles from the Ohio River and twenty-three miles southwest of Cincinnati. Down the length of this valley extended the deep-cut serpentine of a creek. Joined by Dark Hollow Branch and Gum Branch and Beaver Branch, Big Bone Creek was nearing the end of its flow and its juncture with the Ohio. Held within a loop of this stream, a stretch of boggy ground contains a spring where bubbles, rising through murky, chemical-filled water, continually break on the surface of a pool eight or ten feet across. As we stood beside it, amid the dead winter vegetation of the low ground, a faint sulphurous smell filled the air.

Each time Nellie and I have looked forward to one of our extended seasonal trips, we have listed all the things we have long wanted to do, all the sites we have long wanted to visit within the portion of the country we would traverse. High on our winter list of places we especially wanted to see with our own eyes was this Kentucky hollow. For, years before the first white settlers came to "the dark and bloody ground," this out-of-the-way valley was known in the capitals of Europe. It appeared on maps of the New World as early as 1744. In that year Jacques Nicholas Bellin, the French cartographer, exhibited in Paris his pioneer map of Louisiana. On it the site of this salt spring was noted as "the place where they found the elephant bones in 1739." To Benjamin Franklin the valley was "The Great Licking Place." To pioneers it was the "Jelly Ground." To the Indians it was "The Place of the Big Bones." To paleontologists it is "the Graveyard of the Mammoths." To geographers it is Big Bone Lick.

The world first heard of this remote valley more than two and a quarter centuries ago. Twenty-five years before the beginning of the French and Indian War, during the reign of Louis XV, Captain Charles Lemoyne de Longueil, commander at Fort Niagara and later governor of Montreal, set out through the wilderness to explore the valley of the Ohio River. As his birch-bark canoe drifted downstream between the Licking and the Kentucky rivers, his Indian guides told him of a small swampy stretch up a side stream where the ground was strewn with immense bones. According to a legend of the red men, they were the remains of a fabulous race of giant white buffaloes that, long ago, died from drinking the salt water of the springs.

When De Longueil reached the valley, that summer day in 1739, he found a quaking bog impregnated with salt. All across it and around its edge, bleached white by the sun, projected tusks and leg bones and skulls of mammoths and mastodons. These Ice Age elephants had been extinct for thousands of years. Some of the Big Bone tusks measured eleven feet in length. Some of the teeth weighed ten pounds. Some of the leg bones were big enough to use for tent poles. Men sat on vertebrae as on small stumps. What De Longueil saw in this wilderness valley—as Dr. Willard Rouse Jillson, formerly State Geologist of Kentucky, puts it in his book, *Big Bone Lick*—was "the greatest natural depository of the bones of the great Pleistocene mammals that man's eye has ever beheld in any part of the world."

For ages the bog had formed a baited trap. The huge beasts, coming for salt, had mired down in the gluelike ooze and,

dying, had left their skeletons in the little valley. The bones
of more than 100 mammoths and mastodons are said to have
been taken from this one spot. They form prized accessions to
the paleontological exhibits of leading museums of the world,
in London and Paris and New York and Washington. The
great French scientists Cuvier and Buffon studied these prehistoric bones when they reached Europe from the wilds of
America. Thomas Jefferson, when he was President, reserved
a special room at the White House for the 300 items of his
private collection of fossils from Big Bone Lick.

Apparently the first man to realize the scientific importance
of the prehistoric relics was an Indian trader, Robert Smith.
He began collecting tusks and bones in 1744. But all his pos-
sessions were destroyed when his village, on the Big Miami
River, in Ohio, was attacked and burned during the French
and Indian War. Other early attempts to transport Big Bone
fossils to civilization also ended in disaster. Col. George
Croghan, then Indian agent for the colony of Pennsylvania,
started up the Ohio River with a large selection of the relics
in 1765. He was captured by the Algonquins and barely escaped with his life. All his specimens were lost. In 1795 Gen.
William Henry Harrison, later the ninth President of the
United States, visited the lick. He filled thirteen hogsheads
with bones and headed upstream for Fort Pitt. Before he
reached his destination his boat overturned and all the prehistoric fossils disappeared. Even after one early collection
safely reached civilization, it was lost when an ignorant servant
ground up the bones for fertilizer.

Of all the early collectors the most active was Dr. William
Goforth, a Cincinnati physician, a correspondent of Thomas
Jefferson's, the father of a large family, and a doctor with an
extensive practice which, however, was "not very profitable
because of the poverty of the patients." By 1804 he had assembled almost five tons of bones. These he entrusted to an

English traveler who accompanied them to London, sold them and pocketed the money himself. Three years after Dr. Goforth's misadventure, Capt. William Clark, second in command of the immortal Lewis and Clark Expedition, was commissioned by Thomas Jefferson to make a collection of fossils at Big Bone Lick. He remained there for three weeks in the fall of 1807, the year after his return from the mouth of the Columbia. In December of that year he shipped three large boxes of bones down the Ohio and Mississippi to New Orleans, where they were transferred to shipboard for the voyage up the Atlantic to their eventual destination, the White House in Washington.

More than 150 years had passed since Captain Clark stood beside the spring where we now stood. More than 220 years had gone by since De Longueil followed his Indian guides to this little valley. We looked about us with intense interest. What was Big Bone Lick, this spot possessed of so romantic a history, like in the sixth decade of the twentieth century?

The valley itself is only a few hundred acres in extent. Wooded hills of uneven height rise around it. On a slope to the north a few houses and a white church mark the site of the village of Big Bone (pop. 20). In the days of the pioneers, the "jelly ground" of the quaking bog extended over several acres. Today the swampy area around the salt spring covers perhaps an acre or less. The volume of the spring and the oozy character of the bog appear to have diminished from former times when visitors reported picking up bones "from ye mud."

With us as we stood there were William Fitzgerald of Florence, and his wife, Anne. Fitzgerald, the only authentic Kentucky colonel of my acquaintance, is by vocation an instructor of printing at the Holmes High School in Covington, Kentucky, and by avocation a local historian of note. He also has been one of the prime movers in setting aside the spring and the surrounding area—so rich in its historic and scientific associations—as the Big Bone Lick State Park. At the time of our visit the initial grading and construction already had begun.

With Fitzgerald in the lead, we pushed through a jungle of dry weed stems to the bank of Big Bone Creek. Winding in a generally westward direction, its serpentine bisects the floor of the little valley. Here in the rich soil the horseweed or Canada fleabane or prideweed or butterweed or colt's-tail—*Leptilon canadense*—a plant that, depending on the fertility of the ground, varies in height from three inches to ten feet, had attained its maximum growth. Its stems rose as much as four feet above my head.

A week or two before, a sudden melting of the snow on the surrounding hills had sent a torrent rushing down the twisting bed of Big Bone Creek. In places it had cut across loops of the serpentine, leaving all the weeds pointing in one direction, mowed down by the rushing water. Bushes on both banks tilted downstream. They, and the lowest of the tree branches, were festooned with floodwrack, brown leaves and yellow grass and black twigs. Winding in and out among these bushes, each with its burden of flood deposit, we gazed down into the greenish water of the creek and examined the steep banks as we advanced.

For in such a millrace of water, scouring and cutting into the blue clay of the lower banks, prehistoric bones may be brought to light. During summer, when the water is low, Fitzgerald sometimes walks barefoot in the mud of the stream bed in search of fossils. One of the best finds he ever made, a huge vertebra that once formed part of the backbone of an Ice Age mammal, was uncovered in this way. When he kicked what he thought was merely a soft ball of mud, he discovered there was a fossil inside. After lying for thousands of years in the ground, these recovered bones are always dark, almost chocolate in color.

At each turn of the deep-cut stream, we saw how the outer

curve exposed a vertical profile of the soil. Above the solid stratum of blue clay where most of the ancient fossils now are found, there is an overlay of eight or ten feet of more recent material. Geologists calculate it may have taken as long as 10,000 years to deposit this surface soil. From it are recovered mainly the bones of the more recent mammals: deer, elk and bison, as well as domestic cows, hogs and horses. In a cornfield just north of the stream—where we saw a flock of twenty robins flying, calling, hunting for food in the wet ground—a farmer turns up fragments of such bones with each spring plowing.

Slipping on the wet soil and the slick clay, using tangled roots for handholds, we worked our way up and down the steep banks. Once we tight-roped over the precarious bridge of a fallen tree that descended steeply across the stream. Song sparrows and tufted titmice called above us, and a Carolina wren sang from a tangle of flood wreckage among the bushes. Three times we came to muskrat burrows in the stream banks. Once, almost under our feet, a cottontail rabbit bolted from its form. And here, where mammoths and mastodons had fed in ages past, a plump and dark little fieldmouse scurried away among the dry grasses.

For some reason one bend in the creek, where elm trees overhang the water, has proved an especially rich hunting ground for fossils. It was here, in 1960, that Ellis Crawford, Director of the William Behringer Memorial Museum of Covington, discovered the jawbone of a mastodon. Downstream, over the hill toward the Ohio, an immense hollow sycamore stands on the creek bank. Said to be twenty-four feet in circumference, it is a landmark in the region. Another smaller hollow sycamore has contributed a section, three or four feet in diameter, that has been thrust down like a huge tile to protect a bubbling spring on Gum Branch close to its junction with the creek. We watched lines of shining bubbles drift away on the current, floating above a long, almost black, patch of chemical stain that extended over the sandy bottom from this spring. A local belief is that the section of the sycamore rests on the tusks of a prehistoric animal. Fritzgerald views this idea with well-deserved skepticism, as he does the frontier tales of teams and wagons being swallowed up in the mud of the bog.

"How to separate fact from fancy is always a problem," he remarked.

From time to time as we followed the twisting bank of the creek, we stopped to pick off cockleburs, beggar's-lice, burdock burs and pronged sticktights. They all grew in profusion in the valley. The mud of the creek bank was light tan. It stuck to our galoshes, but it never balled up as had the black mud of the Missouri bottomland.

Not far from where Big Bone Creek empties into the Ohio—opposite Big Bone Bar and Big Bone Island—a famous buffalo trace extended in early times from the river to the lick. A boulevard in the wilderness, broad enough for two lumber wagons to pass with ease, this natural highway had been leveled and beaten hard by the hoofs of countless bison over centuries of time. It has now entirely disappeared. All across the Bluegrass Country of northern Kentucky, the trails of deer, elk and bison once led from all directions toward the saline springs. There the herbivores licked up the salt-impregnated ground, sometimes lowering its level several feet below that of the surrounding land. Famed as a hunting ground long before Daniel Boone led his first party of white settlers through the Cumberland Gap, the region attracted Wyandottes, Shawnees and Delawares from the north and Cherokees, Creeks and Catawbas from the south. The clash of warring red men gave the rich territory its name of Kentucky, an Indian word referring to its dark, bloodstained ground. Salt licks, with their concentration of big game and the Indian hunters they attracted, shaped the early history of the region.

Across the open bit of marshland dotted thickly with tussocks of grass we retraced our steps to the edge of the largest spring. As long as Fitzgerald remembers it, its pool has remained about the same size. The bottom is floored with fine, dark, shining mud that extends downward for a considerable distance. A fence rail can be pushed almost out of sight into this watery silt. Once in summer when Fritzgerald slipped from the edge of the pool, he sank up to his hips before he could pull himself out. There is no quicksand in the valley, but the oozy mud clings tenaciously.

Indian hunters camping beside the bog simply boiled their meat in the water of the spring, thus salting it as it cooked. Later, in frontier days two centuries ago, salt was extracted commercially at Big Bone Lick and sold in Cincinnati. In long rows of kettles as much as 500 gallons of water was boiled away to obtain one pound of salt. Much of the surrounding forest was cut for firewood during this period. Besides salt, the water of the mineral springs contains lime and sulphur in solution. Long considered to possess curative properties, the water at one time was bottled and sold by a Cincinnati firm. For a period of several decades, in the so-called Golden Age of Kentucky aristocracy, the valley was one of the most famous health resorts and watering places west of the Alleghenies.

Among the tangles of dry weeds north of the creek we had come upon long lines of half-buried stones. In the 1820's, when the popularity of the resort reached its height, these supported rows of bathhouses where guests enjoyed mud baths while they drank the mineral waters. Nearby stood a fine hotel, named for Henry Clay, and a large open pavilion. Wealthy families arrived by boat, coming down the Ohio, or by carriage, accompanied by numerous servants. For about twenty years, the resort flourished. Each summer the secluded valley became a center of social gaiety. Then the popularity of this frontier spa waned and its big buildings disappeared. Half a century later, in 1870, a new hotel was erected. But the heyday of Big Bone Lick as a watering place had passed.

About the time construction began on the new hotel, one of the mineral springs was dug out to increase its facilities. Within the space of fifteen feet, workmen unearthed a wagonload of prehistoric bones. They included one tusk nearly ten inches in diameter. The fossil lode at Big Bone Lick is far from exhausted. During the summer following our visit, the first large-scale scientific excavations ever attempted in the valley began under the direction of Dr. C. Bertrand Schultz, paleontologist and director of the University of Nebraska State Museum. Working at a leased five-acre tract just north of the creek, the team of scientists removed more than 60,000 cubic feet of surface soil and recovered approximately 2,000 bones during the first season of a five-year project. Eventually they may descend as deep as twenty feet into the fossil-bearing blue clay beneath. All the uncovered bones are being taken back to the Nebraska laboratories and subjected to scientific tests to determine their age.

As we looked around us for a final time before leaving—at the valley, the winding creek, the surrounding hills—I considered all that long parade of visitors that had come to this place of ancient bones before us—Indian hunters, English traders, French *coureurs de bois*, scouts and trappers, settlers pushing west into the wild "Kentuckie Country," frontier scientists, ladies and gentlemen of fashion. Here in the 1750's Mrs. Mary Ingles, known as the first white woman in Kentucky, had escaped from her Shawnee captors and had begun her wilderness Odyssey of hardship that eventually carried her home to Virginia. Here the Father of American Ornithology, Alexander Wilson, had delighted in the flashing colors of innumerable Carolina parakeets—a bird now extinct. Here in 1841 that eccentric naturalist of the frontier, Constantine Samuel Rafinesque, had arrived in search of prehistoric bones. Here, the eyes that had seen the Rockies and the far-away reaches of the Columbia River, the eyes of Captain Clark, had

searched the ground for fossils. Here Gen. George Rogers
Clark and his leather-stockinged Indian-fighters had replenished their provisions. And here, at the height of his fame, Sir
Charles Lyell, the English geologist, had arrived on a pilgrim-
age to this remote bit of land so closely linked with prehistoric
times. They all had been part of the long and varied pageant
that—like ourselves—had been drawn to this one small and
still secluded valley.

TWENTY-FIVE

HIGH WATER

THE month of February—"February the short, the woorst of al" as an old English writer described it—had almost reached its end. Around the Salton Sea, spring wildflowers were now in bloom. Off the Silver Strand, gray whales were plowing northward again. And here in Kentucky, melted snow and days of rain had raised the water level of all the creeks and branches.

As we had moved eastward along our wandering course, the rhythm of night and day had subtly altered. At first imperceptibly, then noticeably, the nights had grown shorter, the days longer. The tide of light was flowing in. The tide of warmth would follow.

South of the Ohio, in the latitude of Kentucky, the earliest signs of the Midwestern spring were already apparent. We passed a woman, with a brown paper bag in one hand, digging dandelions beside the road. Between the showers, children were flying kites. And one night when we slept in Hardin County the birthplace of Abraham Lincoln, the frog chorus from the flooded lowlands reached *fortissimo*. The frogs call. The lambs arrive. The birds return. This is the way the spring comes back.

In such a pre-spring spring—but well aware of how swiftly the late-winter weather could change—we turned south to Mammoth Cave and Bowling Green and Goodletsville, across the Tennessee line on the old Natchez Trace. It was there that

Alexander Wilson first saw the birds he named the Nashville and the Tennessee warblers.

In falling rain we stopped at Transylvania College at Lexington, Kentucky, once the home of that ill-starred genius Rafinesque. In rain we splashed along the buffalo trace that leads to Blue Lick and, in rain, we rode across the fertile Bluegrass region, that land of racehorses, white-fenced pastures and country mansions. The rain still fell—the late-winter rain, the father of floods—when we mounted the long bridge over the Ohio at Maysville. Flotsam, gleaned from lowlands down hundreds of miles of riverbank, spotted and streaked with lines and swirls the brown water sweeping past below us.

Toward the close of that day, the downpour ended. Openings, ragged and temporary, were torn in the western clouds and the glare of a smoky winter sunset tinted the lonely bluff top along which we walked. We had come some twenty miles north of the river. We were in the hill country of southern Ohio. Below the sheer drop of the cliff that formed the western edge of the bluff lay the curving arm of a creek. Looking over the edge, we followed downward with our eyes the trunks of great sycamores rooted on the stream banks. Behind us, paralleling the lip of the cliff, extended the folds of an immense earthen serpent. Nearly a quarter of a mile long, this work of unknown hands, of a forgotten race of men, is one of the most celebrated of all the relics of the ancient Mound Builders.

From the Great Lakes to the Gulf of Mexico and from the Atlantic to the Rockies, explorers and pioneers encountered the varied earthworks of these Stone Age Americans. Some are round or square or rectangular hillocks. Others take the form of birds or serpents or beasts. Among the latter the most famous is this serpent mound near the community of Peebles, in Adams County, Ohio. Running down the 1,348 feet of its winding length is a central core, or backbone, of stones. Over the stones are ranged layers of different soils, first gray clay, then yellow clay mixed with stones, then dark soil supporting the dense sod that forms the green skin of the serpent. The average width of the body is about twenty feet, its height from four to five feet. Recent evidence indicates that the mound dates back to about the beginning of the Christian era. For nearly 2,000 years, this titanic reptile of earth has appeared to be dragging its length up and down over this rolling bluff top. Still debated is its original purpose, whether it represented a symbol of religious significance or a show-piece to wonder at, a kind of Eiffel Tower of primitive times.

When pioneers settled in the Ohio Valley, forest trees had engulfed the narrow ridge and the effigy mound along its top. Later, when the forest had been cut and second-growth trees had sprung up again, a tornado swept directly over the bluff, leveling the woods at its top. The present state of preservation of The Serpent Mound is largely due to the work of one man, Frederic Ward Putnam, of Harvard's Peabody Museum of American Archaeology and Ethnology. Through his efforts, in 1886 about $6,000 was raised for the purchase of the site. During the three succeeding summers Putnam and his assistants, living in tents on the bluff top, cleared and restored the area. In 1900, Harvard University deeded the site to the Ohio Historical Society. It is now maintained as a State Memorial.

In the stillness of the winter sunset, after the days of rain, we wandered down the length of the winding mound. We heard the monosyllabic "check" of a passing redwing, the "peter-peter-peter" of a tufted titmouse and, far away, the excited barking of a dog chasing a cottontail. Then there was silence again. The sounds, the silence, the sky flaming a darker red, the chill at the end of the February day—all these were parts of a timeless world, features of other ages as well as of our own. We could imagine ourselves in that remote period, beyond the threshold of written history, when this earthwork was raw and new, when an unknown race of men completed their task and left their mark on the earth to tell other races of men, unknown to them, that they once had lived.

How many years went by before its completion? How many men and women contributed their days of strength to the labor? Their names are unknown. Their history is forgotten. But this work of their hands remains, more permanent than the victories of Napoleon. What in the lives of modern man will endure so long?

Among those mounds of the Old World, the barrows on the heaths of England, W. H. Hudson—as told in *Hampshire Days*—and Richard Jefferies—as recalled in *The Story of My Heart*—spent hours contemplating, in imagination, the existence of the primitive men whose hands had raised those tumuli. To both came the emotion of being very close to the builders who had known the earth in another, long-ago time. So, in the stillness of the winter sunset on this ridgetop in Ohio, I felt very close to those ancient men who had chosen a spot so beautiful for their master labors. Remotely distant, infinitely far removed from life today, they too, perhaps, had been stirred by sunsets, by all the beauty of the scene outspread below this eminence.

As we advanced down the writhing length of the earth-serpent, we saw how the inside of each curve imprisoned a half-moon of collected water. A pool had formed where the open jaws grasp a mass of rocks, supposed to represent an egg. Below the vertical western face of the ridge, water spread out over the lowland from the creek, catching the light of the sky, glowing with tintings of red between the branches of the sycamores. Everywhere the ground was soggy and streams were overflowing. All across the countryside around us, each twisting rivulet and creek was hurrying its water toward the same destination, the brown expanse of the Ohio.

Next day we turned south and east toward this same destination. Our general plan was to follow for 150 miles upstream the wanderings of the northern river bank, from Portsmouth to Ironton and Gallipolis and Parkersburg. It had been days since we had last seen a paper and we rarely listened to the radio. We had never experienced an Ohio River flood. So we drove lightheartedly on.

Our first surprise came when we reached U.S. 23, which follows the Scioto River south from Chillicothe to Portsmouth. Beyond the highway as far as we could see stretched a tan-colored lake of muddy water. The rising Ohio had backed up this tributary, and miles of lowland were already flooded. Not long afterwards, a highway truck blocked the road ahead. Beyond it, the concrete dipped downward and disappeared entirely under water. We shunted off onto a detour that eventually brought us out on U.S. 52, the main highway along the Ohio. We came to Portsmouth over a bridge only a few feet above the rising flood.

Down side streets, as we rode through town, we glimpsed the great concrete flood wall that rose high above the lower windows of the factory buildings. Beyond Portsmouth, roadmen were flagging down cars and turning them off onto a rough, muddy, pothole-riddled detour that was to carry us "a little way around a hill." The little way extended itself interminably. And the hill seemed to us a mountain.

"When does a hill become a mountain?" Nellie asked.

So, for a time, we diverted our minds from our troubles with such distinctions and dividing lines. We remembered some of our queries later on, after our trip was over, and sought the answers. A hill, according to one definition we found, becomes a mountain when it rises above 1,000 feet. Disintegrated rock becomes soil when it supports rooted plants. Rainfall becomes a cloudburst when the downpour descends at the rate of four inches in an hour.

After bumping along for almost ten miles, going around the hill, we found ourselves back on U.S. 52 not far from Hanging Rock. At Ironton we crossed back to the Kentucky side and, in the early twilight, in falling rain, came to Ashland. There we got the last motel room in town and settled down to read the alarming headlines and flood news in the local paper.

More rain was predicted. The crest of the flood was expected to reach sixty feet. Telephone service had been knocked out. Communities were cut off. Floodgates were going in at all the river towns. Pumping stations had been turned on in Ashland and across the river at Ironton. This was our first taste of a real flood. Would we be cut off? Would our trip be delayed? We pored over maps that evening. Early in the morning, we decided, we would return to Ironton, double back and try to go inland away from the floodwaters of the river valley. Then, across higher land, we could head east for the upstream bridge to Parkersburg. Before we went to bed, we looked out. It was still raining. We went to sleep wondering what the morrow would bring.

The first thing it brought was more rain. We were up at five and away, after a hasty breakfast, at six. The sky, heavy, hanging low, trailed the slate-colored vapor of its clouds across the tops of the higher buildings. Morning papers were filled with flood and disaster. Crossing the Ohio, we noticed even greater accumulations of debris drifting by on the rising water. On the outskirts of Ironton, I pulled into a Soho filling station. The owner, in a slicker and rubber boots, filled my tank.

"Can I get north on 23 this morning?" I asked.

"No. It's under water."

"How about 52 west of Portsmouth?"

"It's out. The bridge is flooded."

"Is there any way of going north?"

"No. There's only one road open out of Ironton. That's the one you came in on—52 going east."

Already backwater covered the open fields on either side and pressed close to the filling station. Creeping up the side of a nearby telephone pole, it had edged an inch or two higher since the station opened. This was not the flood as I had imagined it. There was no rushing torrent. There was no menacing sound. There was only the slow, still, steady rise of the tan-hued water. But soon the filling station would be surrounded. The water was creeping closer even while my tank was being filled. I was the last customer. The owner was locking up as we left.

We swung around and sped upstream, where the ever-widening river was leaving its banks. We passed the bridge to Ashland and got as far as Chesapeake, twenty miles beyond, before we met a barricade set up by highway workers. Ahead the road was flooded and impassable. But here a bridge carried us across to Huntington and the West Virginia side. Perhaps, if we could not go inland in Ohio, we could go inland in West Virginia and so escape from the river at last.

How about the road to Charleston? We might have trouble, we were told, but we should be able to get through. It had been open an hour ago. We started out. The trouble was that, in this hilly country, all the roads followed the valleys of tributary streams and they, too, were in flood. Waterfalls poured down the rock faces of the highway cuts. Time and again we slowed down to ford sheets of brown water fanning out across the roadway. At Barboursville, a bridge was under water and we negotiated another rutted and devious detour. Twice rock slides narrowed the road.

When we came to Milton, we found water from Mud River backing up into the town. A long row of houses, lower than the highway, ran like a chain of islands, each surrounded by water that rose as high as the porches. The red brick building of a consolidated school was set as though in the midst of a lake. Near it a jet trainer, a surplus warplane mounted on a concrete pedestal, barely cleared the flood. People were taking pictures, and schoolboys, giddy with freedom from classes, were calling:

"No pictures! Restricted area!"

On the far side of Milton the highway dipped and disappeared under water. Once more we detoured, zigzagging among back streets until we were released on the open highway again. A few miles outside of town we overtook a trailer truck loaded with new automobiles. The sight encouraged us greatly. Such a valuable cargo, we reasoned, would be transported with care. The driver apparently knew that the road ahead was open. Dark clouds still hung low but the rain had stopped. Three times in half an hour we encountered mud slides. Once, a good-sized embankment, rocks and soil, had come down, bringing a pine tree with it. But we were gaining altitude, going inland. The real threat of the flood had receded behind us.

Somewhere along our route we went through a Deerwalk and a Wolf Summit. Side roads stretched away, rutted and miry. Under the lowering sky, we turned east, winding among bare winter mountains, threading narrow valleys, coming out on great vistas of tumbled and rolling land. Sometime that afternoon we passed a side road leading to a community that had originally been called Molehill but that had changed its name to Mountain. By now, a parade of telephone trucks was passing us, hurrying toward the stricken areas.

The air grew colder as we followed mountain highroads toward Clarksburg and Grafton. At the top of one turn we found ourselves surrounded once more by trees encased in glittering ice. Not long after four o'clock that afternoon, we stopped for the night at Grafton. The uncertainty of the flood hours was past. High water was behind us. Roads ahead were clear. We slept soundly, free from worry, that last night in February. When we awoke, we were in the first day of the last month of the season. We tore the second sheet from the calendar of the year. Only three weeks remained of all our winter days.

TWENTY-SIX

AUDUBON'S SALAMANDERS

D OWN from the Appalachian Highland, down among the bare apple orchards of the Shenandoah Valley of Virginia, then out onto the Coastal Plain and across the swollen Potomac River, we made a leisurely advance the next day. We came to Washington in the early dusk. Swept like a chip in the torrent of traffic at the capital's perimeter, blinded by streams and whirlpools of headlights, we finally escaped to the north as though released from another flood. Before we settled down in a country motel, at the end of this initial day of March, we looked up at the sky. Both Leo and the variable star that has meant so much in the life of Leslie Peltier were hidden behind clouds.

The following morning began in a way no other dawn of ours had ever started. It commenced with a breakfast of hotcake sandwiches—griddle cakes with ham between and a fried egg on top. Thus amply fortified against the cold, we whirled around Baltimore on a new expressway. Speeding along the multilane concrete of this bypass, we envisioned a future when a whole succession of such highways, like the growth rings of a city, may extend in ever wider curves around expanding urban centers.

North of Baltimore, we returned to a region filled with memories. Here the trails of our four journeys converged. When we stopped for the night at Havre de Grace, at the head of Chesapeake Bay, we slept in Cabin No. 7 at the Chesapeake Motor

Court. It was part of all our travels with the seasons. In this identical cabin we had spent our first night when we had ridden south to meet the spring. Here we had stayed when we returned from our journey into summer. Here we had spent the night when we came home from the Pacific after crossing the continent through autumn. And now, in these latter days of winter, we returned to this same cabin once more.

The morning we left Havre de Grace and crossed the Susquehanna River, our wheels rolled over roads in portions of four states—Maryland, Delaware, New Jersey and Pennsylvania. They carried us past Valley Forge, where Washington's Continental Army spent the miserable winter of 1777–1778, and—five miles west of Norristown, near the community of Audubon, in Pennsylvania—they brought us down a long lane to the house at Mill Grove.

More than a century and a half have passed since Mill Grove formed John James Audubon's first home in America. Although he spent hardly two years here—about the same length of time that Thoreau lived at Walden—his name is linked to this rolling land along Perkiomen Creek almost as indissolubly as Thoreau's is to the pond he made famous. The art of each provided a kind of unique and permanent possession. During the comparatively short period Audubon stayed at Mill Grove, the direction of his life became fixed. There he began his study and painting of American birds. There he conducted the first bird-banding experiment made in America. There he met the girl he married; Lucy Bakewell, the most important influence in his life.

Today the ivy-covered brown fieldstone house, now more than two centuries old, is a museum holding relics of the adventurous life of the American Woodsman. In 1951, exactly 100 years after Audubon's death, the 120 acres of Mill Grove were added to the Montgomery County Park System as a sanctuary and permanent historical shrine. The curator, J. d'Arcy Northwood, a friend I had last seen at an osprey's nest on Cape May, welcomed us and installed us in his cottage down a side lane from the main house. Quickly we all changed into warm tramping clothes and started out on trails that wind for more than four miles over the hills and through the woods and along Perkiomen Creek.

Audubon used to refer to Mill Grove as "that blessed spot." Even on this chill, overcast winter day, its charm was evident. We walked among great trees, beech and hemlock and shagbark hickory. In only six weeks or so these wooded hillsides would be carpeted with the wildflowers of spring, with trillium and hepatica and Dutchman's-breeches and jack-in-the-pulpit. Then all the woodland paths would echo with the song of Audubon's favorite bird, the wood thrush.

The birds of Mill Grove probably are more varied today than they were when Audubon observed them. The land is more open, more diversified in habitat. Northwood's list for the area includes 155 species. Evening grosbeaks come in winter to feed on the seeds of the box elders. In summer, swifts nest inside the stone-and-brick chimney of the abandoned copper smelter far back in the woods. The cave on the Perkiomen where Audubon banded phoebe nestlings disappeared more than a century ago, but these birds, perhaps even descendants of the occupants of that historic nest, still return. For sixty years at least, phoebes have nested on a ledge under the back porch at Mill Grove.

Although the Perkiomen is called a creek, it is larger than the River Thames during most of its flow through England. We watched mallard and widgeon and mergansers swimming on the open water below the dam where the old mill once stood. It was on the Perkiomen that Audubon saw a bald eagle pursuing fish on foot in shallow water. And it was here, one day in winter, that he nearly lost his life when the ice broke under him. A few days before we arrived, Northwood had observed eleven common mergansers fishing together, swimming upstream almost abreast, the line stretching from bank to bank.

By bracing ourselves against first one tree and then another, we worked down a zigzag trail along the face of a fifty-foot cliff of reddish rock. It drops almost perpendicularly to the bank of Mine Run near the spot where this smaller stream empties into the Perkiomen. At its base the wall is pierced by the openings of two ancient mine tunnels. We peered into the dark interiors. The timbers have rotted away. Cave-ins have occurred. From each opening flows the clear water of springs that miners long ago encountered deep within the rock of the cliffs. Even on the bitterest days of winter, the temperature of this flow remains at about fifty-two degrees F. Such spring water and the damp darkness of the old tunnels comprise the winter world of slender, moist-skinned, cold-blooded creatures we especially hoped to see. For Mill Grove provides a sanctuary for long-tailed salamanders as well as for wildflowers and birds.

When autumn nights grow chill, these winter-born amphibians migrate under the cover of darkness from the vicinity of Mine Run and Perkiomen Creek to the underground streams that flow through the two man-made caverns of the cliff. There, mainly in November and December, they lay their eggs. It is usually in January, at a time when the outer world is frozen and blanketed with snow, when life seems at its lowest ebb, that the eggs hatch and existence begins for the larvae of each new generation of long-tailed salamanders. For this species, the period of reproduction is over at a time when, for most other salamanders, the breeding season is just beginning.

In 1952 Charles E. Mohr, in his continuing studies of cave life, made extensive observations of the salamanders of the Mill Grove tunnels. At frequent intervals he kept track of the activity and movement of the amphibians. Nature, he found, had marked individuals in a kind of code using lines and spots. No two of the amphibians exhibited precisely the same pattern of markings. By recording the arrangement of black splotches on the yellow to orange-red ground color of the skin, he was able to recognize individuals when he encountered them later on. At times, he discovered, the salamanders would remain in the same place day after day. At other times, they would wander along the floor of the tunnel as far as 300 feet from the entrance. The studies which Mohr made at Mill Grove provided the first precise record of the movement of long-tailed salamanders in their winter home.

As its name implies, this species is distinguished by an abnormally long tail, often half again the length of the body. Its scientific name, as well as its tail, is long—*Eurycea longicauda longicauda*. At Mill Grove it is approaching the northern limit of its range, which extends just above the Pennsylvania line into New York. Adults usually measure from four to six and a quarter inches in length. The record for this species is seven and one-eighth inches. Nowhere else in the world are salamanders as varied and numerous as in the eastern United States. The Appalachian plateau is the world center of abundance for these shy and secretive creatures.

In only two places at Mill Grove, about a mile apart, are long-tailed salamanders known to spend the winter and reproduce. One is, as we have seen, the twin tunnels beside Mine Run. The other is in an artesian well whose clear, cold water flows from Triassic shale in the basement of Northwood's cottage. At the tunnels the creatures enter directly from the out-of-doors, but to reach the artesian well the procedure is not so simple. First the salamanders follow upstream a brooklet that descends for a quarter of a mile to Perkiomen Creek. Then they enter the lower end of a small iron pipe that, day and night the year around, carries away the overflow from the artesian spring. Fighting against the rush of the water, they work their way up this pipe for 100 feet. At its upper end they emerge into the covered concrete box sunk into the basement floor, within which the water of the spring wells up continually.

Back at the cottage we shed our sweaters and woolen gloves and earflap caps and descended to the well. But here, as at the tunnels, we saw no salamanders. We had arrived just too late. By early March the larvae and the adults have already begun spreading away from their winter quarters. To see them, I returned a few weeks earlier the following year. Then, as I leaned over the well, the beam of Northwood's flashlight ran along the concrete at the water's edge. One after another, it glinted on the moist, shining skins of half a dozen salamanders. Most of them clung to the rough interior of the well box just above the water line. One was almost hidden where it had squeezed itself into a crack in the concrete. Others were resting on stones or riding on the floating pieces of wood that, each autumn, Northwood places in the well. All were very thin. It had been months since they had eaten. Moreover, the females now had deposited all their eggs.

More than 100 of these gelatinous spheres, each about the size of a pea, were still unhatched in the well. Most were clinging to flat stones or to the undersides of floating bits of wood. At one place where a spray of fine, feathery box-elder rootlets, after reaching the well through a small crack in the concrete, swayed back and forth in the currents of the spring, a score or more of the globes were thickly strewn throughout the mass. I had arrived, I found, just in the nick of time. For, even as I bent closer, the most dramatic event of the salamander's winter was taking place. The eggs, one by one, were disappearing as the larvae hatched and swam away.

I fished one almost transparent egg from the spring and held it in the water cupped within my hand. Inside I could see the bowed form of the gilled, fishlike larva. It resembled a quarter moon. As I watched, the larva wriggled, the shell of the globe seemed to dissolve, and a new salamander was launched into its watery world.

Within the well, as soon as a larva hatched and swam away, it vanished. It became invisible against the darker bottom of the spring. On emerging from the egg, the hatching salamander is about three-quarters of an inch long. Before it disappears down the overflow pipe by early March, it has nearly doubled its size and has developed a yellowish tail.

The water in which salamander life begins in this artesian well remains, the year around, at almost a constant 50 degrees F. Like all cold-blooded creatures, salamanders are made less lively by cold and more active by warmth. When Northwood caught one adult in his hand and we were bending close to examine it, it warmed up in contact with his skin. In a sudden leap it sailed downward for a yard or more and splashed back into the water of the well.

About these soft-bodied, moist-skinned creatures there is a kind of helpless innocence and charm. They seem to have crept directly from the pages of Charles Kingsley's childhood classic, *The Water Babies*. And young salamanders are, in truth, water babies. With their tiny tufts of gills, they can live only under water. The air-breathing adults—usually found secreted in such places as under rotting logs or beneath streamside stones—also require moist conditions to survive. On several occasions Northwood has come upon the dry bodies of wanderers that have strayed from the well onto the concrete of the basement floor and, unable to return, have become desiccated and died.

In the main, salamanders avoid direct sunlight and tend to prefer cool to warm weather. They are often abroad at times of heavy mist and after thunderstorms. Some species are able to remain active even in icy water close to the freezing point. Although at first glance salamanders seem frail, defenseless, vulnerable to their foes, these creatures have endured for more than 100,000,000 years. Moreover, for them the loss of a leg or tail is no great matter. Unlike the higher animals, they grow another in its place.

Each winter the colony returns to the flowing well in the basement of the cottage. How did it become established? How did its annual migration up the brooklet and the long iron pipe commence? As Nellie and I sat with Northwood on that evening of our winter trip, we discussed these questions. His logical explanation was that the spring long antedated the cottage. The salamanders had been used to following the brooklet to its source and there laying their winter eggs. When the house was built and the iron pipe installed, they continued moving up against the flow until they reached the well.

While we talked, the barometer was falling. Later, when we returned from examining the elephant folio and the many other items of interest at the house where Audubon once lived, we walked down the lane in a rising wind. The thermometer was going down. Gale winds and heavy snow were predicted on the radio before we went to bed. When we awoke in the crepuscular light of a leaden dawn, we could see branches lashing in the wind and almost horizontal lines of snow being hurled past our bedroom window. A howling blizzard raged outside. The barometer continued to fall.

As we ate poached eggs and buttered toast for breakfast, we watched chickadees and tufted titmice being tossed about by the gusts at a feeding tray beyond the window. We debated what to do. The sensible thing was to stay put until the storm was over. But, as Audubon long ago observed: "Time is ever precious to the student of nature." The days of our winter trip were running out. The lane leading from the cottage was narrow and steep; the road it joined would be one of the last to be plowed out. We might be snowed in for days. If we could get out of the Pennsylvania hills onto the flat land of New Jersey, we could be sure of being able to go on as soon as the storm had ended. We looked out at the snow. Although it was building up fast, it was no more than a couple of inches deep. We should have a few hours. We decided in favor of the calculated risk. With considerable misgivings all around, we said goodbye to our friend. Then we headed our white car out into the white gale. When we looked back from the road, Audubon's first American home was already lost in the scudding snow.

On a gale-swept road where branches, here and there, were coming down, we skirted the open slopes of Valley Forge. The log cabins, replicas of those occupied by the Continental troops, were gray and indistinct in the storm. This was Valley Forge as the history books depict it. By the time we climbed the approach to the Pennsylvania Turnpike, the flakes were larger, the snowfall steadily increasing in density. On the elevated roadway the gale, sweeping out of the north, pounded us with redoubled violence. Our windshield wipers labored against the long gusts and the snow that battered the glass at a velocity of more than fifty-five miles an hour. Few other cars were on the highway. For long stretches we were alone in what Ralph Waldo Emerson referred to as "a tumultuous privacy of storm."

Only a few days before, in the changeable fortunes of winter weather, we had been escaping from the flood. Now we were creeping ahead, groping our way through a blinding blizzard. At times we could see no more than a few car lengths before us. All the highway signs were obliterated by snow. So we advanced for ten miles, twenty miles. When I felt my way into the snowed-in driveway of a turnpike filling station, an attendant, bundled up in a huge overcoat and a fur cap, red of face and with snow plastered to his eyebrows, materialized out of the storm. Electricity was off. All the main fuel pumps were out of commission. Only one, operated by a small gasoline-motor generator at the rear of the station, was functioning. Over a wide surrounding area, telephones and electric current had been knocked out by the gale. Trees were down along the side roads. Beyond the Delaware River bridge, the attendant told us, a fallen high tension line was blocking all traffic. His advice was to get out of the storm as soon as possible. Six miles ahead, just before the bridge, we would find a motel.

It took us nearly half an hour to creep those last six miles. All the time the blizzard closed tighter around us. Once, in the very heart of the gale, I glimpsed for an instant a crow hurtling on the wind across the highway and into the woods. By ten o'clock we were almost forty miles from Mill Grove. The Dela-

WHITE FOREST, its hills and hollows filled with drifted snow, forms a fairyland of midwinter beauty.

CHICKADEE perches on a birch stub with a seed in its bill. In the winter woods it is the spirit of good cheer.

ware lay just ahead. Suddenly, looming out of the storm on our right, rose a large, lighted motel sign. We took the first exit, turned the wrong way, groped about in sheets of wind-blown snow, found our lodgings and there, in safe harbor, settled down to wait out the storm.

All day the blizzard continued. From time to time we peered out to see the snow mounding up higher and higher on our car. Each time as we turned back we congratulated ourselves on all the things that might have happened that had not happened. Toward six o'clock that evening the wind slackened. The snow ceased, then began again. At nine o'clock we looked out for a last time. The sky was clearing.

TWENTY-SEVEN

THE WHITE FOREST

THE path of the blizzard receded behind us as we followed the long diagonal of the New Jersey Turnpike northward. The wind had sunk to a gentle breeze. The sun shone and the shadow of a slowly circling turkey vulture curved and recurved across the snow-covered fields. Once more, as we had done in following the spring north, we skimmed upward onto the Pulaski Skyway and rode toward New York amid the smoke and tinted chemical fumes of a maze of factories. But this time, instead of dipping into the Holland Tunnel and burrowing under the river to Manhattan, we turned up the west bank of the Hudson. We continued north toward the white, snow-filled forests of the Adirondacks.

We left behind the Passaic River. It recalled a day in spring when I had stood on the bank of that stream in the midst of a curious mineral-water boom with the derricks of well-drillers rising all about me. We left behind the turn-off to the Lincoln Tunnel. I rode on, remembering the hiss of air in the compression chamber and the chill damp of the dimly lit caissons when, to obtain material for a magazine article, I had gone down under the river with the sandhogs who were digging the tubes. We left behind a side road leading west into northern New Jersey. Somewhere along its length I could visualize a lake where, each year, the winter ice is put to work clearing the bed of unwanted waterweeds. In advance of freezing weather, the level of the water is lowered until the weeds are just covered.

Solid ice forms around them. Then the water level is suddenly raised. The ice floats, lifting the attached waterweeds and ripping out the root systems in a quick and economical clearing of the lake bottom.

The lake, the river, the turn-off, the skyscrapers of Manhattan all were far to our rear and we were winding our way among snow-mantled slopes in the highlands along the Hudson above Bear Mountain when we came once more to the highway we had encountered so often in our transcontinental travels—U.S. 6. We turned off and followed it inland for a dozen miles. This swing to the west was no aimless digression.

On each of our seasonal trips, some small book has been stowed away along with the little leather-bound volume of James Thomson's *The Seasons*, some book to pick up when we were in the mood, in which to read a few pages at a time, in varied places along the way. Once the book had been Robert Louis Stevenson's *Aes Triplex*. Another time it was Emily Dickinson's poems. On this occasion, through all the thousands of miles of winter, we had been accompanied by a pocket-sized, green-clad copy of a book first published in London in 1782. It was Hector St. John de Crevecoeur's *Letters From an American Farmer*.

We had read it little by little as we had crossed the continent, some pages at Imperial Beach at the foot of the Silver Strand, some on the desert at Indio, some by the Grand Canyon, some on the Gulf Coast, some beside the Mississippi, others in West Virginia after the flood. We had come to the last words of the last page while the blizzard swept its wild curtains of snow around us beside the Delaware.

When we read of any bit of ground that has meant so much to someone else—a Selborne or Walden, Sabine Farm or Slabsides—it arouses our special interest. We wish to see it ourselves. So we had turned aside on this March day to observe with our own eyes that pleasant land of hills and streams and valleys, of elms and sycamores and sugar maples that had formed the setting of Crevecoeur's enjoyment.

Born of an old Norman family near Caen, France, on January 31, 1735, the author had emigrated to America as a young man. He traveled widely, married Mehetable Tippit of Yonkers, and in 1769—six years before the Revolution—purchased Pine Hill Farm, about twenty miles west of the Hudson, near the present town of Chester, in Orange County, New York. There he spent his happiest years. His book, a record of that period, presents an idyllic account of the life of a pioneer farmer. It achieved wide circulation in Europe and played an important part in stimulating emigration to the New World. As the *Encyclopedia Britannica* points out, his volume was "perhaps the most delightful book of the American colonial period." St. Johnsbury, in Vermont, is named in his honor.

An inquisitive delight in the natural history of his surroundings forms an important element in Crevecoeur's book. He records his amazement at the multitudes of passenger pigeons that alighted in his woods. He looked forward to his annual outing, when he tracked down wild bees to hollow tree trunks in the forest. He set up birdhouses around his dwelling and, when winter came, scattered grain and chaff for quail in the protected angles of the fences, "the one to feed them, the other to prevent their tender feet from freezing to the earth." Once, near his hives, he tells us, he took 171 honeybees from the craw of a kingbird. He laid them all out on a blanket in the sun and was astonished to see fifty-four "return to life, lick themselves clean," and fly away.

It was mid-afternoon when we came over a rise on a side road northeast of Chester and stopped beside a line of sycamores that stand where Crevecoeur once lived. Behind them hills rise steeply in a rampart against storms from the north and northwest. Before them the ground slips downward into a wide valley extending away to the south and east. The changes since Crevecoeur's time, no doubt, are many. The old pines of Pine Hill Farm are gone. The road that passes the sycamores is hard-topped. On the far side of the valley cars and trucks race down the four-lane concrete of a superhighway. But the hills and the far horizon met our eyes that winter day just as, so often, they had met the eyes of the American Farmer when he was putting down on paper the words of the book for which he is remembered.

After a time we turned back and again followed the Hudson north with the white-robed Catskills, the "Wildcat Creek Mountains" of the Dutch settlers, on our left. The Indians gave them a better name: Mountains of the Sky. We rode the rest of that day and the next through mild, melting, springlike weather. We came to Albany and Glen Falls and Lake George. The mountains rose higher. The snows grew deeper. We were in James Fenimore Cooper country, the land of the Algonquins, when we turned west on a wide circle that carried us for nearly 200 miles through the white fairyland of the Adirondacks.

Sometimes our roads were icy, sometimes rough with frozen snow, sometimes strewn with heaves and potholes. But always they were passable. And always they were surrounded by the crystalline beauty of snow in the forest.

What wildflowers are to summer and tinted leaves to autumn, snow is to winter. It is the chief ingredient in the beauty of the months of cold. We saw it mantling the forest floor, sweeping down the troughs of the hollows, cresting over fallen trees, lifting in cone-shaped peaks above old stumps. Molded by the wind, it ran on, smooth and flowing and streamlined. Dense evergreens rose sheeted and ghostly, their twig-tips spread like fingers clad in thick white gloves, sometimes dripping with the glitter of small icicles. Where broken branches were entangled or tree trunks lay moldering, the snow mounded up into bizarre shapes that brought to mind the castles of gnomes and the galleries of fairies. They seemed nature's own illustrations for the pages of the Brothers Grimm. And everywhere, on these days of sunshine, shadow-patterns of twigs interlaced on the white expanse that sparkled and shimmered, bringing added light to the forest, dark and shaded in leafy midsummer.

The snows of the north country bring a winter-long succession of clean white pages on which are written, with paw prints and feather marks, a record of the activity of wildlife. We read these stories in snow as we advanced. Squirrel tracks linked tree to tree. Around an open hole in a frozen river we saw the lacework of paw prints left by a mink. A little later we came upon the larger tracks of an otter, extending like a chain from hole to hole along the rapids of a mountain stream. Again we read a story of the forest night where a fox had hunted. Its tracks wandered among fallen trees, twisting sharply this way and that. They left a visible trail that had been dictated by invisible scents, by the smell of small prey that reached the keen nose of the hunting predator.

Somewhere beyond Indian Lake we halted to watch a dark forest bird, a ruffed grouse, unhurriedly ascending a snowbank. It left behind the impressions of its winter feet. For each fall the toes of the grouse undergo a dramatic change. Comblike fringes develop along their sides, providing the bird with natural snowshoes for winter travel. These are molted when spring arrives. On more than one occasion I have seen such tracks curving away from a hole in a snowdrift where a grouse had taken shelter during a night of bitter cold or while a blizzard raged. When dawn broke or the storm ended, it had emerged again.

The efficiency of snow as an insulating medium has been demonstrated in numerous experiments. In one simple test a thermometer that stood at twenty-seven degrees below zero F. in the open air rose to twenty-four degrees above zero when it was buried only seven inches below the surface of a drift. A difference of fifty-one degrees was produced by a little more than half a foot of unpacked snow. In another experiment, when the air above a snowbank was thirty-two degrees below zero, the temperature one inch below the surface was one degree below zero and at one foot below the surface it was thirty-one degrees above zero. The grouse that dives into a snow-drift to spend the coldest nights of winter is instinctively taking advantage of the insulating efficiency of the snow.

In astronomical numbers, tiny cells or pockets hold the air within a blanket of snow. Men who have been buried deep in drifts have found ample air for breathing. It is this multitude of minute air spaces that gives snow an insulating efficiency two or three times that of loose sand. They almost eliminate the passage of heat. The warmth stored up in the earth in summer is thus lost less rapidly because of snow. It forms the jacket, the winter overcoat, of the northern earth. So important is it in preventing winterkill in vegetation, as well as in watering and fertilizing the land, that one of the oldest of the farm adages runs: "A year of snow, a year of plenty."

The same tiny air pockets that are responsible for making snow so effective as an insulating medium also deaden sounds. Like the small spaces within Fiberglas or rock wool, they trap the sound waves, reflecting them back and forth until their strength is dissipated and they are no longer audible. Even a thin blanket of snow, I am told, is likely to cause a blind man to lose his bearings on the most familiar city streets. It absorbs the sounds and deadens the echoes of his tapping cane upon which he depends for guidance.

The season of the year that finds the grouse walking over drifts on snowshoes also finds the fur-bearers of the forest clad in heavier coats. In a swift spurt of growth, as cold weather arrives, their pelts become thicker. Which wears the warmest coat? At the Canadian National Research Laboratory in Ottawa a few years ago, scientists tested the insulating properties of various kinds of fur. They compared the pelts of the red fox, the black bear, the white-footed mouse, the wolverine, the red squirrel, the hare, the wolf and the muskrat. Of all those tested, they found, it is the wolf that wears the warmest coat. Like the plumage of the ptarmigan, the fur of a number of animals becomes white in this season of white snow. It is then that "the weasel steals in silver suit, the rabbit runs in gray." But if the "rabbit" is the snowshoe or varying hare of the north, it too is clad in white.

"There's a certain slant of light on winter afternoons"—so runs a line in one of Emily Dickinson's poems. For us a magic light filled the woods on stretches of our road to Indian Lake and Blue Mountain Lake and Tupper Lake and Saranac Lake. It glittered on Niagaras of ice that poured as in stilled motion down the faces of cliffs. It swept across climbing pastures and around lonely farmhouses, each shut up like a snail in its white shell. It streamed along the winter aisles where the only sound was the hollow telegraphy of woodpeckers tapping on branches of the trees.

We had been traveling for hours amid such scenes when our road climbed and turned sharply where an ancient barn, weathered by at least a hundred mountain winters, leaned awry at the edge of an isolated hayfield. The nearer end had fallen away, revealing the hay stored within and the huge pegged and hand-hewn beams. We halted nearby. How many winter gales had pounded its roof and sides! What myriad mice that barn had sheltered in its time! How often had the fox and the weasel hunted there! A whole book could be written about the natural history of an old barn. Riding on among these snowclad Adirondacks, I recalled in vivid detail the barn I knew best in boyhood. I remembered it at Lone Oak, in the Indiana dunes, at winter milking time—an oasis, a shelter from wind and cold, where mice sometimes ran along the beams and gusts banged at the door and the smell of the kerosene lantern mingled with the odors of the loft and the stable.

As we continued our circle past Slim Pond and Panther Mountain, we encountered comparatively few birds. We passed crows scavenging along a river. Once we caught a glimpse of a dark robin appearing and disappearing among the snow-clad trees. Occasionally we heard the nasal calling of a nuthatch. But the most commonly seen bird of these winter woods was the black-capped chickadee. Small bands appeared at the edge of the road, trooping among the trees, darting from twig to twig, hanging upside down, bright eyes seeing all, little wings exploding them into sudden flight. Now and then, amid the "day-day-day" chorus of their calling, we heard the drawling, whistled "phoe-bee" note like the voice of coming spring. On the roughest days of winter, when life seems overwhelmed by storm and cold, watch a chickadee, observe its good cheer and take heart.

In recent years, ultrahigh-speed motion pictures have revealed a number of remarkable things about the activity of the familiar black-capped chickadee. Its wings beat with a frequency of about thirty times a second. This is approximately three-fourths the speed of wing movement of a ruby-throated hummingbird. When a chickadee is alarmed in mid-flight, it can begin altering its course of direction in the incredibly short time of three one-hundredths of a second. After strenuous exercise, the heart of this little bird may beat 1,000 times a minute. Even when it is asleep, the rate of its heartbeat is about 500 times a minute.

With the flame of its little life burning so intensely, how soon does the chickadee use up its store of energy? How long does it live? In one instance, a bird banded in Massachusetts lived under natural conditions for nine years, a span as great as that enjoyed by many far larger creatures. Not only is a chickadee able to inhabit varied types of woodland but it is more prolific than most songbirds. A chickadee lays from six to eight—sometimes ten—eggs. And in southern New England it may have two broods in a season.

We were nearing Saranac Lake when we came out of the

white forest to skirt a pond where ice cutters had been at work. The cakes, stacked along the shore, caught the light—glowing and green-tinted. Close by, a hairy woodpecker was bathing in the snow. It was tossing the light, dry flakes about as though it were in dust or water. Once I observed a blue jay on the snow-covered limb of a maple tree engage in a similar activity. Such midwinter bathing is but one of the uses that birds make of snow. Not infrequently it forms their drinking water. In the midst of a snowstorm I have seen cedar waxwings catch falling flakes in the manner of phoebes snapping summer insects from the air.

Winter is a time when many wild creatures are improvising, sustaining themselves by recourse to unusual fare. All through the Adirondacks, white-footed mice gnaw on the shed antlers of deer. *The Journal of Mammalogy*, some years ago, published the picture of a catsup bottle that some camper had left overwinter in a forest of northern Pennsylvania. Much of its surface was scarred and roughened by the teeth of a gnawing porcupine. As the glass of such bottles contains as much as 18 per cent soda, one scientist suggested that the animal may have been in search of alkali.

From time to time in our swing through the Adirondacks, we encountered signs proclaiming that we were in lands forever wild. In 1894, in a history-making step, the New York State Constitution was amended to provide permanent protection for the wilderness in vast areas of these forests and mountains.

After a night at Saranac Lake, we followed an eastward-turning road. Now skis were strapped to racks on top of almost all the cars we met. We were in a region famed for winter sports. Whiteface Mountain lifted its ski slope to our left. A little later the Olympic bobsled run was to our right. Soon afterwards our road twisted down in a long decline. With safety belts snapped tight, we seemed riding on a bobsled run of our own. In the deeper cuts, new signs appeared: "Fallen

Ice Zone." And high above us long scars on the mountain-sides recorded the paths of previous snowslides.

In such wild surroundings we followed an icy spur to a lonely farm set among white mountains. Its red clapboard house is now maintained as a shrine by the state. For here John Brown, the abolitionist, rested between efforts to free the slaves; here he lived from 1849 until his fatal raid on Harpers Ferry. Here, in a simple grave marked with a boulder, John Brown's body lies. On this March day, the surrounding prospect seemed aloof and wild. The winter mountains rose on all sides, like his spirit, austere and untamed.

One of our last memories of the Adirondacks in winter is of hundreds of chips scattered over the snow at the base of a large tree. The chisel bill of a pileated woodpecker had hewed in the trunk a deep rectangular groove. It revealed the hidden galleries of a colony of carpenter ants. Such dormant insects form the main winter food of this largest of our northern woodpeckers. These black ants also are relished by a variety of other creatures, including, in some instances, man. Lumberjacks on the upper peninsula of Michigan used to eat the insects as a preventive of scurvy. One Midwestern university professor was in the habit of nibbling on a few as a kind of pickup in late winter. I even remember seeing an advertisement for such ants packed in glass jars and offered for sale as a spring tonic.

A few years ago a scientific mystery in connection with the winter life of these ants was solved by a team of biochemists at the University of Minnesota. What keeps the tissues of the insects from freezing in subzero temperatures? The answer apparently is that their bodies contain the equivalent of the antifreeze used in automobile radiators. When cold weather arrives, the carpenter ants manufacture glycerol, a chemical closely resembling that used as the basis for a number of antifreeze preparations. During the period of its hibernation, one of these insects may contain as much as 10 per cent glycerol.

If the ant is brought into a warm room and becomes active, this antifreeze chemical disappears completely. If the insect is subjected to cold again, it quickly reappears. The glycerol is present in winter when it is needed; absent in summer, when it is not required.

TWENTY-EIGHT

SNOWFLAKE COUNTRY

WE stopped at the top of the hill. Outspread below us extended the wide lower valley of Lake Champlain. Beyond rose the Green Mountains, now white, lifting in a line of rounded summits like shining clouds low along the horizon. Our descent carried us into a land rich in history. Riding among apple orchards that ran up and over the lower hills, we passed Crown Point and Fort Ticonderoga. At the far end of Chimney Point Bridge, we entered Vermont, our first New England state. Now all the winter of the Pacific shore, the western deserts and mountains, the Gulf Coast, the Mississippi and Ohio valleys, the Appalachian highland and the Adirondacks lay behind us. Ahead remained the final days of the season drawing to its close in this northeastern corner of the land.

Among the drifts of the open fields, Vermont farmers were already spreading manure from their stables. Horned larks, and once a flock of more than a hundred redpolls, flew wildly down the road before us. Osier clumps, vividly red against the snow, rose above the ice of swampy tracts. The red of osier, the green of pine, the pale tan of winter leaves on sapling beeches, the blue of late afternoon shadows on the snow and the play of sunrise and sunset tintings across the mantled fields—such are the colors of a New England winter.

When, about noon, we reached the ice-locked marshes of the Dead Creek Waterfowl Sanctuary, I swung into a turnout beside the road. We sat in the winter sunshine eating our lunch. After a time, something white among the silvered branches of a distant dead tree caught Nellie's eye. We turned our glasses in that direction. The creature we saw magnified in the round windows of our binoculars had first tried its wings over the tundra of the Great Barrens of the far north. It was that large and striking bird of prey, a snowy owl.

It may have come south as far as 1,000 miles. Yet its movement was not a true migration. With warm plumage and feather "boots" that extend down over its legs and feet, a snowy owl is well adapted to withstand the arctic cold. It is scarcity of food that drives it south. Periodically the lemmings, the northern rodents on which it depends mainly for food, reach a low point in the cycle of their abundance and the white owls move down, invading the northern United States in search of other food. During the winter of 1945–1946, more than 13,000 snowy owls are known to have flown south from Canada.

In *Stray Feathers from a Bird Man's Desk*, Austin L. Rand tells of the Scotch factor at a Hudson's Bay Company post who was liberal with credit to the natives some years and who refused all credit in other years. He was watching the snowy owls. Their abundance meant that the lemmings—on which arctic foxes and other furbearers also depend for food—were at a peak and that the trappers would bring in a rich haul the following winter. Scientists who have studied the snowy owl on its nesting ground report that the birds lay twice as many eggs in years when lemmings are abundant as they do when they are scarce. During the breeding season these owls sometimes produce a loud sound by clapping their wings together.

When the white owl left its distant perch, we saw it move through the air with deliberate strokes of its broad wings. One of the largest of the owls, with a wingspread of as much as five feet, it is—like one of the smallest, the pygmy owl we saw in Arizona—a diurnal hunter. Its flight is smooth, noiseless, deceptively fast. A snowy owl has been seen overtaking and killing a wild duck in flight. One winter day, while riding with Allan and Helen Cruickshank among the low dunes on the south shore of Long Island, I saw one of these birds lift into the air beside the road. For two and a half miles it flew just ahead of the car. We watched the speedometer. Considering the headwind it was meeting, we calculated it was cruising along in easy flight with an air speed of more than fifty miles an hour.

This deceptive speed of the bird, with its unhurried wing beat, brought me what was probably my closest brush with blindness. I was standing at the far side of a large museum room while a photographer friend shot close-ups of a snowy owl that had been removed from a temporary cage before being released. Without warning the bird launched itself in my direction. It seemed at one end of the room one instant and a wing beat later passing above me. I snapped my head to one side. But the movement of the owl was quicker. As it swept by, before anchoring its claws in a roller shade at a window, it dropped one leg in passing and flicked with its needle-sharp talons a triangle of scratches on my cheek. One was no more than three-quarters of an inch from my left eye.

In the out-of-doors any relatively small object covered with fur attracts the attention of a snowy owl. On one occasion a bird darted down and gripped the fur glove worn by a farmer working in a field. Another time one of these birds dived on a waving raccoon tail that was attached to the radio antenna of an automobile. And in the far north, a startled trapper once had his fur cap snatched from his head by a snowy owl.

The dead tree and the white owl had been left a dozen miles behind when we halted to look up a long lane toward a yellow frame house just north of Ferrisburg. Here had lived and worked Rowland Evans Robinson, one of New England's famed nature and regional writers of the last half of the nineteenth century. Born in the village of Ferrisburg in 1833 and dying there in 1900, he achieved most of the work on which his reputation depends after he had become blind. We looked around at the magnificent scene that extended away in the March sunshine—the lake stretching its unbroken plain of white toward the west and the Adirondacks rising beyond. To lose the sense of sight in such surroundings, in a land so beautiful, seemed an even greater tragedy, as when a vibrant bird is blinded. How much more was lost by becoming blind *here!*

In the best of his nature books, such as *In New England Fields and Woods*, Robinson reflected the evolution from hunter to naturalist. At first he was "the sportsman-farmer." His gun and the game he killed played prominent roles in his nature sketches. But with the passing of time the appreciator became ascendant. We find him writing "A Plea for the Unprotected" and "A Century of Extermination" and entitling one of his last books *Hunting Without a Gun*.

"Back and forth across the land, in swift and sudden alternation," Robinson noted in one of his essays, "the March winds toss days of bitter cold and days of genial warmth. . ." As he had known it long ago, we were now experiencing the winter of northern Vermont. This was March, the month of continual change. The sunshine spread its brilliance across the white fields as we drove north from Ferrisburg. But before nightfall the wind had veered. The smell of snow was in the air. I remarked this fact to the waitress who served us in a restaurant at Essex Junction.

"Snow! " she exclaimed. "*Who wants it?* "

Well, children do. Skiers do. Artists do. Plants do. Many kinds of wildlife do. And on a farm less than fifteen miles away, beyond Jericho, under the shadow of Mt. Mansfield, a man had lived who took such passionate delight in it that he devoted virtually his entire life to snowflakes.

When we turned in that direction the following morning, our wheels rolled through a two-inch blanket of white that had descended in the night. Those two inches apparently

BLIZZARD SNOW plastered on trunks and branches
of a woods by the gale winds sweeping out of the north.

BIRD TRACKS in the snow. Tree sparrow, top left; crow, right. Lower left, quail; lower right, ruffed grouse.

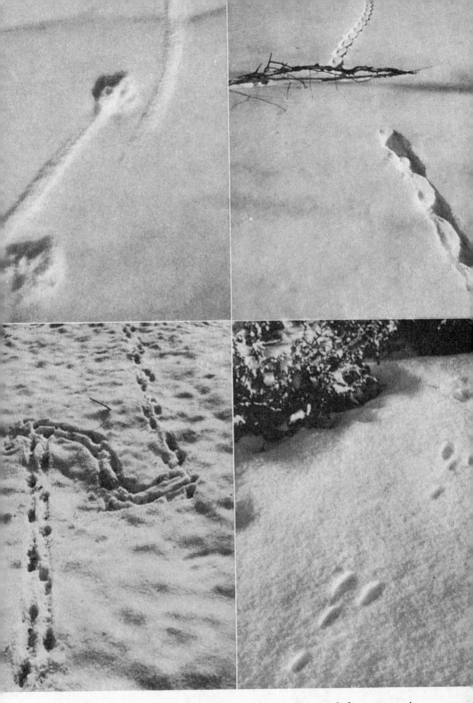

ANIMAL TRACKS in the snow. Opossum, top left; gray squirrel in soft snow, right; skunk, lower left; cottontail, lower right.

TRACKS across the snow left by white-footed mice among drifts covering juniper bushes on a hillside.

were part of a widespread snowfall. For when we switched on the radio we heard an announcer in Montreal, Canada, reporting a curious fact about the snow that had arrived there. In one part of the city, meteorologists had found, the snow contained four times as much water as it did in another part. The general rule is that it takes about ten inches of snow to equal one inch of rain. But flakes vary greatly. It requires only six inches of the large, soft and soggy snow that is usually called "goosefeathers" to be equivalent to an inch of rainfall. On the other hand, it may take a full thirty inches of dry and powdery flakes to equal one inch of rain.

Wildly beautiful was the snow-mantled scenery of northern Vermont through which we drove that day. Our road twisted among the hills. Then, with the highest of the Green Mountains lifting its white-topped bulk above us, the road straightened out and cut across level land. About a mile farther on, I turned into a drive leading to a farmhouse set among shade trees. We saw a design painted in white on a dark triangle under the eaves. We had reached "the house with the snowflake on it."

I think that among the men who have lived in my time one of those I regret most never having met is Wilson Alwyn Bentley, the farm boy who became world famous as the Snowflake Man of Jericho. The writer of the Book of Job asks the question: "Hast thou entered into the treasures of the snow?" No one has ever entered more fully into these treasures than the man who had lived under this roof in this remote section of Vermont. Although Bentley's education stopped at grade school, he was commissioned by the *Encyclopedia Britannica* to write its section on snow and frost. Although his camera equipment was restricted to the barest necessities, and his money was always limited, his immense collection of snowflake photographs remains unsurpassed.

One winter day, eleven years after he was born on February 9, 1865, his mother let him peer through a cheap microscope at the fragile beauty of a snowflake. That was the beginning of his lifelong delight in these frail crystalline creations of winter, so delicate that a breath will cause them to dissolve and disappear forever. In 1885, when he was twenty, his mother persuaded his farmer father to buy him a compound microscope and a heavy studio camera. They cost about $100. As long as he lived, his father looked back on this outlay as an unnecessary extravagance. But for almost half a century afterwards, as each winter arrived, this same cumbersome outfit was set up in an unheated shed to record on large glass plates the magnified images of snowflakes. Every storm, for Bentley, filled the whole sky with falling jewels. Make haste as he would, he could catch and photograph but a minute proportion of the infinite number of separate and distinct designs. He congratulated himself all his life on having been born in northern Vermont where the snows are frequent and the types of flakes particularly varied. Vermont winters are long, but they were never too long for Bentley.

The next best thing to meeting a person often is visiting the place where he has lived. When we were shown through the house where Bentley had spent his years, the occupant, Mrs. F. H. Monty, pointed out a heavy homemade tripod. She had found it in the attic where she had been busy sweeping up cluster flies when we arrived. These elongated insects are part of every north-country winter. According to the position of the mercury, they are attracted to or repelled by light. When autumn comes and the temperature falls below a certain point, the flies seek out darkened crannies. They squeeze themselves into buildings, particularly into the garrets of farmhouses. When the temperature rises inside the buildings, the insects are attracted to light and cluster on the inside of windowpanes; hence their common name. Although hundreds die, some survive through the winter, mate and produce larvae that are parasitic on earthworms.

Everyone I talked to who had known the Snowflake Man

described him as a quiet, gentle man, kindly by nature. His neighbors thought him a little queer, "chasing snowflakes in every storm." He was slight of build, only five feet, four inches tall, with a prominent New England nose. He never married. His was a poet's emotional response to the beauty of the snow. Long years afterwards he spoke with regret of one particular flake, one of the most beautiful he had ever seen, that broke before he could record its image. "But beauty vanishes, beauty passes, however rare, rare it be" and the snowflake is beauty in its most fleeting form. Its fragile ice shatters or melts away and no one will ever see its like again. Its design is lost forever.

Few flakes reach the ground in perfect condition. Often they bump or cling together in the air. Each descends according to its shape. Some spin, some drift, some slip sidewise. It was Bentley's habit, when a winter storm began, to stand at the door of the unheated shed, holding out a smooth board about a foot square and painted black. To prevent transmission of any heat from his mittened hands to the wood, he held the board by wire handles. Inside the shed, he examined the accumulated snow crystals through a magnifying glass, holding his breath as he did so. Damaged flakes were brushed away with a feather from a bird's wing. Perfect ones were transferred with extreme care to microscope slides. With the camera pointing toward a window, each picture was taken through the microscope with the light passing through the snowflake. A combination of wheels and ropes, formed from odds and ends, enabled Bentley to focus his unwieldly apparatus while watching the ground glass at the rear. There the images of the flakes appeared magnified from sixty-four to 3,600 times. Exposures were long, ranging between ten and 100 seconds. In this manner flake after flake was photographed during a storm.

Some of his finest photomicrographs were taken, three years after he had obtained his camera, during the famous blizzard of 1888. But of all the storms that he enjoyed, the one that brought him the greatest yield occurred forty years later, in February 1928. The snow began falling on February 9, his sixty-third birthday. Before it stopped he had added to his collection a hundred photographs of new snow crystals. He used to refer to them as a "birthday gift from kind winter." All of his glass plates, as soon as they were taken from the fixing bath, were washed in the ice-cold running water that flowed from a spring in his backyard.

Each delicate flake of snow that he photographed had the same beginning. It developed, as does a raindrop, about a nucleus. This might be a speck of dust or, in the case of the snowflake, a frozen cloud-droplet floating in the winter sky. Once started, the snow crystal continues to grow. By the addition of a vast number of infinitesimal particles of ice, it builds up to its final form. Meteorologists have calculated that a single snowflake may contain a million or more such ice particles. The diameter of a flake, when it reaches the earth, may vary from one one-hundredth to about one-quarter of an inch. Its thickness usually is about one-tenth of its width.

The design of each of these fragile creations records, in symbols of ice, the story if its birth and growth. And, as Bentley once wrote in an article contributed to the *Annual Summary of the Monthly Weather Bureau Review*: "Was ever life history written in more dainty or fairylike hieroglyphics?" At a glance Bentley could tell in what part of the sky a snowflake came into being. He divided the crystals into high-altitude and low-altitude flakes. The cold upper regions of the heavens produce the fine, dry snow so highly prized on ski slopes. It descends in small flakes, usually in the form of plates or prisms. But it is at lower elevations in the sky that the most beautiful designs are formed. There the flakes, feathery, star-shaped, drift downward through warmer and moister air. Rarely are such flakes created at sky temperatures much below zero. In fact, the heaviest snowfalls do not occur in the coldest weather. In the United States, they usually come at times when the thermometer stands between twenty-four and thirty degrees F. The record for the highest average annual snowfall in this country—575.1 inches—and the greatest amount of snow to fall in any one winter—1000.3 inches— both have been reported from the Paradise Ranger Station on Mt. Rainier, in Washington.

Through his lifework, Bentley preserved in his photomicrographs the forms of nearly 6,000 snow crystals. Nowhere else is the immense prodigality of nature's innovation more vividly demonstrated than in the production of these creations of ice. In his nearly fifty years of searching, Bentley never found two of them alike. It was his belief that each snowflake is unique, that nowhere else on earth would another be found that would be identical. Yet it has been calculated that in a ten-hour storm a million billion flakes may fall on a single acre of land.

The pictures Bentley recorded at this remote farmhouse among these winter hills have been used in college textbooks. They have appeared in illustrated periodicals in many parts of the world. They have been employed in teaching science and art. They have been included in encyclopedias. Artists turn to them for inspiration. Fifth Avenue jewelers base designs on them. They are found in leading museums in many lands. To Bentley they brought such honors as membership in the American Association for the Advancement of Science and a fellowship in the American Meteorological Society. His magnum opus, *Snow Crystals*, prepared in collaboration with Dr. W. J. Humphreys, of the U.S. Weather Bureau, contains more than 2,000 of his finest snowflake pictures. It appeared in 1931, in time for Bentley to see and enjoy this climax of his half-century-long labors. He died three weeks later, on December 23, 1931.

According to local tradition, the Bentley home, where we were shown one of two secret closets, was a station on the Underground Railroad that aided fugitive slaves in escaping to Canada. Here, in this quiet land nestled at the foot of the mountains, far removed from great cities, the Snowflake Man had contributed something of lasting value to the world. Even though his home is on a back road and not on a superhighway, it should be honored, as it is not now, by a state historical marker. For his life and work honored Vermont.

We drove away, turning east through the winter beauty of the state, winding among mountains surrounded by sparkling air and sparkling snow. We saw last year's bird nests mounded over with white and thought of all the thousands of separate flakes whose individual forms no one would ever see, ever know. We dined on salmon chowder. The human population seems to shrink in winter. People disappear indoors with the onset of cold weather. We traveled for a long time through wild scenery on a road that we had virtually all to ourselves. Then we came to one of the most incredible moments of the trip. On the edge of the village of Tunbridge, lost among the mountains, a sheriff halted us. For fifteen minutes we sat, no other person in sight, no other car coming down the road. Then a signal sounded. The practice air-raid alert in the village was over!

Not far from Bentley's home, we had seen our first sap buckets attached to the trunks of sugar maples. Now, as we followed the Connecticut River southward, they were all along the road. Once we passed a cow industriously licking the bark of a tree where maple sap had trickled down. We saw children sucking sweet icicles. This was March, a time of cold nights and warming days. Vermont's famed maple sap was running. The liquid harvest was in full swing. It promised for us another winter experience we had never known before.

TWENTY-NINE

NIGHT IN THE SUGARBUSH

THE path we followed in the frosty night ascended a slope of moonlit snow, vanished in the black shadows of a clump of evergreens, reappeared crossing the white glitter of another snowfield, and ended at the door of a long, low structure crouching beneath billowing clouds of steam that rose luminous in the moonlight. Five miles away Rudyard Kipling had written *The Jungle Book*. Two miles away John Kathan, the earliest settler in this part of the Connecticut River Valley, had encircled his cabin with a log stockade to ward off Indians. Half a mile away Murder Hollow Brook followed its deep gulch to join the river. Around us, in dark and immense columns, rose the trunks of ancient sugar maples. We were at Pine Grove Farm, south of Putney, in the oldest sugarbush in Vermont.

When we pushed open the door of the weathered building, warm, moist air swirled around us. We heard the roaring of a wood fire and another sound like the spatter of falling rain where maple sap bubbled in shallow pans. Two gasoline lanterns spread a diffused, watery light through the steam-filled interior. The humid air we breathed was sweet with the perfume of the boiling sap. For the first time in our lives we were in the midst of that fragrant annual rite that heralds the close of the New England winter and the coming of the New England spring—sugaring time, when maple sap is boiled down into the exquisitely flavored syrup that pioneers knew as "Indian molasses." Night in the sugarbush in a never-to-be-forgotten memory of winter in Vermont.

As we came in and closed the door behind us, a wiry man wearing a plaid cap and with his hands encased in thick leather gloves straightened up in the glare of the open firebox door. He was George Ranney, the owner of Pine Grove Farm. In quick succession he fed half a dozen four-foot lengths of wood into the flames. As a rule, he told us, it takes about five cords of wood to boil down 100 gallons of syrup. The most prized fuel for boiling sap is quick-burning slabs from a sawmill. But this year highway construction had provided free odds-and-ends wood that filled a large shed opening into the sugar house. The last stick to go in was an unusually crooked section of a tree limb. Ranney worked it inside among the flames and slammed the door.

"That," he remarked, "will straighten it out."

We had met him that afternoon when—to watch the gathering of the sap—we had driven down from Windmill Hill, west of Putney, with Edward H. Dodd, Jr. Ever since *Grassroot Jungles* days, more than a quarter of a century ago, "Tommy" Dodd and I have worked on books together. No other friend has opened so many doors going in the direction I wanted to go. As editor and later president of the century-and-a-quarter-old publishing house of Dodd, Mead & Company, he has played an all-important part in almost every manuscript I have produced. Where else, as in *Of Nature, Time and Teale*, has a publisher written a book about an author? On retiring early, when many kinds of life were open to him, he and his wife, Camille, had chosen the simple existence of the country year. Except for trips to the South Seas for a long-continuing study of Polynesian art, they make their home in the Vermont hills, at the end of a country road, in a house built in 1776. Over the years, in many ways, he has become one of the most admired of all my friends. Together we had planned the four American Seasons volumes and now, in the fourth and final journey, together we were riding on one of its adventures.

Up the slope of a ridge and over the top ran the great maples of the sugarbush. In the sunshine of the afternoon, we followed sled roads plowed through the snow and winding among the trees. We had arrived, on this bright March day, during the excitement of a sap run. The clear, shining liquid, the "sweet water" of the Indians, was falling drop by drop into more than 1,900 metal buckets hanging from metal spiles driven into shallow holes bored in the tree trunks. Ranney told us each bucket holds about sixteen quarts. When full, it weighs more than thirty pounds.

Several times I lifted one of the hinged metal lids that keep out rain, snow, animals and falling bark and watched a quick succession of drops form at the tip of the spile. When I timed them, I found they were forming and falling at the rate of more than one a second. During the heaviest runs, they follow one another so rapidly that 150—even, for short periods, 300 —have dropped into the buckets in a minute's time. A tree a foot in diameter may contribute thirty quarts of sap in twenty-four hours, and there are records of as much as eighty gallons of sap flowing from one taphole in a season. While the average seasonal yield of a mature sugar maple is about twelve gallons, the sap yield of exceptional individual trees has gone as high as 250 or 300 gallons. Where is the best place to tap a tree? That is a question endlessly debated in sugarbush country. On the south, or sunny, side; above the "instep" of a main root; on the lower side of a leaning tree; on the side where most branches grow and the bark is thickest—all these beliefs have staunch adherents.

Nellie and I caught some of the falling drops on our forefingers and licked them off. The sap was cold and refreshing, faintly but deliciously flavored. Draughts of this fluid allay the thirst of many a worker following his rounds among the trees. It may even, at times, provide a drink for weary horses. In pioneer times, when uncovered wooden buckets were used, it was a rule to hang them four feet above the ground. This kept deer and cows from drinking from them. When writing his classic *Sylva of North America*, François André Michaux noted: "Wild and domestic animals are inordinately fond of maple juice, and break through their enclosures to sate themselves; and when taken by them in large quantities it has an exhilarating effect upon their spirits."

From time to time we stepped aside to let a sturdy horse-drawn sled go by. On it rode a 1,000-gallon tank in which the sap is collected from the buckets and transported to a storage tank on the slope above the sugar house. On this same March day, all across New England and in New York and Pennsylvania and Michigan and north across the line in Canada, similar activity was in progress. As many as 20,000,000 sugar maples are tapped annually in this $50,000,000 winter's-end industry.

All maples have some sugar in their sap. But it is from the hard or rock maple, the true sugar maple, *Acer saccharum*, that the yield is sweetest and the flavor best. On the average, I was told, the sap of this tree contains about 3 per cent sugar. However individual trees run as low as one per cent or go as high as 12 per cent. For some unexplained reason, New Hampshire's famous sugar maple, "Sweet Sue," produces sap with three times the sugar content of that of similar trees that grow around it.

Not only from tree to tree and from grove to grove, but from run to run and year to year the richness of the sap varies widely. In a sugarbush of a hundred trees, John Burroughs once wrote, there is as wide a difference in the quantity and quality of the sap produced as among that number of cows in regard to the milk they yield. Sometimes thirty gallons of sap will produce a gallon of syrup; at other times fifty gallons of sap will be required.

"How sweet is the run today?" I asked Ranney.

He did a little calculating and found that, although the flow was copious, the sugar content was rather low. He was having to boil away forty-four drops of water to obtain one drop of syrup.

The sugar that contributes its sweetness to maple syrup is synthesized by the leaves in summer and stored in the root systems of the trees in winter. About the beginning of the present century, studies carried on in Vermont showed that the total yield of sugar by a tree is likely to be roughly proportional to the area of its summer leaves. One characteristic of the trunk of a sugar maple is an abnormal abundance of sapwood. The cross section of one of these trees a foot in diameter is likely to show a central column of heartwood hardly thicker than a man's thumb. It is this feature of the trunk that speeds up the flow of sap and aids the tree in carrying nutrients rapidly to its buds as spring approaches. Yet the precise manner in which that sap moves upward is still imperfectly understood.

But to New Englanders the rising of the maple sap each year is like a rising barometer. Their spirits lift with it. "Sap's running" and "sugarin' time" are words of good cheer. They usher in a harvest time, a time of sugar parties in the snow, a kind of festival of winter's end.

"How often do runs occur?" I wanted to know.

They may occur, Ranney told me, from the middle of February to the first of May. The richest and heaviest flows come when the temperature seesaws violently, when frosty nights are succeeded by brilliant days, when the weather seems to leap from spring back to winter, then to spring again. "Sap weather" is a series of freezing nights and sunny days with the temperature standing, roughly, at twenty degrees at night and rising to forty-five degrees at midday. The sap ceases running if the thermometer falls below thirty degrees or rises to about fifty degrees F. Usually the strongest flows are brief, lasting from two or three hours to a day at most. During a season there may be one run or a dozen runs or only "drizzles." The weather, not the date on the calendar, is important in stimulating a run of sap. Everything depends on the weather —and that, in New England, is proverbially unpredictable.

Yet it is because of this changeable climate, as well as its latitude and altitude, that New England and especially Vermont and New Hampshire provide the right conditions for strong runs of sap. When sugar maples were introduced from America into Europe, where the climate is more uniform, the changes less sudden and excessive, sap runs of importance failed to materialize. The sweet and deliciously flavored syrup of the sugar maple is a product of North America alone. The great sap runs that characterize the end of the New England winter are peculiar to the New World.

Some sugarbushes now employ a maze of plastic tubing, letting gravity transport the sap directly from the trees to the sugar house. In a few places, on steep slopes where collection is difficult, Ranney has installed such tubes. But they have their drawbacks. Squirrels and porcupines sometimes bite into them, as they do into maple twigs, to get to the sweet fluid flowing within.

America, as we had seen in our travels through the four seasons, is the land of beautiful trees. And one of the most handsome of all is the sugar maple. With the flame of its foliage it ushers in the winter, and with the sweetness of its sap it draws the winter to a close. Near the far edge of the sugarbush we came to two immense maples growing side by side. They were encircled by twin necklaces of buckets. I counted fifteen catching the sap of these two trees alone. The larger the tree, the more buckets it will support; the more open its surroundings and the more sunshine its foliage receives, the richer the sap is likely to be. For years, Ranney told me, he has been cutting hickory and butternut trees and weeding out the poorer maples to open up his sugarbush. The same taphole is never used a second time. The opening is filled in by the tree in four or five years.

Not far from the twin giants, we came upon the remnant

of another immense maple. It lifted its massive, shattered bulk, a gnarled and lichen-covered stub, to a height of perhaps forty feet. Its top had been carried away. Only the four lower branches remained. Great scars, made by the axes of pioneers in the crude early methods of tapping, extended as high as my head. Before the Revolution, this tree was producing a harvest of sweet sap. It is the last survivor of Vermont's first sugarbush.

The Indians, who had used such primitive means of obtaining sap as breaking off the end of a branch, had taught the men of the Massachusetts Bay Colony how to produce maple syrup. It is one of the oldest of America's agricultural products, made by the Pilgrims as early as 1723. Only forty-one years later, in 1764, John Kathan's son Alexander—who built a cabin in a clearing on what is now Pine Grove Farm and lived there to the age of ninety-five—tapped trees of the virgin forest and boiled down the sap in an iron kettle over an open fire in the first recorded instance of the making of maple syrup in the state.

It was Kathan's habit to make small notations after dates in his almanacs. In March 1803 he wrote: "What a sight of pigeons did fly all the 13th"; on March 5, 1804: "Sea two robins"; in February 1811: "Killed 110 rats in the corn house in one day"; on July 22, 1811: "Had new tatoes"; on April 5, 1781: "A man and a horse crossed the river on the ice." How such simple entries bring the long-ago past to life! Earlier, in his historic note set down on March 19, 1764, Kathan recorded: "Tapped trees. Made 21 pounds of molasses."

A century and a decade later, in 1874, twenty-three of the original trees of this pre-Revolutionary sugarbush still were standing. By 1924 only four were alive. Now only this single venerable stub of a tree remained. Its four branches still put forth leaves in spring. It still tenaciously clung to life. But we were seeing it in the last days of its long, long span of years.

But other trees, descendants of those ancient maples of the virgin forest, still supplied an abundant harvest of sap. We saw it boiling and bubbling in Ranney's sugar house when we returned that evening. We watched the clear liquid flowing by gravity from the storage tank higher up the slope into the first of a series of four shallow, slightly tilted and interconnected boiling pans. It came in as colorless fluid and was finally drained away as amber syrup.

Ranney called our attention to the corrugations that run the length of the pans to increase their heating efficiency. At the elevation of the sugar house, the sap boils at about 220 degrees F. As it boils, it is moved slowly by gravity from one to another of the interconnecting pans. We noticed how the bubbles forming across the surface of the boiling liquid were first white, then more and more yellow or amber-tinted as the gradual flow advanced from pan to pan. Ranney's rig will boil about six barrels of sap into syrup in an hour.

In the first unit, where the fluid is thinnest, the boiling is most violent. As we peered into it, the sound of the bubbling suddenly rose in volume. The seething contents of the pan mounted toward the rim. We stepped hastily backward. Ranney said:

"I'll take care of that."

He reached calmly for a small container of cream and poured in no more than a drop or two. Almost magically the rushing sound subsided into a steady murmur. The small addition of fat had broken the surface tension. A little white of egg or a piece of salt pork dipped into the boiling sap will produce the same result. In all, as it becomes thicker and darker, the sap travels thirty or forty feet, boiling its way from pan to pan, before it is drawn off as syrup. To produce maple sugar, the thickening fluid is stirred or beaten while the boiling continues.

At intervals Ranney drank milk from a vacuum bottle, and his son Robert refreshed himself with water from a canteen. Sometimes during the long days in the sugar house, they boil eggs in the sap. For the duration of sugaring time each year, workers around the boiling sap lose all desire for sweets.

"I notice," Ranney remarked, "that I always crave sour food, pickles and dishes with vinegar in them."

Apparently, sufficient sugar is obtained from the inhaled steam. In fact, at the end of a long day during the boiling of a sap run, workers often observe that their eyebrows and eyelashes have become sticky.

Hour after hour in the night, the crackle and roar of the fire, the drowsy sound of the bubbling sap continued. Often either Ranney or his son added wood to the fire. Occasionally a great gust struck the sugar house and drove down swirling clouds of steam through the long, rectangular openings where two hinged sections of the roof had been folded back on either side of the ridgepole. When heavy rain falls, boiling is suspended and these sections are closed. Otherwise, too much rainwater would reach the pans. Just before a storm, when the atmospheric pressure is lowered, Ranney has observed that the sap boils noticeably faster.

Helen and Scott Nearing, in *The Maple Sugar Book*, tell of a Vermont farmer who wore a pedometer during a busy day in his sugar house. At the end of seven hours he found he had taken 29,090 steps. Ranney and his son seemed always occupied. They kept constant track of the boiling sap. They fed the fire. There was rarely a lull in their activity. The final pan received the most frequent attention. There the syrup was checked with a hydrometer to determine if it had attained the desired density. A time-honored, rule-of-thumb test is to pour some of the syrup from a ladle; if it tends to thicken and form an "apron" along the edge, it is ready to remove from the pan.

We watched Ranney, before he packed the hot syrup into waiting containers, strain it through felt-and-flannel cones to remove the gritty residue, largely lime deposits, called sugar sand or niter. We watched him hold up a sample of the syrup and compare it with the tinted liquid in a series of glass vials, grading it according to color: Fancy, A, B or C. Then he poured the batch of syrup, still hot, into the sterilized containers in which it is sold. Packing it while hot insures against fermentation. Also, in cooling, the contents contract slightly, leaving a vacuum which permits the syrup to expand in hot weather during storage. The filled cans formed rows, and the rows lengthened. Held within each container was the rich sweetness, the delicate flavor that had been extracted amid these clouds of fragrant steam.

Returning home from a visit to the New World in the eighteenth century, an English traveler reported that farmers in Connecticut made it a rule to leave one sugar maple at the edge of every field so that "in the heat of midsummer the weary reaper could tap the trunk and obtain a cool and refreshing drink." Such arboreal soft-drink stands, of course, represent a humorous misconception. Usable sap no longer flows when the maples are in leaf. As soon as the buds begin to unfold, the fluid loses its sweetness and becomes viscid. If collected too late in the season, the sap produces syrup with an unpleasant, rather bitter "taste of buds." Especially prized by connoisseurs is syrup made from first-run sap. It has a delicate bouquet and flavor unequaled during the later runs.

It was late at night when Ranney banked the fire and ended the long day's work at the sugar house. The next morning he would have to rise at 2:30 A.M. to supervise the machines that milked his 120 cows. Then by nine he would commence boiling sap again. The harvest of the sugar maples has to be gathered when it comes or, as Ranney put it:

"When the sap runs, we boil sap. It's work that can't be spread out to a more convenient time."

As we descended the moonlit slope, with Ranney's collie Cinderella Boots racing about in the snow before us, I saw a few far-scattered lights—perhaps marking the location of other sugar houses—glimmering faintly among the dark New Hampshire hills across the river. I turned for a last look at the low building crouching under its thinning clouds of steam,

WHITE-FOOTED mouse peers from the entrance hole of a birdhouse which provides it with a snug winter home.

under its tall smokestack where a swarm of small sparks, like red fireflies, still whirled away to expire on the air or come down harmlessly on the snow.

Driving back to Windmill Hill along wooded roads, with a can of new-made syrup beside me, I noticed how my headlights picked out small, tan fluttering moths among the trees. According to an adage of the region, when "moth millers" become numerous, sugaring is almost over. In spite of the lateness of the hour when I went to bed, I lay awake a long time remembering all that I had seen. Never again would news that sap is running in New England be a mere item in a paper. Always now it would evoke memories of our experience, inerasable memories of the sights and sounds and smells of day and night in the sugarbush. Like the remembrance of the honking of wild geese flying north, they would form nostalgic links with the near approach of winter's end.

THIRTY

THE WITCH-HAZEL GATHERER

I REMEMBER once walking down a New York street on a summer day with an explorer from the American Museum of Natural History. He had just returned from nearly a year in the jungles of the Malay Archipelago. Suddenly he stopped on the sidewalk.

"By Jove!" he exclaimed. "A cobbler's shop! How long it seems since I smelled that smell before."

At the close of World War II, a hero of the Marines was welcomed home in western Pennsylvania. At one point when the parade of automobiles came to a halt, he leaped out and entered a corner building. His explanation was:

"I just wanted to smell a grocery store again."

Anthropologists have suggested that the brain may originally have been a smelling organ. Below the level of consciousness odors revive long-buried emotions and memories or, as Kipling expresses it: "Smells are surer than sounds or sights to make your heart-strings crack." Those vague, indefinable shifts of mood, those passing feelings of elation and depression for which we can find no plausible reason, may well be the products of faint scents and fragrances of which our minds are unaware. So profound and universal is the effect of odors on emotions that a Harvard scientist has suggested the possibility of devising a language based on smells to provide a means of communication in case inhabitants are discovered on other planets.

It is a common experience to have some passing scent bring to sudden, vivid life a whole period of the past. Odors are the great scene shifters on the stages of memory. I remember we had just turned east in southern California when, in one swift leap, for no apparent reason, I was in retrospect a small child again, wandering in an abandoned, weed-grown gravel pit. As we rode on I became aware of the smell of some dusty plant beside the California road, a nostalgic scent, an olfactory link with those former days. At Terre Haute, where we stopped on our way through Indiana, I stepped out into the winter night to get something from the car. I paused in the dark, breathing deeply, feeling that I had lived this moment before, lived it with the puffing of steam locomotives passing by. Then I realized that this leap through time, swifter than the speed of light, was the product of the odor of soft-coal smoke in the air, a scent that dominated winter nights when I was young.

In his *Adventures With a Texas Naturalist*, Roy Bedichek recalls how, as a young man, he used to pass a large produce house on his way to lunch. On each occasion, he was leaving behind disagreeable office routine and approaching the enjoyment of a meal. Always afterwards the smell of decaying vegetables revived in his mind a sense of pleasure. Napoleon said his memories of childhood were linked with the smell of the *maquis*, the dense scrub that covered much of Corsica. In a chill bedroom, with woolen blankets pulled up to his chin, Ralph Waldo Emerson first read the dialogues of Plato as a young man. Throughout his later life, he associated Plato with the smell of wool.

In their laboratories chemists have tracked down and translated into cold symbols the sources of even the most emotionally potent of smells. They have explored the world of odors and catalogued the varied chemicals that produce them. It is diacetyl that gives the odor to butter, ketene to the pickle barrel. The rich smell of plowed fields and spaded gardens in the spring arises from a chemical by-product given off by invisible bacteria in the soil. The scent of carnations and violets, of cedar and fir, of ripe apples and grapes, even the olfactory enchantment of fields of new-mown hay, misty in moonlight, has been traced to its chemical origin.

The source of the smell the scientists can pin down. The effect, the depth of the emotions stirred—who can measure this? The thing that I remember most vividly about the dedication of Henry Thoreau's statue at the Hall of Fame in New York, some years ago, is the sudden, nostalgic smell of rain on hot dust that rushed through the open windows of the crowded auditorium.

One New Year's Day, a friend of mine gave up smoking. When that spring came, and flowers returned, he was amazed at the new world of smell that opened up for him. In his years as a smoker he had been unaware of how much he had missed in the subtle variety of odors around him. His experience was reminiscent of William Wordsworth's "vision of paradise" when the poet sat in a flower garden after a temporary loss of the sense of smell. Man's ability to detect faint odors is poor at best. We can only dimly imagine the olfactory magnificence that surrounds the bloodhound and the fox. Among the four divisions of the year, winter is the most barren in scent. But even it—with its smell of snow in the air, its drifting woodsmoke, and, in its latter days in maple-syrup country, the redolence of sugaring time—has its olfactory pleasures.

On such things I reflected next day as we crossed the Connecticut River below Putney and cut at an angle downward through lower New Hampshire and into Massachusetts. We rode in thawing weather. At times, cars tore past us and went racing down the road with small winter rainbows glowing and flickering over sheets of muddy spray. They carried our minds back to all the rainbows we had seen in the four seasons—over the ocean off Bull's Island on the Carolina coast in the spring; over the Black Hills in South Dakota in summer; on the breaking waves of the Oregon coast in autumn; low above Aransas

Bay on our visit to the white cranes in winter.

Some places, like some people, make an instant and indelible impression. There are turns and barns and hillsides all over America that we have seen in our trips and that remain alive in our memories even though we have no idea where to place them on the map. Such a turn lies somewhere in the lower valley of the Connecticut. We came to it by a twisting course that carried us south and brought us to the river again almost 200 miles downstream from Pine Grove Farm and its historic sugarbush. A little farther on, where the flowing water had less than ten miles of its course still to run, we came to the outskirts of Essex, Connecticut. Suddenly we were back in a world of memorable odors. The air we breathed was filled with another richly evocative scent. It recalled things as dissimilar as sore muscles in boyhood and rain among the creosote bushes near White Sands. For we were approaching the plant of the E. E. Dickinson Company, the source of most of the world's supply of witch-hazel.

Long before the coming of the *Mayflower*, Indians boiled the wood of the witch-hazel to extract a fluid valued for relieving sore muscles. The Pilgrims learned about witch-hazel— as they had learned about syrup-making—from the red men. For generations, from Pilgrims to early settlers to modern times, this aromatic fluid has been employed as a household remedy for sprains, frostbite, bruises, wounds, burns and muscular stiffness. When I pulled in at the Dickinson office, I learned that it requires several million bottles of witch-hazel to meet the annual demand.

Out in the woods, on that March day, a dozen men were still following the ancient craft of witch-hazel gatherers. In the trade they are known as brushmen. The veteran of them all, I discovered, is Stanislaw Gula of my home village of Hampton, Connecticut. For more than thirty-five years he has been spending his winters in the woods—not as a hunter, not as a trapper, not as a lumberman, but as a collector of witch-hazel. He has supplied thousands of tons to the Essex plant. On a bright morning in a later March I accompanied him in this winter harvest.

We worked, that day, in a hundred-acre woods that ran over hills and down into lowland stretches. Hemlock and white pine and hickory were mixed with the dominant red maple. Underneath these larger trees, among the rocks and mossy logs and melting drifts of the woodland floor, rose sprawling clumps of witch-hazel. Their trunks, covered with speckled bark, leaned apart in crooked growth. A lack of symmetry is characteristic. For the witch-hazel is a botanical individualist. It is not linked with any special environment. It grows on dry slopes and hilltops as well as in wet and swampy woodlands. At times, the clumps appear singly and widely spaced; at other times, they cluster together like alders in a swale. Not infrequently a tract containing witch-hazel will be close to similar woodlands that hold none. Rarely can Gula predict where he will find it.

Each fall, before his winter work begins, he follows back roads for upwards of 500 miles in a search for likely stands. All told, he has ranged over 500 square miles in the hill country of northern Connecticut and across the line into Massachusetts. Owners of the land are paid so much a ton for cutting privileges.

My first surprise, that day, was the entire absence of the smell of witch-hazel. I had imagined that the woods would be redolent as the cutting progressed. But the operation was odorless. It is heat, during the steam distillation under partial vacuum at the factory, that brings out the aroma that had scented the air as we approached Essex. The cambium layer, not the sap, is the source of the soothing lotion.

Watching Gula move from clump to clump, I saw his short-handled axe rise and fall. Each slender trunk is severed in the same way. A downward gash into the yellow-green wood on one side near the base is followed by a reversal of the implement and a blow with the head of the axe that knocks the trunk free. In this way nicking the cutting edge on the numerous boulders of the rock-strewn woodland floor is avoided. For, as Gula explained:

"An axe can get old fast in this work."

Almost everything about the witch-hazel is a source of surprise. All during the flowering time of the year, spring and summer, it shows no signs of blooming. It is only after its own golden autumn leaves have fallen, only after the woods grow bare and winter cold is drawing near, in late October and November, that it proves itself an exception to all the rules. Then it bursts into bloom. Then its leafless limbs bear the feathery, golden clusters of the long-delayed flowers. In New England woods, the pussywillow stands at one end of the annual parade of tree-flowers and the witch-hazel—the last of all to bloom— at the other.

The four petals of its flowers extend outward like tiny shavings or ribbons of gold. On the same limbs the blooms may be both pistillate and staminate. Even after snow fills the northern woods, a few of the flowers still cling in place. On this March day, near the end of winter, I came upon two, shriveled and dry but still yellow in hue. Because of this endurance of its flowers, one common name bestowed upon the witch-hazel is "winterbloom."

About the time the flowers appear, the seed capsules that have slowly matured from the blooms of a year before are ready to provide another surprise. Within these rounded, blunt, woody capsules, the seeds are hard and polished and pointed like bullets. In moist weather the capsules remain tightly closed. But in the drier days of fall they suddenly split open. The constriction of the elastic, incurving lining forces the seeds out violently. They shoot away like slippery orange pips squeezed between a thumb and forefinger. This ejection is accompanied by a faint but audible report. A few days of dry, cold weather in late autumn will discharge the whole battery of these capsules. Many of them, empty and gaping, still clung to the branches in March. Several times when I have brought twigs of witch-hazel home from the woods in fall, the dryness of my room at night has triggered the little mortars of the capsules and I have been awakened by the sound of the seeds striking the walls and windows. In the woods they are fired in all directions, sometimes to distances as great as forty-five feet.

Throughout its range in the eastern half of the United States —as far south as Florida and as far west as eastern Minnesota —the witch-hazel, *Hamamelis virginiana*, is always angular and crooked in form. Early travelers mistook it for the witch-elm, or "wyche-hasill," of Old England. Gula has noticed that its development seems most crooked when the growth takes place beneath high trees. We visited one part of the woods where all the taller trees had been felled about two decades before. Here many of the witch-hazels were older than the second-growth trees around them. The shrubs were noticeably straighter, they grew closer together, and many rose to a height of eighteen or twenty feet.

It is only when the leaves are off the twigs that the witch-hazel can be harvested. Lotion made from branches that are in leaf has different characteristics and is considered unacceptable by the National Formulary of the Food and Drug Administration, which controls its manufacture. Gula works in the woods from November to April. He has gathered witch-hazel at twenty degrees below zero.

The green 1½-ton Ford truck that he uses to haul his harvest out of the woods was manufactured in 1931. Several people have offered to buy it as an antique. But he refuses to part with it. Its great advantage is its high chassis. Without difficulty it passes over stumps and rocks that would halt a lower, modern machine. Almost always he finds the remnants of some old woods road running through the area where he is working. Only a little clearing out makes it passable. With the truck laboring along such a road, he hauls a ton or more of witch-hazel from the woods on a good day. I saw the load rising higher, the sticks all pointing butt-forward with the tops to the rear. Outside the woods, they were run through an engine-driven chopper that noisily reduced them to short lengths for delivery to the factory. I noticed that every shred of grapevine was disentangled from the shrubs that Gula cut. The whole load must be pure witch-hazel. A single stick of spicebush or alder or black birch, cut by mistake, will contaminate an entire batch so that it must be discarded at the factory.

From the stubs that Gula leaves behind, new witch-hazel sprouts appear. His winter cutting does not kill the roots, but growth is slow. More than two decades may go by before the shrub reaches its former height. As I have been writing these pages, I have brought home from the woods that stretches to the south beyond our pond at Trail Wood part of an old witch-hazel trunk. Its four-inch cross section shows forty-one growth rings. This slowness of development has made it unprofitable to raise the shrubs as a commercial crop.

As we ate our lunch that noon, the witch-hazel gatherer recalled some of the wild creatures he had encountered in the woods. Once he looked up and saw a gray fox watching him intently over the top of a nearby stone wall. Ruffed grouse frequently burst from the underbrush and, when he is working in swampy woods late in the season, woodcock sometimes fly up almost at his feet. Half a dozen times deer have been pursued by dogs in woods where he has been working and twice does, heavy with fawns, have come close as though for protection. While he chased the dogs away, they stood panting, regaining their breath, without making any effort to go farther. One rested for nearly five minutes within a hundred feet of him before it moved away.

Probably the oddest form of life he encounters appears during midwinter thaws. Then the snow is sometimes patched with what looks like spilled gunpowder or moving dust. Each

tiny grain is a living insect, a snow flea or springtail, a creature, Thoreau wrote, "whose summer and prime of life is a
thaw in winter." So hardy are these minute creatures that
one species has been found inhabiting desolate glaciers in the
antarctic 6,000 feet above sea level. Besides its ability to survive under harsh conditions, the springtail is famed for its
curious form of locomotion. It moves about, not by walking
or flying but by catapulting itself into the air. Its slender,
spinelike tail is bent under its abdomen, then released suddenly. This hurls it in an arc through the air. During some
winter thaws, Gula has seen his footprints in the snow become
black from the myriad snow fleas that have fallen into the depressions.

The sky remained cloudless and the day became milder as
the harvest of witch-hazel continued. Sunshine streaked the
tree trunks and spotlighted the moss-covered logs wet with
melted snow. Bluebirds called along the edge of the woods.
And so the hours passed. This was another experience like the
day with the herb woman of Kite Hollow in the southern
Appalachians, like the day with the fern gatherers in the forests of Washington. As I followed the winding track of the
mossy road that led us out of the woods for a final time that
day, I stopped frequently to examine the winter buds. I ran
my fingers along the plump green buds of the sassafras; the
brown, twig-tip clusters of the oaks; the red-tinged buds of the
swamp maples; the slender, spearhead shapes of the beeches;
the blunt, velvety buds of the shagbark hickories. Within each,
folded and tucked and compressed like a packed parachute,
was the leaf of another summer. On this day when the feel of
winter's end was in the air, I reveled in the shape and texture
and promise of the winter buds.

A friend of mine once showed me a copy of Emerson's
essays that John Muir had carried during his wanderings
through the wilderness of the Sierra Nevada of California in
the 1870's. On the margins of many pages he had penciled

his own reflections after reading Emerson's words. Where Emerson wrote: "Nature is transcendental, exists primarily, necessarily, ever works and advances yet takes no thought for the morrow," Muir had underlined the last words and had written: "Are not buds and seeds thoughts for the morrow?"

As far as I could see up into the tallest trees, each twig held such thoughts for the morrow. Protected by waxy scales or tough, waterproof coverings, they had been unaffected by the roughest storms of winter. Slowly swelling, they stood ready, when the warmth of spring has come, to burst their shells and expand in sudden growth.

It is, in fact, during the early weeks of summer that trees do almost all their growing. Twigs lengthen, leaves unfold, new rings are added to the trunks. A tree does not continue increasing its size all summer. Even before the Fourth of July, in most cases, growth has virtually ceased. The warmest weeks of the year, the "harvest time" of the tree when its leaves are producing their greatest supply of food, are mainly devoted to the creation of the winter buds. From about the end of August—sometimes for as long as nine months—these buds remain almost unchanged. Like Sleeping Beauty of the fairy tale, awaiting release from a spell, they await the coming of spring. Then all through the woodlands come millions of silent explosions, millions of bursting buds. The leaves unfold and expand with the power of their inherent growth. All this would happen in a time that was drawing near, in the days succeeding winter's end. Then a few swift weeks pass and the activity is over. The trees are covered with outspread leaves. The work of the winter buds is finished.

THIRTY-ONE

GREAT SWAMP

W HEN we crossed the line into Rhode Island, about
eleven o'clock in the morning, we entered not only the
smallest but the most densely populated state in the Union.
Only one Rhode Islander in ten lives in the country. Nine-
tenths of the inhabitants are urban dwellers. Their state forms
one link in that vast "megalopolis" that now extends down the
eastern seaboard from southern New Hampshire to northern
Virginia. This constellation of towns and cities and suburban
developments represents one of the greatest concentrations of
population in the world. One-sixth of the inhabitants of the
United States live on less than 2 per cent of the land area.

Yet, paradoxically, when we came to a stop ten miles inland from the sea and a dozen miles east of the Connecticut
line, we found ourselves, even in this small state of many
people, surrounded by a scene of ancient wildness. Ten thousand years before, retreating glaciers had scooped out a shallow
bowl behind the curving line of their terminal moraine. This
ridge of higher ground is one segment of the great moraine
that forms the hills of the north shore of Long Island and the
headlands of Cape Cod. Blocking direct drainage to the coast,
impounding water in the shallow bowl, it created the historic
Great Swamp of southern Rhode Island, a 2,600-acre morass
that even today is the home of mink and deer and otter. Here,
on a winter Sunday in 1675, a Colonial army of 1,000 men
crossed the ice and surprised the island stronghold of the

Narragansett tribe. The three-hour massacre that followed, called the Great Swamp Fight, played an important part in ending the Indian uprising known as King Philip's War.

On that December day, the morass had been frozen solid. On this March morning, nearly three centuries later, the ice was gone, the snow was melted. Our swampy road seemed overarched by a swampy sky—moisture-laden, filled with a fine, cold drift of mizzling rain. We pulled aside and ate our lunch, watching the trunks of the red maples grow darker, the green of the lichens brighter, watching moisture gather on the brown of the dead bracken, on the early silver of pussy-willows, on the red berries and the shining, pointed leaves of the American holly, here near the northern limit of its range.

As we sat there, gazing about at the rain-washed scene, visualizing the summer lushness of the wild gardens of the swamp, first vaguely, then more sharply, there took shape in the background of my memory the image of an artificial vine spreading its artificial twigs and its artificial leaves across the ceiling of a banquet room in a New York hotel. Under that spectacular decoration I once addressed a meeting of eastern horticulturists. Speaker after speaker before me talked of formal gardens and new insecticides. They emphasized that a garden is "something *you* have created," a fiercely personal achievement, a victory over undisciplined nature, a bringing of order in a world of disorder. Then I, like some Man from Mars arrived on earth by mistake, arose as a representative of the weeds, one with a kind word to say for insects. The consideration shown me was great, but I still recall the puzzled look in many eyes. Cultivated flowers I enjoy. But wildflowers, weed flowers, unplanted, untended, growing in their natural setting, making their way without benefit of rakes or hoes or DDT— these I enjoy better.

Among the multitudinous wild plants that made up the flora of the swamp around us, one seemed best able of all to make its own way, to extend its range and hold its own. It rose in

dense stands along the muddy road we followed. We had encountered it all across America. It is familiar to Europe and
Asia as well as to the New World. This is that primitive and
remarkable plant, the cat-tail.

Frayed by the winds of winter, bedraggled in the rain, the
cat-tails of the Great Swamp rose above the matted pale-tan
mass of the last year's leaves. As many as 300,000 seeds are
packed into one head, sufficient to plant a dense new stand
over six acres of marsh. Individual seeds are so minute that it
takes nearly 100,000 to weigh an ounce. To each are attached
from forty to sixty slender hairs. They form the parachute
on an air-borne journey that may carry a seed for a few feet or
for hundreds of miles. As an acre of cat-tails often contains
80,000 seed-heads, such a stand alone may send forth as many
as 24,000,000,000 seeds in an annual aerial distribution that
has spread the species wherever the habitat is suitable. In
the open spaces of the West we had come upon small isolated
pools edged with these far-flung plants, often fifty or a hundred
miles from the nearest other cat-tails.

Beneath these many-seeded plants, rhizomes push out in all
directions. They form an interlacing mat of roots from which
other plants arise. As many as thirty-five new shoots may spring
up around a cat-tail plant in a single growing season. It has
been calculated that in some instances more than an acre of
cat-tails may be judged to be one gigantic plant. Beneath an
acre stand of such plants there may lie as much as 140 tons of
starch-filled roots. The Indians, who employed the leaves of
the cat-tail for weaving mats, its fluff for lining moccasins and
the pollen for making cakes that were considered a special
delicacy, harvested the roots as a vegetable crop. The white
man, who quickly adopted the red man's maize, has never
seriously turned to cat-tails as a source of food. Yet the dried
roots produce a palatable flour, rich in starch and containing
approximately the same amount of protein as rice or corn flour.
An acre of cat-tails will yield about three tons of such flour.

As we came out beside one stand of the dry and yellow plants, the air was filled with sounds of spring. A flock of male red-winged blackbirds, arrived in advance of the females to stake out nesting territories, whirled into the air. Irrepressible, unaffected by the chill or the drifting rain, the scarlet of their epaulets brilliant even in the dull light of that sodden day, they heralded the approach of spring with their ringing "Okale-e-e-e!"

Below them, silent and hidden, still lost in hibernation, another form of life lay in snug retreat deep within the soft down of the cat-tail heads. This was a minute, pale-yellow overwintering caterpillar. In the warmth of spring, it would awaken, spin a white silken cocoon and transform into a tan-colored moth with a wingspread of only a quarter of an inch. Wherever cat-tails grow, you find this tiny moth, *Lymnoecia phragmitella*. It lays its eggs on the flowers, and the larva feeds on the tissues of the plant. Both in immature and adult form, the whole life of this insect is associated with cat-tails.

In other parts of the Great Swamp, that rainy day, we encountered the plundered hiding places of two less fortunate overwintering insects. On higher ground, at one edge of the morass, we saw where a round gall on a goldenrod had been cut open by the chisel bill of a downy woodpecker. The insect occupant was gone. A little later, we came upon the large silken cocoon of a cecropia moth. It stood out against the rich green of nearby rhododendrons. As we drove past, we saw that it had been torn open and rifled. Was this, too, the work of the downy's bill? We backed up and looked more closely. A woodpecker attacks such a cocoon from the front. Here the silk gaped open at the bottom. This tear was the handiwork not of a bird's bill but of the little teeth of a white-footed mouse.

Throughout the swamp, as throughout America, such large-eyed, soft-furred, big-eared mice, sometimes called country mice or vesper mice or wood mice, fill a niche in many habitats. Wherever we had traveled in the four seasons, there had almost always been a white-footed or deer mouse. No other North American mammal is found over so wide an area. In varied species such mice range from the Great Barrens of upper Canada as far south as Panama. They embrace the golden mouse of the Okefenokee Swamp and the gray piñon mouse of the dry Southwest. In California, white-footed mice are encountered two miles high in the mountains and 200 feet below sea level in Death Valley.

Arrested in the beam of a flashlight, the nocturnal white-foot, with its great black eyes and its long, sensitive whiskers, presents an appealing picture of shy, wild charm. Timid and gentle under ordinary circumstances, the mother white-foot is brave when her young are endangered. On several occasions, when I have accidentally uncovered a nest, I have seen the mother mouse overcome her panic and wait until all the baby mice had attached themselves to her body. Only then did she run away, dragging the litter to safety.

Like the chipmunk and red squirrel, this provident mouse stores up nuts and seeds for winter use. It leaves its signature on each nut it opens by gnawing into the shell from opposite sides. Many of the stores laid up are never used, for the mortality of mice is great. The white-foot is one of the chief prey species of the continent. Because, unlike the meadow mouse that tunnels under the snow, it runs over the drifts, it is often caught by owls. Sometimes in midwinter the pellets of these birds contain nothing but the bones and fur of such mice. The only "singing mouse" I have ever encountered was a white-foot. Ordinarily the sounds produced by these small rodents range from a squeak to a high-pitched buzz. This musical mouse would repeat over and over a sustained and melodious trill.

For these home-loving creatures, the area of their activity is usually only 100 or 200 feet across. However they possess an excellent sense of orientation. In tests, individuals have found their way home from distances as great as a mile and a half. Home, for them, may represent a wide variety of places. Readily able to climb trees and bushes, they sometimes install themselves in abandoned woodpecker holes. Often in the woods I have come upon some low bird nest, such as that of a catbird, and found it mounded over with shredded leaves and bark to provide a snug home for a white-footed mouse within. In the Great Swamp, the nesting boxes put out for wood ducks provide a windfall for the home-hunting mice when winter comes. Each spring, field men of the Rhode Island Division of Fish and Game, which maintains the swamp as a sanctuary, have to clear out the grass and bark and vegetable fibers carried in by the mice. This is particularly true in the northern portion of the swamp where white cedar predominates.

It is in this area that the white-tailed deer congregate in years when the snow is deep. During the especially severe winter of 1947–48, the Rhode Island animals "yarded" here as deer do in the forests of Maine, trampling down runways and feeding areas that gave them solid footing amid the drifts. To visit a snowbound deer yard deep in the woods of northern Maine had long been a dream of ours. Now, in these last days of our winter adventure, that hope was nearing realization. North of Moose River, close to the Canadian line, we were to travel to one through a forest where snow lay four feet deep, riding on the caterpillar treads of a Weasel, a surplus army vehicle designed for arctic use. Toward this far-off destination we turned when we left the Great Swamp behind.

Soon we also left the rain behind. In the sunshine of a March thaw, we came to Walden Pond and Concord where, a century ago, Ralph Waldo Emerson wrote: "The inhabitants of cities supposed that the country landscape is pleasant only half the year. I please myself with the graces of the winter scenery and believe that we are as much touched by it as by the genial influences of summer." In the sunshine of the same widespread thaw, we reached the Massachusetts coast and saw the open

Atlantic rolling beyond the wave-lashed rocks of Cape Ann. There we watched old squaw and red-necked grebes and European cormorants with those choice companions, John and Margaret Kieran. But mercurial March was back with a flurry of snow when we drove north from Rockport in the morning.

Now we traveled colder roads leading to a colder region. But winter cold, the enemy of the easy life, is not the enemy of all life. Scientists have demonstrated, in fact, that it is essential to the proper development of many buds and seeds and insect eggs. In order to sprout, some seeds require months of cold just as they do days of warmth in spring. Unless they are subjected to cold, the eggs of the tent caterpillar and the Rocky Mountain locust fail to hatch. Many apple trees need from 900 to 1,000 hours below forty-five degrees F. to break their rest period. If the tree is not exposed to that amount of cold, the buds fail to open properly when spring arrives. Blossom buds on numerous fruit trees require less cold than do leaf buds. Hence, the blossoms open before the leaves unfold. Even mammals may require cold for their welfare. The collared lemming and arctic fox of the far north are unable to live much below the Arctic Circle. In one experiment, a lemming died of heat prostration at an air temperature of only seventy-seven degrees F.

It was ten-thirty in the morning when we crossed the Piscataqua River into Maine, that last state of our long, wandering journey through the fourth season, the state where our winter would end. Snow now rose so high on the center strip of the turnpike that we could see only the tops of cars moving in the other direction. Over Nonesuch River and under the bridge of Cat Mousam Road, we paralleled the coast. Then, beyond Portland, we turned inland, up the map, on the long run north to the forested top of the state.

In sharp little vignettes winter scenes along the way return in memory: white birches bent like drawn bows under their weight of snow; icicles, formed in a high wind, tilting in the same direction all down the edge of a cabin roof; an expanse of sproutland stretching away like a cotton field with every bush holding up small boll-like masses of fluffy snow; the winding chains of snowshoe tracks leading from lonely cabins into the forest; and always, as we advanced, long vistas of snowfields and woodland and pointed evergreens. Late in the day, the shadows of the trees all lay blue on the white snow. I remembered E. B. White's observation: "I am always humbled by the infinite ingenuity of the Lord, who can make a red barn cast a blue shadow."

Near the end of his life, Henry Thoreau wrote to his Bangor relative, George Thatcher: "I should like to see those woods and lakes and rivers in midwinter, sometime." For him that sometime never came. We were more fortunate. We, too, had seen Maine only in summer; we had visited it in winter only in imagination. Now it lay around us in all the variety of its mantle of white. This was the beautiful winter of Maine.

Up the Arnold Trail and through Skowhegan we followed the turnings of the ice-and-snow-covered Kennebec. Scavenging crows and herring gulls, with now and then a black-backed gull, turned above the wide, white river as it wound through the white landscape. Once, where open water tumbled along a rapids, we pulled to a halt and watched half a dozen female golden-eyes diving among the ice floes or drifting sidewise in the swift current. Now farmhouses and barns and sheds were all linked together—a design for north-country living in a time of winter winds and high-piled snow. We passed one barn with an open door revealing a deep-freeze and a cat curled up in the straw sleeping in the sunshine. The sun had climbed far since that December day beside the Silver Strand. The cloudless sky was almost azure. To look at the snow-covered ground was to be in winter, but to look at the sky was to be in spring. The grip of winter was surely lessening. All over New England these days, people talked of the nearness of spring.

But when we drove into Solon the drifts beside the road were eight feet high. We advanced as in a deep white groove. Years before, I had spent a day in Solon with Charles Holway, the famous snowshoe designer of upper Maine. In a little shed attached to the rear of his house he produced special shoes to individual specifications, shoes that carried woodsmen, trappers, game wardens and timber cruisers through the winter wilderness. So pleased had he been with the magazine feature I wrote about him that he had sent me a pair of his timber-cruiser shoes. They rode with us now in the trunk of the car.

At Bingham we were half way between the equator and the pole. Beyond we entered what is always for us romantic country—lumber-camp country, big-game country, snowshoe country, the great northern forest. Mountains of pulpwood logs appeared on the river ice, awaiting the breakup of spring to be carried downstream. We came to the log cabins of the Canadian Trail Camps, now deep in snow on the shore of Wyman Lake. A flood of memories came rushing back. There we had spent our vacations summer after summer before the war, with our son, David, sharing the wilderness with us. For miles beyond, we were in familiar country in an unfamiliar season. There was Carney Brook, and there was the trail we had followed long ago when we spent a week in a trapper's cabin deep in the forest, and there was the path along which Bruce Gilbert, the Maine guide, had led me on a camping trip to a remote beaver bog. All along the way, that day, he had lopped off an overhanging branch here, clipped off a sapling there. Beside the campfire that evening he explained:

"I aim to leave the trail a little better than I find it."

I was snapped awake from these remembrances by a near tragedy on the ice of the river below. Scattered across it were small wooden shacks in which men were fishing through the ice. Suddenly two men tumbled from one and raced away. Behind them the whole building disappeared in a mass of rolling flames. Apparently their oil stove had exploded and they had escaped just in time.

Somewhere beyond Caratunk we came to a large and ancient white pine, a friend of ours that we had stopped to see on many summer days. We halted now to inspect it in a different season. Beneath its boughs, a fine drift of rust-red needles lay on the snow. But when we glanced up, we saw rising above us, rank on rank, the green of the living foliage. The secret of the winter greenness of pine and spruce and other conifers lies in the toughness of the surface of the needle-leaves, giving greater protection to the chlorophyll within. While each needle of a pine is sliverlike in form, presenting but a small surface to the sun, the cumulative effect is great. The total surface area of the needles of a white pine may be fifteen times the area which its extended boughs overshadow.

When the highway that carried us northward beyond the pine was constructed in the nineteen-thirties, blasting operations exposed unusual mineral deposits in small caverns in a cliff near The Forks, where the Dead River joins the Kennebec. Each cavern contained powdered hematite, or red ocher, the same material that is found in the graves of the mysterious Red Paint People who once inhabited Maine. Under their stone cairns the burial places of these prehistoric men invariably have yielded this material, sometimes less than two quarts, sometimes as much as a bushel. In such far-distant parts of the world as France and Australia, other paleolithic graves have also contained the powdered hematite. Anthropologists believe that the red ocher was employed in primitive burial customs because its color suggests blood, the symbol of life.

The Forty Mile Woods, with its Enchanted Pond, Shutdown Mountain, Cold Stream and Bean Bog, stretched northward beyond The Forks. We crossed a height of land where all the evergreens glittered with frost and snow. A sign beside the road read: "Motorists Caution. Fifteen Miles of Deer Crossings."

"I don't see any tracks," Nellie said.

And no deer tracks were anywhere in the great Maine forest that day except in the widely spaced yards where the deep snow was packed into solid footing. In the wilder country, as we advanced, the rise and fall of our highway took on increased amplitude. Ahead rose mountains blanketed in snow, like the Never-Summer Mountains of Colorado.

Late in the afternoon, down a long last descent through the snow-filled forest, we came to Jackman and Moose River. The Canadian border cut through the wilderness hardly a dozen miles to the north. We looked at the winter world of forest and frozen pond and evergreen-clad mountainside about us. Somewhere out there lay the deer yard we would visit. We wondered where. In the morning we would know.

THIRTY-TWO

THE DEER YARD

THE Weasel squatted at the edge of the forest, its two tons of metal resting on wide caterpillar treads. We walked around it, the snow squeaking under our feet in the near-zero weather. Eight solid wheels, revolving in line, turned each endless tread. The rectangular, steel-walled box of the body, ten feet long and five wide, extended over the treads and rose almost as high as my chest. Above it a metal framework supported a roof and side curtains of thick brown canvas. Everything about this awkward-appearing vehicle was heavy, ponderous, rugged. It had been designed for use by the U.S. Army in the far north, in Greenland and Iceland and Alaska. But it could roll over mud and shifting sand as well as over snow. Weasels had lumbered across the soft volcanic dust on Iwo Jima. We looked at the vehicle before us, its faded red paint scuffed and scratched, and wondered what service it had seen.

After the war, Henry Duquette, owner of a Jackman restaurant, had purchased the Weasel as army surplus for winter travel in the forest. No matter how deep the snow, it rolls over the top, packing it down with its treads, making its own road as it advances. Such a road would carry us into the snow-filled forest to a deer yard that Tilford McAllister, game warden in the Jackman region, had been observing that winter. West of Moose River, beyond Gander Brook, near Burnt Jacket Mountain, it occupied a cedar—or arbor-vitae—swamp extending along the shore of a forest-rimmed lake about five miles away.

Duquette, a mild-mannered, soft-spoken man, took his place behind the steering levers and gearshifts of the driver's seat. He looked ahead through the heavy glass of the windshield. At his right, a panel of instruments ran along the metal housing that enclosed the engine, a ninety-five-horsepower Studebaker Champion. Bearpaw snowshoes, ready for walking out of the woods in an emergency, occupied a rack overhead. He switched on the ignition and stepped on the starter. The motor ground, volleyed, settled into a steady roar as it warmed up. Nellie and McAllister and I clambered into the rear where three bucket seats were ranged side by side across the metal body of the Weasel. Ahead of us I saw our lunch and a large vacuum bottle full of hot coffee braced in the midst of a jumble of snowshoes and odds and ends.

With a metallic clatter of treads, we backed, swung about almost in the length of the machine, and charged a six-foot wall of ice and snow beside the road. The Weasel reared upward, then leveled off and headed away across an open stretch of snow that funneled into the winding white ribbon of an old logging road. Clouds of fine surface snow swirled up on either side. I looked back. Wide, twin, parallel tracks extended away behind us across the white surface. The treads were sinking a foot into the snow. This is about as far as they ever go, no matter how deep the drifts beneath them.

The top speed of a Weasel is between twelve and fifteen miles an hour. Its cruising speed is five. The engine consumes a gallon of gasoline every three miles. On the twenty-four gallons in its fuel tank, the machine can run for eight hours and cover approximately seventy miles. Except for the vibration and chatter of the machinery, we traveled smoothly over our highway of snow. We crossed Gander Brook, locked in ice. All around stretched an uninhabited winter wilderness.

Ahead of us to the west, hardly six miles away now, the

Canadian boundary dipped down through the forest. To our left lay Little Big Wood Pond and to our right, less than three miles off as the raven flies, Crocker Pond with its cluster of quiet log cabins where we had spent our vacations after each of the seasonal books was finished. This was the country of Sandy Stream and Slidedown Mountain. We knew it well, but only in summer dress. Off there in the forest there had been a lumber camp we had once visited where lumberjacks, wolfing down their noon meal, chose the food they desired— one heaping up his plate with nothing but boiled potatoes, another mounding his high with doughnuts drowned in maple syrup.

In the winter of 1913, Slidedown Mountain received its name. Toward the end of the season days of rain and days of cold alternated. Water repeatedly froze in the age-old cracks in the cliffs, expanding by one-eleventh of its volume and exerting a pressure of 2,000 pounds to the square inch. This pressure mounted as the mercury fell. At eight degrees below zero the force exerted on the rock was 34,000 pounds to the square inch. Under the terrific leverage of this repeated thawing and freezing, the whole weakened mountainside fell away. With an earth-shaking roar that brought people out of their houses in Jackman, ten miles away, hundreds of thousands of tons of rock let go. The first visitors to the spot found the sheer wall of a new-formed cliff, hundreds of feet high, with a quarter-mile jumble of great blocks of gray rock below. One August day, at the end of a trail through the forest, Nellie and I had come out among this titanic rubble. Some of the blocks were as large as a good-sized room.

All day, all night, the week before our Weasel ride to the deer yard, snow had fallen. Fourteen inches piled up on the drifts already covering the forest floor. Everywhere we went, our treads unrolled the first man-made tracks on this virgin snow. No human being had been this way before us. No snowshoes had left their telltale marks on the new drifts.

Only the tracks of wild creatures of the forest were imprinted on its surface.

The most common tracks we saw were those of the snowshoe hare. Able to make tremendous leaps and attain speeds as high as twenty-five miles an hour, these forest dwellers have two other advantages in their winter living. They can run lightly over the drifts. Wide-spreading toes on their hind feet form their snowshoes. Their alternate name—varying hare—refers to the second advantage. When winter comes the animal changes from brown to white. To see a snowshoe "rabbit" suddenly bolt away in the midwinter woods is like seeing a small portion of a drift disengage itself and go bounding off. Now, in the month of March, the hares had reached their breeding season. Later, unlike baby cottontails, the precocious young would arrive in the world fully furred and with their eyes open. The growth that would follow is so rapid that in eight days their body weight would double, in twelve it would triple and by the end of the first month they would weigh nine times their weight at birth.

At intervals among the tracks of the hares there ran the dainty, in-line pawprints of a fox. And more than once along the logging road we came to cat crossings, places where the large furry paws of wildcats had left a trail across the snow. That autumn, when a deer was killed on the highway, McAllister had dragged it to a clearing in the forest. For a long time wildcats fed on the carcass. Two had remained in the vicinity all winter. That larger cat, the Canada lynx, is no longer seen in this part of Maine. On this day, wherever we went, no animal had stirred without writing the story of its activity on the surface of the drifts. Snow is the great revealer. It cannot keep a secret. All through the woods around us it was filled with the gossip of the night. For most of the creatures whose tracks we saw are nocturnal.

As we advanced deeper into the forest, travel grew rougher. The Weasel reared and plunged, yawing, slewing suddenly sidewise as we rode over large obstacles in the way. But this machine was made to travel over rocks if need be. We had been riding for about an hour when we came to a forest hunting cabin, half buried in snow. Ahead we saw a stand of cedars. We were at the edge of the deer yard. Duquette swung the Weasel around in a pivoting turn, heading back the way we had come. Beside the cabin he cut off the ignition. The sound of the motor, the clatter of the treads ceased. Instantly the great silence of the forest rushed in upon us.

"Haven't we scared everything within miles?" I asked McAllister as we unloaded the snowshoes.

"No. That's a curious thing. Deer have become so used to power saws and logging trucks that they are less frightened by mechanical sounds than by the sight of a single man walking silently in the woods. In fact, where lumbering is going on, the sound of the power saws seems to attract them. They come to feed at night on lichen in the tops of the felled trees."

McAllister told us he had been born in Solon. As a boy he had lived next door to Charles Holway, and the snowshoes he had used for fifteen years, wearing out four rawhide webbings, had been specially designed for him. The ones we buckled on Nellie's feet were long and slender, pickerel snowshoes. In his Jackman hardware store Harry Sopp—who with his wife, Ann, have been friends of long standing—first fitted her out with bearpaws. Then he decided that Ann's pickerel snowshoes would suit her better. The choice was right. For, although never on snowshoes before, Nellie got along amazingly well. McAllister broke trail and we started off.

For nearly a mile the cedar swamp followed the shore of the lake. It extended back into the forest about half a mile. It was here the deer had yarded. Each year, as soon as the snow begins to pile up in the north woods, these animals gather into bands—usually from six to thirty—and, choosing some area protected from the cold winds and provided with such food as twigs, bark, tree lichens and evergreen boughs, settle down for the winter. Most frequently cedar swamps are selected. In soft snow, the small feet of the deer provide little support. Individual animals flounder, almost helpless, in deep drifts. By banding together, trampling down the snow to a solid footing, they are able to get about, escape their enemies and reach food until spring releases them. Then the groups disband and scatter through the forest. How long they remain in their winter quarters depends upon the severity of the season. During mild winters, the deer may be confined to their yards for only a few weeks; during severe ones, they may remain there for three or four months.

Since that March day I have asked many friends what they thought a Maine deer yard is like. Most have described—what I had assumed and several books in my library imply—a large area trampled down as cattle pack down the snow in a barn-yard. But wherever we went among the cedar trees, nowhere did we come upon such a scene. Instead we found ourselves in the midst of a maze of narrow, winding, interconnecting trails. Each was merely a rut in the snow only a few inches wide and perhaps a foot and a half deep. Traveling single file along such trails, the animals walked on solid footing. Sometimes large concentrations of deer do trample down half an acre of snow and produce paths "as wide as Main Street." But most often a deer yard is comprised entirely of such a network of narrow trails. Even when a band is starving, the animals rarely make any effort to reach additional food by breaking new paths through the surrounding drifts.

Taking our time, walking over the top of the snow—sometimes with Nellie along, sometimes, on the more rugged slopes, McAllister and I alone—we followed the trails of the deer yard. They led us beside the pond, over rolling hills, along a nameless forest brook. One path ended where this stream fell over rocks in a tumbling rapids. Here deer had come to drink. At another point along the course of the brook, the animals had used their sharp fore-hoofs to break a hole through relatively thin ice. Like birds, deer can also obtain water by eating snow. Along each path twigs were nipped off as far as the animals could reach. Even after the snow is gone in spring, the interconnecting trails of such a yard must be clearly evident, blazed by the browsing of the deer.

"How big was the biggest yard you've seen?" I asked McAllister.

"One I remember," he replied, "was three miles long. It covered about one and a half square miles of woods."

In any given forest, the number of yards tends to vary from year to year. As a general rule, the heavier the snow, the smaller the yard and the greater the concentration of animals in it. In the White Mountain National Forest of New Hampshire, some years ago, field biologists studied twenty deer yards. Their areas ranged from one to 1,000 acres. Some were temporary, some had been used for a decade or more. In New Hampshire, as well as in Maine, the twigs of the cedar provide a principal source of food. Sometimes in summer, while paddling across a forest pond bordered by a cedar swamp, McAllister has noticed how deer in previous winters have browsed as far as they could reach while standing on their hind legs. The result has been an almost ruler-straight line running along the lower branches of the trees.

As the morning advanced, the weather grew milder. Snow no longer squeaked beneath our feet. This sound, produced by the sharp edges of the frozen crystals rubbing together, fades away when the thermometer rises and the crystal edges become less solid, more easily blunted. Surrounded by the brilliance of the sunshine, we were once more, as we had been in the Adirondacks, in a white and shining forest. "In the range of inorganic nature," John Ruskin once wrote, "I doubt if any object can be found more perfectly beautiful than a fresh new snowdrift, seen under warm light." Snow mirrors back as much as 90 per cent of bright sunshine. All the hills and glades of the forest, the edge of the pond, the cedar swamp and its maze of trails, were filled with this reflected light.

As our snowshoes carried us over the drifts, around fallen trees, beside stumps crowned with high peaks of snow like inverted ice-cream cones, past outstretched branches that seemed as hard as iron, we noticed in several places where the deer had walked beneath tilted tree trunks that stretched no more than two or two and a half feet above their trails. Sunk in these narrow ruts, with their chests level with or below the surface of the snow, they passed with ease under such obstructions. Four or five times beside the trails we discovered round or oval depressions in the snow. They were about a foot deep and roughly the size of a dishpan. Here deer had slept. The animals seem to have no special places for resting and sleeping in a deer yard. They lie down wherever fancy dictates. The same place apparently is not used a second time. The heat of the animal's body melts the snow in contact with it and leaves the bowllike depression lined with ice, making it unsuitable for later use.

When we returned to the cabin about noon, Duquette had a fire going in the pot-bellied stove. Lunch was ready. And we were ready for lunch. By then our 6 A.M. breakfast of pancakes and maple syrup seemed an event of the remote past. As we ate roast beef sandwiches and doughnuts and drank hot coffee, Duquette reported that while we were away he had measured the depth of the snow. On the level it was four feet deep. The greatest depth either he or McAllister could recall was seven feet.

We were buckling on our snowshoes again when the ringing sound of chopping, as though some lone woodsman were wielding an axe, came from the deer yard. A few minutes later, as we came over a rise, there was a flash of red and black and white and a bird as big as a crow disappeared among the trees. This was the woodchopper—a pileated woodpecker. We came to the stump where it had been excavating a deep rectangular hole in a search for carpenter ants. Spreading in a wide apron around its base lay a bushel or more of yellow chips.

Wherever we went along the meandering trails we were
alert for the sight of a deer. Once, as I rested beside a fallen
tree at the top of a slope, listening intently, I heard a snorting
in the woods beyond. But whichever way we turned, the deer
melted away before us, moving off down their interconnecting
trails. They were warned of our approach by whispers of sound
caught by their great, uplifted ears, by faint scents detected
by their sensitive nostrils, by subtle changes in the tempo of
forest life. In one part of the deer yard, a red squirrel unwound
its sputtering, barking monologue each time we came near.
Chickadees, the state bird of Maine, greeted us with drawling
"phoe-be" notes and followed us from tree to tree along the
trails. Rarely were we beyond the sound of the calling of the
red-breasted nuthatch and once we heard the sweet chatter of
crossbills among the evergreens.

In the afternoon, the still air that had hung over the forest
all morning began to move. The breeze freshened, became a
wind. The trees around us were filled with long creaking and
sudden rushing sounds. Meteorologists who have studied the
effect of woodland on wind velocity have found that 1,000
feet inside a forest the speed of the moving air is reduced 90
per cent. They have also determined that the effectiveness of
deciduous trees as a brake upon the wind is decreased as much
as 40 per cent when the boughs are bare in winter.

As we were heading back toward the cabin and neared the
edge of the swamp where it meets the pond, we felt the
strength of the wind increase. It swept toward us unhindered
over the wide snow-covered expanse beyond. Once, McAllister
recalled, he had been fishing through a hole in the ice on this
pond when an otter went loping past him over the snow, paying hardly any attention to his motionless form. Rushing
through the trees, the long gusts came in quick succession.
They drowned out all sounds of our approach as we drew near
the shore. Our scent was whirled away behind us. It was thus,

without giving warning, that we came upon the deer.

They were sunning themselves at the edge of the trees, a doe and a buck. Bucks may, or may not, yard with the does during winter; in this instance they had. The two deer stood side by side. Their coats shone in the sun, their heads were held high. The winter had been relatively mild, and the animals had come through it in excellent condition. When we first caught sight of them, they were looking intently out across the pond. Their graceful forms, their uplifted ears, stood out against the immaculate whiteness of the level snow beyond. For perhaps two minutes they remained motionless. Then the buck swung his head in our direction. Some slight movement may have caught his eye, for with a great bound he whirled toward the trees. The doe followed. In three or four leaps, made with the grace characteristic of the deer family, they gained the woods and disappeared. On a previous visit, at this same spot, McAllister had watched a single-file parade of five deer following the edge of the pond.

Ahead of us, as the Weasel clattered its way back along the trail and out of the woods, every clearing was swept by luminous sheets of windblown snow. Already the deep tracks we had made coming in were disappearing. At the edge of the forest where we had started, we tilted down the snowbank, flattened out and came to a stop. We had seen the winter deer yard. And we had seen more. We had seen the beauty of the Maine forest in its season of snow. Bidding our companions good-bye, Nellie and I turned south toward the rocky headlands of the coast. Of all those roaming days of freedom that had stretched across the continent before us when we had left Death Valley, less than a week now remained.

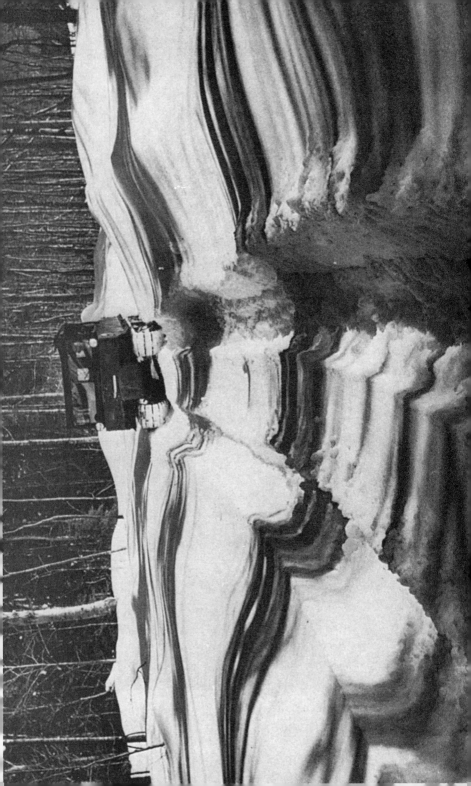

DEER-YARD trail winds among trees in the Maine forest. A maze of such paths interconnects to form the yard.

THIRTY-THREE

COAST OF THE HIGH TIDES

WHERE the Maine coast meets the winter sea in a boundary-line of rock and ice, the shore is pierced by innumerable coves and inlets. It abounds in points and promontories. It is fringed with chains of rocky islets. So convoluted and broken is it that although the air-line distance, from Kittery on the south to Calais on the north, is only 225 miles, the length of the coastline is more than ten times that distance, 2,379 miles. This is almost twice the length of the shore line of California.

This was the coast we followed north in the final days of the final season. Nosing out onto promontories and curving around arms of the sea, we progressed along a shore armored with rock. Both geographically and scenically we were at the opposite extreme from the flat, sandy, sunny beach of the Silver Strand. There we had looked out on the silky swells of the early-winter sea. Here, where great tides rose and fell and where combers exploded and shattered in foam against the cliffs, it was the late-winter sea we observed in action. The four-foot snows of Moose River had been left far behind. In the milder climate and the saltier air of the coast, the white blanket covering the open fields was at most a few inches thick.

Somewhere in his writings, Maurice Maeterlinck maintains that: "The best part of traveling is the before and the after, the least pleasant is the traveling itself." But not for us on these journeys with the seasons. From beginning to end, it was the present moment, the present scene, the present beauty, the present interest that absorbed us. We experienced and enjoyed the hours as they came.

And never had the gift of the days seemed sweeter than in these closing hours of our long adventure. At times we resembled a child with an ice cream cone that is almost gone. We appeared trying to save every minute as we followed this winter coast that is known to millions of visitors only in summer months. When we spanned the Kennebec at Bath, we rode above ice cakes floating downstream to the sea. Beyond we veered south on a side road that carried us for nearly a dozen miles down a series of islands connected by bridges until we reached the village of Georgetown.

Half a dozen years before I had received a letter postmarked: "Georgetown, Me." It came from Josephine Newman, a woman nearly eighty years of age, a remarkable naturalist who lived alone in a 200-year-old farmhouse on a wooded promontory nearly surrounded by the salt water of Robinhood Cove. She had, she wrote, just come in from following on snowshoes the miles of trails through her woods. More than a hundred times chickadees, and several times red-breasted nuthatches, had alighted on her hands and shoulders while she fed them sunflower seeds. "In order to save my 400 acres for nature study," she explained, "I have to sacrifice nearly everything else in my life. I snowshoe to the well for water and I am writing this note by kerosene lamplight while I wait to turn on my battery radio to listen to the Secretary of State." Her absorbing interest in nature began when, as a young teacher, she had walked three miles each way to a stone schoolhouse in the Maine woods.

We found the deeply-shaded lane that climbs among evergreens to her house. It was clogged with drifts and imprinted with the tracks of snowshoes. Pulling on high-topped leather boots, Nellie and I plowed up the hill. The woman who answered our knock at the double-Christian doors of the old house was five feet, two inches tall. She weighed about 100 pounds. She had slipped into her constant companion in the woods, a thirty-five-year-old jacket with long yellow fur. It was this jacket that the chickadees recognized. Of all the people we met from the Silver Strand to Caribou, few, if any, seemed enjoying life so much as Josephine Newman. She chopped wood for her kitchen range and, in summer, raised vegetables in the garden behind the house. Still active and energetic in her eightieth year, she skated, ran like a deer and scooted over the drifts on her snowshoes like a waterstrider on a summer pond.

Where the light of one window fell upon it, we saw a worn brass microscope, shiny from years of use. Peering through its eyepiece, Mrs. Newman has carried on a long study of the mosses of her region. Her hobby has added a new species of the genus *Pseudisothecium* to the list for Maine. At the Boston Flower Show one year, she received a bronze medal for her exhibit of native mosses.

"People talk about my being all alone up here," she said as we walked toward the edge of Robinhood Cove. "But I never feel alone. When I feel alone is when I am among many people, none of whom shares any of my interests. Then I really am alone."

Among the rocks of the cove, where the icy surf was pounding, she pointed out a dense, many-branched seaweed, reddish-purple in hue. This was Irish moss or carrageen, *Chondrus crispus*. Each year along the Maine coast, tens of thousands of tons of this marine alga are collected. When boiled, it swells and dissolves and produces a jelly that absorbs from twenty to thirty times its weight in water. This gelatine when dried is used in soups and desserts, in cosmetics and shoe polish, in curing leather and sizing cloth. Some years ago, Mrs. Newman heard that the men engaged in the rough work of collecting the carrageen rarely have cracked or chapped hands. She put a boilerful of the Irish moss on her kitchen range and cooked it into a gelatinous mass. Straining off the jelly, she added a little coloring and a dash of perfume to overcome the rank sea-smell and then put it up in odd bottles as a remarkably effective skin softener. When, with regret, we parted company at the end of our stay, she presented Nellie with a bottle of the green-tinted lotion. Carefully packing it away in the car, we turned north once more and continued up the coast.

Everywhere the sea dominated the land. Its influence was reflected in such place-names as Head Tide and Starboard. Near its mouth, we crossed the Penobscot, a river born in the north woods near Sandy Stream. We passed snowmen melting in village yards, redpolls seed-hunting among the alders, logging trucks bouncing along, mud-spattered and decorated with necklaces of tire chains draped over their front bumpers. On our right, toward the sea, we saw the snow-covered bulk of Mt. Cadillac, rising to a height of 1,532 feet in the Acadia National Park, the highest point on the Atlantic coast north of Brazil.

All this we saw in the light of lengthening days. The sunset that had brought to a close that short December afternoon along the Silver Strand had ended a period of sunshine only nine hours and forty-eight minutes long. At Bitter Lake, the home of the cranes, sunrise and sunset were ten hours and ten minutes apart. By the time we reached the Vermont sugarbush, the period had extended to eleven hours and thirty-nine minutes. Here along the Maine coast we were nearing the time when day and night would be equal and then, as spring advanced, when the days would be longer than the nights.

One old New England custom I had read about as a boy was having mince pie for breakfast. We decided that for once in our lives, when we came to Maine, we would do as the New Englanders do. But we found the New Englanders no longer do it. Pie for breakfast seemed unheard-of. So we contented ourselves with what no doubt was a better diet, an old-fashioned lobster supper at a restaurant beside a cove. While we ate, a woman at another table observed to her companion:

"She never seems to realize that as you get older your circle keeps getting smaller."

We ate on and as we dipped bits of lobster into melted butter we ran over in retrospect varied things we had overheard in restaurants along the way, fragments of conversations, not infrequently compressed expressions of human attitudes and experience.

In a California town: "Christmas is the worst time in all the year when you are poor."

Among the foothills of the Rockies: "The view *is* beautiful but my wife keeps telling me: 'You can't eat the view'."

On the Texas coast: "I know people hate him. But one time he explained it all to me. He said: 'This is what I was faced with: Would I have a lot of friends or half a million dollars?' "

Near Cherryfield, while crossing the Narraguagus River, we looked to the north and saw a large bird with stiffly outspread wings soaring in wide circles over the woods and open fields. Even without our glasses we perceived its head and tail were white. It was a mature bald eagle, a bird we had last seen 1,200 miles away, where the Illinois River joins the Mississippi. Later, from a restaurant overlooking the bay on the main street of Machias, we sighted a second eagle—or, possibly, this same bird—descending in a long curving glide to the top of a distant tree. I pointed it out to the waitress. Her immediate reaction was:

"Is that a sign of spring?"

All along this northern coast, thoughts of the new season were uppermost in everyone's mind. Its arrival was now hardly more than forty-eight hours away. When tomorrow had become yesterday, winter would be gone. Everywhere we went, as we advanced up the coast, we saw news of spring published by pussywillows shining above the snow, by later sunsets, by children playing ball and skipping rope in schoolyards. The owner of a filling station remarked, as a sign of the season, that there appeared to be more cars on the road—or, as he put it, "more cahs on the rudd."

This same highway that we followed, in the spring of 1833 had carried John James Audubon by carriage and mail coach to Eastport and the beginning of his voyage to Labrador. Along this route, in another season of the year, more than a century and a quarter later, we passed the turnoff to a community with the picturesque name of Meddybemps. Better a thousand times, to my way of thinking, a Meddybemps or a Cat Mousam Road than all the stereotyped "News" of the New World, than all those innumerable New Viennas and New Berlins and New Lisbons that are so familiar to our maps.

Another side road wandered off in the opposite direction. It led toward the scene of a curious event of natural-history interest that had occurred some years before. The story was related to us by a man we talked to along the way. Near the end of summer in 1931, he recalled, he had visited his friend, the keeper of the lighthouse on Petit Manan. In the twilight, as he stepped into his boat to leave the island, he glanced up. The lighthouse light was out. At that time, the lamp used a mantle and burned liquid fuel. Hurrying to the top of the tower, he and his friend found the mantle shattered. Beside it they saw the singed body of a monarch butterfly. When the lamp was burning again, they counted 127 other monarchs within the top of the octagonal tower. All had squeezed inside through the one-inch louvers that ventilated the light. Massed together on the outside of the tower clung thousands of additional monarchs. On the mainland these insects often collect for the night in immense numbers on "butterfly trees." Here, on this small offshore island, they had collected instead on a "butterfly lighthouse." The keeper, later on, often speculated on what officials at the regional office in Boston had thought when they received his report that the Petit Manan light had been off on such and such a date for so many minutes—extinguished by a butterfly.

Near the top of the coast, on our way to Eastport, we dipped into the valley of the Dennys River. Under ancient elms on the farther slope, a large yellow house caught our eye. Under its roof had lived Thomas Lincoln, the adventurous young man who had accompanied Audubon to Labrador. Ten thousand miles and more away—as we had traveled—beside the Sonoita River, on the Mexican border at Patagonia, we had seen the handsome little Lincoln's sparrow that had been named in his honor.

As we had progressed north along the Atlantic coast, we had seen the range of the tides increase. At Baltimore, Maryland, on Chesapeake Bay, the average range between high and low water had been only one foot, one inch. At New York City, it was four feet, five inches; at Portland, Maine, eight feet, eleven inches. When we circled Carryingplace Cove and came to Eastport, on Passamaquoddy Bay—only half a dozen miles from the easternmost point of land in the United States, West Quoddy Head—we found ourselves in the presence of one of the great tides of the world. Here, at its ebb, the water had dropped more than eighteen feet from the level of its flood. At Calais, Maine, less than twenty miles to the north, the range is even greater, as much as twenty-three feet, and to the east, at the head of the Bay of Fundy between Nova Scotia and New Brunswick, a combination of certain astronomical conditions may produce tides in the Minas Basin with the record range of fifty-three and a half feet, a rise and fall equivalent to the height of a four-story building.

From this coast of the high tides, on June 6, 1833, the 106-ton schooner, *Ripley*, sailed north with Audubon and his party. One of the birds Audubon observed at Eastport before his departure was "the Bonapartian gull." On this March day, we watched this smallest of American gulls sweep in buoyant flight above the incoming tide. Black-headed in mature breeding plumage, it was now, in winter, white of head, with a single round spot of black behind its eye. A few bufflehead and black duck and surf scoters rode the waves among great rocks shaggy with seaweed. Eiders fed farther out, among the offshore islands. In dark contrast to the white of the gulls, a small band of crows hunted along the tide line. Here, too, were a few ravens. When winter comes, each year, there is a noticeable movement of these larger birds from the interior to the coast.

Across the rise and fall of the great tides, hardy water-birds easily survive the cold. But when winter gales come raging in from the sea, particularly those from the southeast, they often carry pelagic birds from the open ocean far inland. All along the upper coast of Maine, after such a storm, the bodies of dovekies are sometimes found scattered across the snow-covered fields and even in the woods. A year or two before, when the weather cleared after an onshore gale, a horned grebe was encountered walking down the main street of Dennysville.

I talked to one veteran outdoorsman of the region about these winter birds. He proved to be a cautious Down-Easter given to qualifying his statements. He would say: "fully one-half—well, let's say one-fourth" or "as many as 1,000 eiders —well, let's say 800 eiders" or "ten years ago—well, let's say seven years ago." But he knew well the many islands of the bay and his mind was stocked with observations. He remembered winters when gyrfalcons came down from the north, sometimes snatching up waterfowl before the eyes of hunters who had just shot them. He recalled Bohemian waxwing years. He remembered snowy owl invasions when he had seen as many as twelve of the large, white, round-headed birds scattered like snowmen across a single field. In former times, he recalled, bald eagles wintered all along this northern shore.

A few weeks hence, above the tides of this coast another tide, a living tide of returning birds, would flow in from the sea and up from the south. The immense concentrations of breeding birds on the shore and cliffs and islands of this region amazed the early explorers. More than three and a half centuries ago, James Rosier, in his *A True Relation of the Most Prosperous Voyage Made this Present Yeere 1605 by Captaine George Waymouth*, refers to the Maine coast with its "many birds of sundry colors, many other fowles, in flocks, unknown." Soon, now, the returning waterfowl would be scattered across the bay and the returning seabirds would be nesting on the islands. Once more, so many years later, Rosier's quaint description would be apt for "much fowle of divers kinds breed upon the shore and rocks."

Between Eastport and Calais there are two small rocky islets known as The Wolves. They have the distinction of lying almost exactly on the forty-fifth parallel. Once again, as we drove north, we reached and crossed this halfway point between the equator and the pole. That night we stayed at Calais and the next morning, in the last dawn of winter, with the hills of New Brunswick on our right, we commenced the 147-mile run to Caribou. Our ascent to Jackman had been at one side, our ascent to Caribou was at the other side of Maine's more than 16,000,000 acres of forest.

The day was mild and melting. Beyond the higher ground of Topsfield, in a lowland stretch where frost-heaves had broken the hardtop, puddles caught and held the color of the sky. For a mile or more we advanced along a road bounded by white snow and dark-green spruce and decorated throughout its length with hundreds of small pools of shining blue.

We looked at our thermometer. The mercury stood at thirty-eight degrees F. Half a century ago, the researches of Dr. Ellsworth Huntington revealed that human beings produce their greatest physical activity at sixty degrees F. and their greatest mental activity at thirty-eight degrees F. I rode on remembering this and reflecting on how pleasant it would be to record some transcendent thought occurring under these propitious conditions. My thoughts, I must report, remained earthbound. But this had its compensations. For the earth, that day as always, was filled with fascination, with interest fresh and varied.

Beyond Dark Cove and Peekaboo Mountain, north of Danforth, we observed the looming white shape of Mt. Katahdin lift higher into the sky to our left. To our right, beyond the St. John River, in New Brunswick, we could visualize a unique one-tree orchard we had visited years before. In a lifelong hobby, the owner had grafted onto the branches of this single tree all the species of apples growing in the province. Spruce boughs, the natural winter insulation of the north-country, were banked high around each isolated house we passed along the way. Once, as we went by a cabin in a forest clearing, we caught sight of a pair of bright red snowshoes thrust upright into a drift beside the door.

After Mars Hill the forest fell back. The country opened out. Immense fields extended across undulating land. Beside the road huge storage sheds were banked with earth to their eaves. We were in Aroostook County, in the famed potato empire of northern Maine. Instead of the blustery, windy weather of the usual March, the weather we had expected, on this day that brought the winter to a close we experienced calm, mild air and sunny skies. Across a rolling, brightly lighted land we drove the final miles to Caribou.

THIRTY-FOUR

NORTH OF CARIBOU

MORE than a hundred times, since we had left home, the land around us had rolled downward into darkness and upward again into the light. At the close of this twentieth day of March, on the final downward ride of the season, we saw all the drift-covered fields tinted under the swirling flames of sunset. Near a barnyard we watched a cream-white cat walking on pink snow. Then, almost suddenly, the ball of the sun dropped behind the black pointed trees of the remote horizon. The still winter night closed around us. The moon, one day short of full, lifted into a clear sky above the dark New Brunswick hills.

We drove north on U.S. 1 over Caribou Stream and Otter Brook, Hardwood Brook and Halfway Brook. We left behind the lines and chains of tiny twinkling lights that, like some greater constellation, outlined the huge Loring Air Force Base. We rode alone on a lonely road. The twin beams of our headlights on the curves of the winding highway swept from side to side. Birches leaped out in shining lines of white. Red osiers stood spotlighted above the snow. Once, where the moon-shadows of poplars barred the roadside drifts, an owl in swift, low and silent flight slipped in and out of the headlights' glare. The snow grew deeper as we went north. We glimpsed one farmhouse in the moonlight buried to its eaves, and where a side road dipped to join the highway it cut through a drift ten feet deep.

It was after nine and we were on a height of land somewhere north of Caribou when we turned back again. The town was a mere pinhead of neon colors on the horizon. Orion glittered far to the west. Its position marked the old age of the season. Each evening during the months of our diagonal course through the winter we had seen this constellation shining a little higher in the sky. Now in the west it appeared and disappeared, was brilliant one second, obscured the next, the light of its stars winking on and off among the black spires of the roadside spruces. Out in the open, between wooded stretches, it raced along above the dark horizon line. It seemed keeping pace with us, accompanying us as it had accompanied us through all the wanderings of our winter journey.

In that journey, so short a time ago, 10,000 miles of the fourth season lay before us. Only yesterday, it seemed, 1,000 miles still remained. Now on this deserted road amid the snows of this far northeastern corner of Maine, in this still moonlit night, our wheels were rolling down the very last of those winter miles. The months and weeks and days, once untouched, were now reduced to minutes.

I pulled to the side of the road, stopped close to the face of a high drift, and switched off the motor. The only sound we heard in the intense stillness was the fine ticking of my wrist watch. In the beam of a small flashlight we followed the movement of its hands, the same hands that had indicated the moment of the season's beginning a continent-span away beside the Pacific. We watched them plod along the dial. They advanced to 9:25; 9:27; 9:29—the countdown of a season's end.

The hands touched 9:30. Far away from the hush of this moonlit northern night, over the ocean, off the mouth of the Amazon, at that precise moment the rays of the sun shone directly down on the equator. The vernal equinox, that dramatic milestone of the year, the end of winter and the beginning of spring, had arrived and was gone while my watch ticked once. Spenser's "ever-whirling wheele of change, the which all mortall things doth sway" continued its unwearied turning. And everywhere in the northern hemisphere, in city and country, in lands of many tongues, in igloo and ranch home and penthouse as well as here behind the tiny rectangles of the lighted windows of the far-scattered farmhouses rising pale in the moonlight, human beings would be profoundly affected by the changes that would follow.

For us, so long on winter's traces, this moment had even greater significance. It marked not only the end of our wanderings through the fourth season but the end of our wanderings through all the divisions of the year. We had rounded the great circle. We had come to the beginning again. The shift of an apostrophe told the story. What on previous trips had been the season's end was now the seasons' end.

Back in our room at the Red Brick Motel, on the southern edge of Caribou, I opened once more the small, scuffed, brown-leather copy of James Thomson's *The Seasons*. It had traveled with us through all the sequence of spring and summer and autumn and winter. It had ridden with us in four successive cars. It had accompanied us through the Everglades, in Death Valley, amid the rain forests of the Olympic Peninsula, where the Never-Summer Mountains rise in Colorado. I paused at the words I had read at Imperial Beach, below the Silver Strand: "See, Winter comes to rule the varied year." Now, at Caribou, at the season's end, I read again the final lines: "The storms of Wintery Time will quickly pass, and one unbounded Spring encircle all." On the blank page at the end of the book, I set down the date and place and the words: "The end of winter. The end of the four seasons."

The next morning Nellie and I turned south. We headed toward the far-off, oncoming tide of spring. Here amid the miles of drifts in northern Maine the chief sign of the season was highway workers rolling up the snow fences. Yet even here, in this calendar-spring, this winter-spring, we could visualize that tide as we had followed it north in our first adventure with a season. We could see it again, invincible, gathering its forces in the Everglades, sweeping north over the Kissimmee Prairie, on through the Okefenokee Swamp, across the low barrier islands of the Carolinas, ascending the tilted coastal plains and racing up the valleys of the Great Smokies. With color and life and action it was on its way. At the average rate of fifteen miles a day, it was moving up the map, a tide of green, a tide of violets and dogwood and azaleas, a tide of bird song and sunshine and breezes soft and perfumed. The year was beginning again.

Throughout this long flow of the season, life in an infinite variety of forms, life dormant in bur and bud, in burrow and pupa-case, life biding its time, would respond to the increasing warmth. As we rode south through a land of the later spring, we knew that under the ice crystals of the drifts, beneath fields of white and rivers of ice and in the hard and frozen ground, life was waiting, confident, undespairing. Its activity was merely suspended. The stillness, the seeming death of winter, is but an illusion. The apparent conquest of the season is only temporary. Like the moon's waxing and waning, like the tide's ebb and flow, life retreats and is triumphant again. This, as Richard Jefferies noted long ago, is the allegory of winter.

When Nellie and I had come home from that initial journey with the spring, we had wandered for nearly 100 miles after we crossed the Whitestone Bridge onto Long Island. We had turned aside and made delays, loath to have that first adventure end. Now, again, at the conclusion of this last of all our travels with a season, we stretched out our days of freedom. We moved south by loops and zigzags. We followed a laggard's path.

On that first full day of spring, we cut west from Bangor over the hills of central Maine to Skowhegan, on the Kennebec. In the days that followed we roamed across the New

Hampshire line, among the Shelburne birches, past frozen Sunday River where the veeries had sung in the June twilight and down the length of the White Mountains in their white spring. Once more we stood on the green bridge below Mt. Lafayette. With silent emotion we gazed from that eyrie out over the valley of the Gale River still in its winter garb. Here, with twisting rivers of mist tracing the courses of invisible streams in the woods below, we had watched the sundown of our glorious spring and here, in the first dawn of the second season, we had seen the beginning of our most memorable summer.

As we lingered on this homeward trail, at Echo Lake where the mayflies danced in the spring dusk, at the white cabin beside the Pemigewasset where, in starlight, the first season had come to its end, by Mt. Chocorua and along Bearcamp River, our minds were filled with memories of other moments, other times in the quartet of seasons that "fill the measure of the year." We talked, as we rode along, of all that we had seen, of floating islands and underground rivers, of sea otters tumbling in the surf, of the hundred miles of warblers and the night of the falling stars, of painted forests and timberline tundras in bloom, of our million-duck days at Bear River, of migrating butterflies and white cranes in the wind and that magic twilight song of the unseen bird at Sutter's Mill.

Ours had been an adventure unique and we were profoundly thankful. No two other persons in history had ever known the experience we had shared. We had observed first-hand the infinite diversity of the American seasons. We had crisscrossed, from sea to sea, this land unsurpassed for the variety and magnificence of its scenery, for the interest of its wild inhabitants. And, it seemed to us, we had seen it in the nick of time. For during the period of our protracted travels, during the more than twenty years that had elapsed between the inception and completion of our design, the country was steadily changing, becoming less wild, more settled. We had seen its Clear Creeks and Pleasant Valleys when, in the main, its streams were clear and its valleys pleasant.

This we learned from our experience with the four seasons: We want them all. We want the rounded year. We crave no unending Golden Age, no perpetual spring of old mythology. We cherish the variety, the whole sequence of the seasons. In truth, as William Browne wrote in the seventeenth century: "There is no season such delight can bring as summer, autumn, winter and the spring."

And so we came home at last. We came home rich in memories. We drove down the long lane to the 160-year-old white cottage under the hickory trees. We unlocked the door in spring that we had locked in autumn. We found calendars of another year hanging on the wall. That evening, with logs blazing in the great fireplace, we watched the darkness fall beyond our windowpanes. It seemed the final curtain descending at the end of the completed whole of the eternal drama of the year.

Another spring is coming in as these words are written. The white magic of another winter is gone. Another night is falling over our woods and fields and pond. I switch on the lamp above my study desk. Its soft light falls on typed sheets of fieldnotes, on marked maps, on odds and ends, mementos of our winter travels. I am nearly at the end of that self-imposed task that for more than two decades has been my work and my relaxation, my livelihood and my diversion. While I have been wandering across the country and writing of what I have seen—a kind of Plutarch of the seasons—two new states, Alaska and Hawaii, have been added to the Union, the population of the United States has grown by 50,000,000 and the earth has traveled through space 10,000,000,000 miles.

I set down these final words in the dusk of an early spring day. You are reading them when, where, under what conditions? Now the light—my light here, your light wherever you

SNOWSHOE MAKER Charles Holway at work in the doorway of the shop where he created special shoes for forest use.

WINTER'S END, north of Caribou, brings to a close
the fourth and final journey with an American season.

are—falls on the last page of the last book of the last season. We have traveled far together. We have watched the successive seasons flow and merge and intermingle. We have seen the beauty of the land through the whole cycle of the year. To those of you who have journeyed so long, who have traversed the four seasons in our company, to all farewell.

For here ends the story of our travels
through the spring and summer
and autumn and winter of
The American Year.

INDEX